Virgin Capital

Virgin Capital

*Race, Gender, and Financialization
in the US Virgin Islands*

TAMI NAVARRO

Published by State University of New York Press, Albany

© 2021 State University of New York

For information, contact State University of New York Press, Albany, NY
www.sunypress.edu

Library of Congress Cataloging-in-Publication Data

Name: Navarro, Tami, author.
Title: Virgin capital : race, gender, and financialization in the US Virgin
    Islands / Tami Navarro.
Description: Albany : State University of New York Press, [2021] | Includes
    bibliographical references and index.
Identifiers: ISBN 9781438486031 (hardcover : alk. paper) | ISBN
    9781438486024 (pbk. : alk. paper) | ISBN 9781438486048 (ebook)
Further information is available at the Library of Congress.

10 9 8 7 6 5 4 3 2 1

For my mother.

Contents

"Welcome, neighbor," I begin.

Audre Lorde

Acknowledgments

In some form or another, I have been researching the Economic Development Commission (EDC) program since 2003 and have been the recipient of unspeakable grace along the way. *Virgin Capital* began at Duke University where I was gifted with the incomparable direction of Deborah A. Thomas. Deb, you are an incredible mentor, teacher, model, and aspiration. I am an anthropologist because of you. At Duke, I also had the good fortune to work with and learn from Anne Allison, Charles Piot, Orin Starn, Lee Baker, and Mark Anthony Neal. Ian Baucom and Karla Slocum graciously served on my dissertation committee and strengthened my analysis in critical ways. In graduate school, I was fortunate have a deeply committed community of fellow scholars-in-the-making who helped me find my voice: Bianca Williams, Micah Gilmer, Jamaica Gilmer, Attiya Ahmad, and the late Johnetta Pressley were my champions. Your friendship sustained me.

After leaving Duke, life brought me back to Middletown, Connecticut, in the form of a visiting professor stint at Wesleyan University, where I had begun my academic journey and where I was reunited with the brilliant and generous Kehaulani Kauanui and Krishna Winston. I thank them both for modeling what rigorous and engaged scholarship looks like. Thank you to Dorothy Hodgson, who took a chance on my work and offered me an incredibly generative postdoctoral fellowship at Rutgers.

A number of institutions have provided the funding that have enabled me to complete this project: The Center for Latin American and Caribbean Studies at Duke allowed me to conduct much early fieldwork on St. Croix, and a fieldwork grant from the Wenner-Gren

Foundation funded my extended fieldwork. The period of writing is challenging for many academics, and my own such time in the wilderness was made much easier by a dissertation fellowship from the Ford Foundation.

At Barnard College, the community of scholars I encountered—many of whom are now friends—has elevated my work. To Janet Jakobsen, thank you for your consistent demonstration of your belief in my work. Tina Campt is a force to be reckoned with and I continue to learn from her. Thank you for sharing your scholarship, your approach to collaboration, and your razor-sharp wit. Elizabeth Castelli, your dedication to ethical living and community building is an inspiration. One of the happiest surprises of being at Barnard has been working with Kaiama L. Glover. Thank you for joining me in crafting *Critical Caribbean Feminisms* and *Writing Home*. The work we do together is restorative. Monica Miller, Yvette Christiansë, Maja Horn, Neferti Tadiar, Paige West, Pam Philips, Hope Dector, Avi Cummings, Premilla Nadasen, Celia Naylor, Miriam Neptune, Natasha Lightfoot, and Eve Kausch have all made Barnard a welcoming and productive space for me and I am indebted to them all.

In the New York area, I have benefited greatly from the insight and support of Vanessa K. Valdés, Dána-Ain Davis, and David Scott. As a scholar, I believe deeply in the value of intellectual collaboration and have been fortunate to be included in several spaces of cothinking and cowriting: Thank you to the KRUSH writing group (Abosede George, Kimuli Kasara, and Molly Tambor). Our deadlines and mutual accountability are a large part of the reason this book is in the world. To my fellow members of the Virgin Islands Studies Collective (VISCO)—LaVaughn Belle, Hadiya Sewer, and Tiphanie Yanique: your work, zeal, and politics continue to energize me. What a world we are making for ourselves. At Barnard, both the Gender Justice and Neoliberal Transformations working group and the Transnational Black Feminisms working group have been profoundly productive spaces for my present and future scholarship. Over the course of this project, I have shared portions of this manuscript in lectures at the University of the West Indies, Cave Hill, and have been honored by the collegiality and warmth of Tonya Haynes, Halimah DeShong, Veronica Jones, and Charmaine Crawford.

St. Croix is such a large part of my life that it took me many years to find a balance between inhabiting it as "home" and engaging my work there as time in "the field." It remains a tricky balance—a slippery slope in either direction. In any case, my friends and informants on St. Croix are the heart of this project. Nicole Y. Canegata, Ana Castillo, Emily Graci, Deanna James, and Quiana Adams kept me going in the early (and middle and late) days of fieldwork. Anthony Weeks and Governor Albert Bryan gave generously of their time and expertise. We view many things differently, but their insight and perspectives have greatly enriched this book.

This book has been shepherded into the world by my wonderful editor, Rebecca Colesworthy, who has believed in this project from the day we met. Marisa Escolar has also helped to make this a better book, for which I am grateful.

My deepest thanks are reserved for my family, who have endured countless conference hotels, lectures, and drafts. Richard, Ella, and Judah, we have made something together that is larger than any of us. I am humbled every day. To my mother, Ursula Navarro, thank you for making this life possible for me. To Seeranie Seewah, Susi Persaud, and Amanda Bonilla, the love, support, and care you provide keep us moving forward. I became a mother during the course of this project and had no idea how that change would shift my world and ability to write. Clarissa Caban, Keena Utley, and Zaryah Aparicio have done me the honor of minding my children so that I might put these words on the page. Thank you.

The epigraph on page viii is from the poem entitled "Judith's Fancy" by Audre Lorde, taken from The Marvelous Arithmetics of Distance: Poems, 1987–1992. Permission has been granted by W. W. Norton & Company, Inc.

This book has taken a long time to come into the world, but as it has been said, "time is not counted from daylight, but from midnight."

Chapter 1

Introduction

At the outset of fieldwork, the question of methodology loomed large in my mind. My central concern was how to get at the complexity of the Economic Development Commission (EDC) program on St. Croix. In 2007, everywhere I went on the island, this tax holiday program seemed to be all anyone could talk about. There was excitement and optimism around St. Croix's economic future, but there was just as much suspicion and fear surrounding the program and the mainland Americans it had brought to this US territory. How would I construct a methodology that would bring together both the anxiety and anticipation of the EDC program: Would I conduct focus groups? Engage in the "deep hanging out" offered by Clifford Geertz? As these questions swirled in my mind, I dedicated myself to perfunctory tasks: checking the mail was ideal because it afforded me an opportunity to interact with people and, vitally, offered the illusion that I was busy—a person with somewhere to be and something to do, when I was, decidedly, not.

As I walked into the post office one Wednesday afternoon and stood in line to buy stamps, I heard shouting. Although yelling was not in itself unusual, as customers often loudly grumbled about the long wait time or inefficient service, this was different. This was an argument, a shouting match really, between two customers: a middle-aged white woman and a Black man from St. Kitts in his sixties. They were debating the skyrocketing cost of real estate and property taxes on St. Croix. The woman, Karen, insisted that these increases were the fault of the EDC program in general and of "that Stanford man" in particular (Allen Stanford was a billionaire who had recently relocated his considerable business operations to St. Croix—and had been in the process of purchasing large tracts of land across the island since his arrival). The man with whom Karen was arguing, however, insisted that these developments were the fault of unmotivated locals, arguing that it "is we, is we! If we don't buy, we can't get vex." In this debate, Karen was squarely in the camp of St. Croix residents who were critical of this program and its wealthy beneficiaries. Her interlocutor, however, articulated a competing position, that Virgin Islanders were not merely *victims* of global capital and its handlers, but rather that they had a part to play in negotiating the terms of its impact on the island.

After witnessing this exchange, I approached Karen outside of the post office and asked to talk with her about her views on the EDC program. As we walked to a nearby café to escape the scorching summer heat, she told me that, having lived in the Virgin Islands for over twenty years, she was concerned about the rising cost of land on St. Croix (in part, as a result of the astronomical sums being paid by wealthy white families brought to the island by the EDC program), and she told me about her plans to organize a "march for peace" that she hoped would diffuse what she saw as increasing racial tensions on the island as a result of the EDC. This march, she felt, was needed, as the arrival of wealthy white Americans on the island had reinvigorated long-standing anxieties related to race, wealth, and belonging.

The Program

In 2001, the government of the United States Virgin Islands (USVI) established the Economic Development Commission (EDC), a development initiative that closely linked the economic fate of this eighty-four-square mile island to financial developments on Wall Street.[1] *Virgin Capital* addresses the effects of this tax exemption program operating in the US Virgin Islands and engages primarily with its operation on the largest of these islands, St. Croix. The EDC program encourages financial services companies to relocate to the American-owned US Virgin Islands in exchange for generous tax holiday policies, including an exemption from 90 percent of US federal income taxes. While in operation, these companies are expected to stimulate the local economy by hiring local workers and donating to local charitable causes. This program, rooted in attracting American capital to the USVI, marks the emergence of St. Croix as a node in global financial circuits.

However, the inception of this program and the attendant arrival of a number of primarily American financial firms and their Anglo managers brought long-standing racial tensions to the fore and deepened social and economic stratification in this US territory. When I arrived to conduct my fieldwork on St. Croix, the EDC program had been in operation for just over five years, a period of time during which the initiative was dogged by much suspicion, stemming from an understanding that the emergent EDC community, comprised of these recently arrived financial managers and their families, was at best snobbish, and at worst racist.

The suspicion surrounding the EDC program had much to do with the history of racialized wealth accumulation in the Caribbean. This history, including slavery and colonialism, when combined with the unevenness of contemporary neoliberal development, of which the EDC is an instance, came together on St. Croix to produce anxiety about the program's legitimacy. The behavior of EDC beneficiaries also figured prominently in its overall reception: so closely linked are these representatives with the program that they are known in the Crucian community as "EDC people"—a shorthand for wealthy, white, and more often than not, only selectively interested in engaging with the local community. Patterns of residential insularity that saw EDC people purchasing homes on the East End of the island and selective hiring preferences that favored upper-middle-class Crucian women in their twenties and thirties shored up this assessment. These hiring preferences were of great concern in the community, as they deepened existing divisions of class and color in ways that were uncomfortably reminiscent of the race and color hierarchies of slavery and colonialism.

Despite these critiques, EDC companies and EDC people had a tremendous impact on the island, as sources of revenue, potential employers, and topics of streetcorner critique. In its Annual Report, the local governing body charged with regulating this program argued that it "has resulted in the expansion and growth in the financial services industry in the Territory. The creation of high paying jobs for college graduates from the Virgin Islands has partially reversed the flight of intellectual capital to the United States mainland" (Economic Development Authority 2004: 1). This classification of EDC jobs as "high paying" is central to the ambivalence with which the program was received on St. Croix: part of the assumption of lucrative EDC employment is based in fact, as compensation of EDC employees averaged $66,000, nearly double the average income in the USVI,[2] Yet, despite this potential for economic advancement, there were many on St. Croix—like Karen—who pointed to a darker side of this program, citing economic marginalization, increased stratification, and reinvigorated tensions around race and belonging.

The history of the Economic Development Commission program in the US Virgin Islands is one of evolution. While its sister islands of St. Thomas and St. John have both fared well economically,[3] St. Croix has struggled for decades with finding ways to stimulate the local economy because tourism, the economic development avenue pursued by many Caribbean countries since the mid-twentieth century, has not been a significant growth industry. Given these disparate economic realities across the USVI, the government turned to courting US capital through the EDC program in the hopes of stimulating growth on St. Croix. This move is not unusual for the region: since the mid-twentieth century, many Caribbean territories have pursued development through industrialization-by-invitation programs. The 1948 implementation of Operation Bootstrap in Puerto Rico stands as a pioneering example; yet countries like Jamaica, Trinidad, Haiti, and the Dominican Republic have also attempted these types of schemes. Typically, these projects have provoked resentments among sectors of the "host" societies as managerial staff, mostly foreigners and local elites, maintain exclusive social enclaves that are classed and racialized (Douglass 1992; Maurer 1997).

During the 1970s and 1980s the local government of the USVI similarly pursued economic growth through the Industrialization Development Commission (IDC)—the precursor to the EDC—with the primary beneficiaries being working-class Crucians who were able to find employment within the aluminum and watchmaking industries on St. Croix. In the late 1990s, the program began to focus on companies making use of light, flexible labor, in keeping with the paradigm shift that was taking place in the Caribbean as a whole during that decade.[4] This broader shift impacted development attempts in the USVI, with the IDC accepting small numbers of benefit applications from technology and financial companies, most often financial management and investment firms. It was not until the early 2000s that it was formalized, with the IDC being renamed the Economic Development Commission (EDC), focused on attracting primarily American financial management companies to the island, thereby solidifying the US Virgin Islands' entrance into the global competition for development dollars through finance. The new EDC program, however, has been seen as abandoning the working class. In part, this is because it is directed toward financial services and not industrial production, favoring Crucians from backgrounds of relative mobility and privilege.

The EDC program, much like its industrial predecessor, focuses on attracting businesses to the US Virgin Islands by offering tax incentives, perhaps the most enticing of which is the 90 percent waiver on income tax. These islands are hardly the first to offer such incentives, as tax holidays have been offered by a number of countries in the region in an attempt to stimulate their economies. For instance, the Cayman Islands have long been viewed by investors as receptive to their needs, and there is a growing banking sector in the nearby British Virgin Islands. While the USVI fits into this broader pattern of economic development, its status as an English-speaking American territory in the Caribbean makes it uniquely attractive to US-based businesses. Much like neighboring Puerto Rico, the USVI relies heavily upon its political relationship with—that is, its status as a possession *of*—the United States for the success of the EDC program. While the status of the USVI and Puerto Rico as territories of the US has made various economic development initiatives possible, it is this very status that has contributed to the gutting of local economies such as agriculture, often leading to intense outmigration.[5]

A widespread move toward independence in the Caribbean in the 1960s and 1970s followed Operation Bootstrap, and while the 1970s was a period during which many Caribbean islands turned toward increasingly autonomous development plans (largely as a result of frustration with the outcomes of development programs implemented after independence from Britain across the region during the 1960s), the USVI continued to rely on its political relationship with the US. As has been amply demonstrated by scholars in and beyond the region, the development strategies pursued during the immediate postcolonial period did not substantially diverge from those that had been followed before independence and did not fundamentally alter the colonial social and economic hierarchies that characterized the region. During the 1970s, however, with the increasing interest in the nonaligned movement, with Black power movements gaining speed in many Caribbean countries, and with democratic socialist policies being pursued in Jamaica, a sea change was occurring in the formerly British West Indies. Nevertheless, the US Virgin Islands continued to root its hopes for economic development in its status as an American territory. As the global focus changed post-1970s from heavy industry to a regime characterized as more flexible, scholars grappled with what these increasingly global processes might mean for a new world order. In the 1990s, some theorists analyzing those processes through the lens of globalization began to argue that their electronic (or virtual) nature would result in greater global integration, with formerly remote areas incorporated through these circulations. At that time, Arjun Appadurai's (1990) theory of global flows (or "scapes") traveling at "blinding speeds" captured the hope of that optimistic moment, hope that has largely been dashed in the intervening years by the persistence of inequitable power dynamics and—as it relates to the USVI—the continued unfolding of the project of US empire.

For both theorists and residents of the Caribbean, the move toward lighter industry was seen, at least initially, as an attractive alternative to the service-sector jobs provided by tourism, as the local population anticipated training in new skills, and because the financial services companies were to walk with a lighter footprint on the islands. This desire to move away from a tourism-centered approach to economic well-being was informed by objections to both the lower wages generally paid in the hospitality sector (for instance, jobs in this sector in the USVI included a starting salary of $16,350 in 2016)[6] as well as more general critiques of the ways in which this industry trades upon and extends the history of Black service and white leisure in the region (see, for instance, Cohen 2010; Gmelch 2003; Kincaid 1988; Nixon 2015; Sheller 2003) and extends the project of US empire (Gonzalez 2013; Aikau and Gonzalez 2019). Given the reproduction of these problematic dynamics in this industry, the USVI turned to economic development in the form of the EDC program. Yet, EDCs have produced many of the same effects as tourism in relation to racialization and gender, including the feminization of labor and the continued dependence on foreign capital resulting in racialized hierarchies that recall earlier processes in the region. Further, the economic and social vacuum created by the too-numerous EDC companies that continue to leave the island quickly and under suspicion is much the same as that created when "runaway shops," noted by Helen Safa (1981), or tourist markets move elsewhere.

Unlike the earlier IDC, the newer EDC program has been seen as solidifying preexisting hierarchies of privilege rooted in race, class, and color. In part, this is because it is directed toward financial services and not industrial production and, as a result, the program typically hires Crucians who have received their tertiary educations in the United States. This hiring preference on the part of EDC employers has contributed to an entrenchment of status hierarchies that are rooted in education and the ability to migrate, which are themselves tethered to local color and class expectations. It has also tended to solidify biases that position the attainment of education on the US mainland as superior to that which could be obtained locally. Finally, the program has reorganized the ways opportunities are gendered because EDC employers tend to hire significantly more young women than men. Beyond the notion of "EDC people" (an identity tied directly to one's relationship to this tax incentive program—and, thus, capital), these hiring preferences have contributed to the creation of a new social category on St. Croix, the "EDC girl," a subject expected to dress, act, and dispose of her generous salary conspicuously on items such as clothing, cars, and vacations—spending patterns that often frustrate the parents these women now outearn. This emergent identity is central to my analysis, as it demonstrates the fraught relationships between gender, race, color, capital, and processes of subject formation in the current moment. Like other banking sectors across the region, the EDC focuses on capital management as the driver of economic development, an emphasis that creates space for my analysis of the ways in which the financial services model has similar effects vis-à-vis long-term development in the Caribbean as tourism, the very model it was intended to replace.

Virgin Capital examines the impact of the EDC program not only by revisiting the debates among policymakers, program beneficiaries, and Virgin Islands residents about the program over time, but also by paying attention to the ways in which my informants invoked histories of racialized violence. For instance, Crucians' claims about EDC beneficiaries' desired return to the social order of slavery or the invocation, by Black residents, of earlier episodes of race-based violence (including a 1970s murder of a group of white golfers at a St. Croix golf club) serve as moments in which Crucians' theorization of the EDC as an extension of the project of racial capitalism is on display. What is more, this exploration of the raced, classed, gendered, and generational effects of the EDC program on St. Croix allows me to parse the social and cultural effects of new relationships between states, state functions (Trouillot 2001), and markets within territories that are often overlooked, not only within scholarship but also in relation to the global development mandates and opportunities whose terms are set by independent nation-states and multilateral institutions.

Housing capital in the Caribbean has long been viewed as suspicious (an assessment based on the assumption that such invest-ments are intended to evade US tax requirements), and advocates of the EDC program are adamant that it is an attempt by the local government of the US Virgin Islands to build on its American sta-tus and provide an opportunity at legitimate banking and financial management in the Caribbean. Arriving from the US mainland and sometimes employing the requisite number of Virgin Islands residents, the managers of many of these companies have long been viewed ambivalently on the island because they are seen both as potential sources of generous income *and* as social pariahs intent on recolo-nizing St. Croix in the model of plantation slavery. This connection was so clear to my informants that a common response I received to questions about the EDC program and EDC people was, "Slave days over!"[7] I learned, over the course of fieldwork, that this response was rooted in these interviewees' positioning of this economic development program in the long history of racial capitalism and their assessment that it was but the most recent iteration of this project. Rather than viewing selective hiring preferences and housing purchases in solely economic terms, these Virgin Islands residents counted such practices as evidence that EDC beneficiaries desired to return to the social and economic model of slavery. This rendering of an economic program as an attempt to return to "slave days" on St. Croix points to the ways in which these financial transfers, and the grounded, local practices that make them possible, are racialized and tied to long histories of racialization. What is more, the effects of this development program are not entirely new for many Virgin Islanders, as this equation of the EDC with "slave days" names the continuities between this program and exploitative historical processes in the region. While advocates of the EDC program herald its singularity, Crucians remain haunted by all that has come before. Describing his 1982 visit to St. Croix, Danish scholar and diver Leif Svalesen has written, "On a bus stop alongside the Fort I read: 'Free the Black People from the Chain.' This is not a battle cry from the nineteenth century. It has been freshly painted! It appears as if the dissatisfaction among the black population of St. Croix is a never-ending problem" (Svalesen 2000: 207–208). Ongoing racial dissatisfaction on St. Croix in particular may well be the case, but in recent years many scholars have pointed to both the racialization of global processes and the continued—even increasing—racial tensions that mark the current moment (for instance, see Clarke and Thomas 2006). It is in the vast difference between these views of the program—in the space between a feared return to "slave days" and financialization-as-development—that *Virgin Capital* makes its intervention.

Throughout *Virgin Capital*, I argue that Crucians' objection to the EDC program is demonstrative of a larger critique of the project of capitalism and the ways it is undergirded by race and racism, an analysis that is deeply indebted to Cedric Robinson's (1983) theory of racial capitalism. That is, the assessment of the EDC program as an attempted return to "slave days" (and by this Crucians mean both the structural and quotidian continuities between the *system* of enslaved labor and racially segregated daily life under slavery) is rooted in an understanding of processes of racialization undergirding the project of capitalism—a reality made plain in Robinson's *Black Marxism* (1983), as he demonstrated the ways in which capitalism is fundamentally rooted in racism and the exploitation of raced subjects' labor. This is why Robinson writes that the relationship of the transatlantic slave trade and slavery to capitalism was "historical and organic rather than advantageous or synthetic" (1983: 4). This insight on the racialized roots of capitalism has found renewed life in scholarship and activism,[8] both with respect to the historical (that is, as a way to parse both the ideology that justified slavery and the continuing significance of this institution on life in the Americas) and the contemporary (as a way to mount theoretical and action-based responses rooted in the

Black radical tradition). The understanding that there is not only a fundamental *connection* between race and capitalism but rather that capitalism is undergirded by race and processes of racialization makes legible the racialized anxieties expressed by Crucians vis-à-vis the EDC program. That is, the logic of Crucians' positioning of neoliberal "development" in general and the EDC program in particular as an attempt to return to the order of slavery begins to emerge through explicitly linking this project of wealth accumulation to its roots in racist labor exploitation. Seen in this light, the underlying anxiety that EDC people desire a return to the days of slavery is not at all hysterical or indicative of a misapprehension of the program (as its proponents often claim). Rather, this rendering is rooted in a more complicated experience of time, race, and the underlying logic of capital accumulation.

In addition to concerns about racism, much of the suspicion surrounding the EDC program concerns the legality of beneficiaries' business practices. While the pay at EDC companies is generally much higher than that offered in other sectors on St. Croix, these companies are also seen as unstable and illicit—a reputation earned as a result of a number of federal investigations at various EDC companies and further solidified by charges of investment fraud brought against the largest such company on the island during my fieldwork, Stanford Financial. Operating five growing offices across the island and quickly buying up large swaths of real estate, this company's CEO, Allen Stanford (the man whose name Karen invoked in her argument in the post office), was heralded by advocates of the program as the billionaire-savior of St. Croix's long-struggling economy but vilified by many Crucians priced out of the real estate market as a result of his seemingly endless dollars. This company and its CEO served as the embodiment of the ambivalence with which Crucians viewed the EDC program.

In light of the enormous impact that Stanford Financial had on St. Croix, as well as the CEO's avowed commitment to good corporate citizenship (at a 2007 economic forum on St. Croix he described the order of the day as "getting rid of the pirates *in* the Caribbean" vis-à-vis investing), I interned with this company, as well as several other EDC entities, as part of the research on which this text is based. Having returned to the US mainland after fieldwork, I heard from friends quickly when the US Securities and Exchange

Commission (SEC) filed charges against Stanford, alleging that his business was in fact a massive Ponzi scheme and that he had enacted "a fraud of shocking magnitude that has spread its tentacles throughout the world."[9] These developments dealt a stunning blow to the already-beleaguered economy of St. Croix. The arrest of Stanford Financial's chief investment officer as well as the CEO himself made it increasingly difficult for Crucians to take seriously the prospect of employment with this company or any of its kind on the island. For former Stanford employees, many of whom had left the island to attend college in the United States, landing a job within the EDC sector and earning a salary comparable to that earned by financial workers on the US mainland represented a viable opportunity to spend at least part of their working lives back on St. Croix. However, the very public implosion of this company served as a reminder of the long history of circuitous economic practices in the region—circulations of capital that continue to straddle the boundary between licit and illicit.

Allen Stanford held a grand spectacle of a groundbreaking ceremony for his 105,000-square-foot megacomplex headquarters on St. Croix in 2007, replete with the requisite dignitaries and, for added measure, the Antiguan cricket team in full uniform (Stanford's long-term financial presence in Antigua included ownership of that island's national stadium). Given this introduction, the revelation of Stanford's actual state of affairs marked a stunning reversal for this company in particular and the EDC program at large. While Stanford's implosion lends itself to an easy recasting as a Madoff-style scheme,[10] the context here is crucial: until his indictment, employment at Stanford—and the conferral of its coveted company Stanford logo pin (a golden eagle) upon hiring—was a defining status marker on St. Croix. More deeply than that, however, working at this company—and to a lesser degree any EDC—represented the possibility of increased mobility and a new identity for Crucians long overlooked by the standard economic stimulus of Caribbean islands: tourist dollars. The downward spiral of the EDC program as a whole after the 2008 financial crisis and the fiery crash of Stanford in particular drew attention to the long history of economic stagnation on St. Croix and the multifaceted outcomes of its recent insertion into global financial circulations.

In some ways, it is strange to begin this book with the downfall of the EDC program. Coupled with the 2008 financial crash in the United States, Stanford's arrest largely marked the end of the program.[11] In many ways, however, this is the only way to tell this tale of wealth, greed, class, dreams of mobility, empire, and racialized history. This particular beginning, this starting with the ending, would not have been my choice. I would have preferred a linear tale, one that began with setting off into an uncharted anthropological field site and concluded with a few hard-won conclusions. However, this analysis—my analysis—of the EDC program did not unfold in that way. Instead, my engagement with the EDC as an instance of neoliberal development was complicated by my informants' insistence that this program was simply slavery—or, at best, colonialism—reincarnate. Their insistence that this model of economic development, despite the soothsaying of program supporters, was a renewed way for wealthy, white capitalists to increase their wealth by circuiting through the Caribbean challenged any attempt to position the EDC as simply an innocuous instance of the current model of neoliberal development practice. While the EDC is certainly demonstrative of contemporary capital accumulation, it also reveals the problematic assumptions and histories of domination in which this model is rooted. The long and painful histories of slavery and colonialism in the Caribbean broadly and the US Virgin Islands in particular have resulted in great trepidation—articulated as racialized anxieties—around the EDC model of development.

Throughout this text, I have taken seriously the concerns of my Crucian informants who argued that the EDC program is an attempt to return to what they termed "slave days," and I place these concerns in productive tension with the position of its advocates, that it marks an attempt to move the USVI—and specifically St. Croix—forward, to reinsert it into transnational capital flows. It is the argument of this book that this program, and those like it, are not fully captured by either of these renderings, but instead contain elements of both. That is, neoliberal initiatives that advocate the freeing of markets and purport to mark the way toward greater global integration build upon—and often lead to the entrenchment of—existing processes of racialized and gendered inequality. In many formerly peripheral spaces, particularly Latin America and the Caribbean, this relationship to neoliberalism is conditioned by long and violent histories of slavery and colonialism that make the ostensibly novel circulations of European and American capital—and the racialized hierarchies they engender—hauntingly familiar.

Spectral Time

The question of time—of alternate temporalities that complicate a linear notion of time—has been the preoccupation of a number of scholars.[12] Many have argued that the region is best apprehended through analyses that privilege temporality (Harvey 1989; Alexander 2005; Benítez-Rojo 1997) and capital (Mintz 1985; Sheller 2003; Khan 2001). For those working in formerly colonized (or postcolonial) spaces, the interplay of past, present, and future has been of significance; for instance, Achille Mbembe (2001) has turned to the notion of "entanglement" to account for interlocking pasts, presents, and futures that inform life today in postcolonial African contexts. Caribbeanist scholars, too, have thought deeply about the implications of conceptions of time on both the present and the self and have turned to any number of fields of study to address these questions.[13] In *The Repeating Island*, Antonio Benítez-Rojo (1997) enlists chaos theory to theorize the Caribbean as a space defined not by a neat unfolding of events but rather a space perhaps best defined by fluidity and an unpredictable sameness. In her theorization of complex time, Deborah A. Thomas has turned to quantum physics (2016). Citing Ella Shohat, M. Jacqui Alexander (2005) has productively engaged the notion of "palimpsestic time," where time is akin to a "parchment that has been inscribed two or three times, the previous text having been imperfectly erased and remaining therefore still partly visible" (2005: 190). All of this work does much to rightly foreground temporality and introduce alternate temporalities with which to think. For my work on the EDC program, the contributions of Ann Stoler (2016) are particularly useful, as she privileges unfolding anxieties vis-à-vis the past. For instance, in her work on complex time that is not neatly divided into past-then-present, she argues rather that time is unpredictable and that contemporary life is often informed by unexpected realities—what she terms the "uneven sedimentations" of imperial rule. On this point she writes, "We need to do better to understand the nature of imperial duress, the anxieties and fears it produces, the potentialities it short-circuits, the possibilities it enables, and the force it galvanizes to ensure that viable futures are not foreclosed" (2016: 35–36).

This emphasis on the *anxieties* that exist vis-à-vis nonlinear time is key to this project—yet it is not quite enough. Beyond anxiety around what *might* happen—that is, what awful outcome of the EDC

program can be imagined, given past experience—Crucians articulate
a framing of time grounded in haunting. That is, while the EDC
program is viewed skeptically on the island because of public failures
like that of Stanford and other EDC beneficiaries, this is not the
only—or even primary—evidence Crucians marshal in their critique
of the program. Instead, I argue, the positioning of this program
as an attempt to return to "slave days" is rooted in an analysis
that does not separate this instance of neoliberal development from
earlier iterations of racialized wealth accumulation, such as slavery
and colonialism. While advocates of the EDC program dismiss the
situating of this program in this trajectory as nonsense or misapprehension, I argue that this position is one that emerges from an
experience of being haunted by the long history of racial capitalism
in the region—what, borrowing from Bliss Cua Lim, I call spectral
time. In a 2001 essay, Lim employs the phrase "spectral time" in a
discussion of ghost films as historical allegory, writing, the "ghostly
return of traumatic events precisely troubles the boundaries of past,
present, and future, and cannot be written back to the complacency
of a homogeneous, empty time" (2001: 287). This recognition of
the present being not merely informed by the specter of the past
but rather being deeply interwoven with it is a productive framing of
the ways in which Crucians engage the EDC program. In this way
of seeing, it is not merely that wealthy white people have circuited
through the Caribbean before, and increased their wealth by doing
so (although they certainly have); it is rather that that past *is* this
present (or, at the very least, could be). That is, for Crucians whose
response to the EDC program is "slave days over," this neoliberal
development program marks a desired attempt to reanimate a social
and economic order rooted in their marginalization. This framing
is also tied to Avery Gordon's (2008) notion of "ghostly matters"
that *demand* productive examination, as a central underlying premise
of spectral time is that something (and here, that "something" is
the expendability of Black people under racial capitalism) has gone
terrifyingly awry, and not for the first time.

   Throughout this text, I attempt to capture the "haunting" of
the EDC program, the palpable fear of past wrongs reemerging in/
through the present, with the phrase spectral time—a term that I
use to gesture toward the fear and anticipation of violence—here
anticipated as an economic and structural, rather than necessarily

physical, threat. In a text that engages the long history of racism and capital accumulation through the lens of haunted time, it is, of course, impossible to overlook Marx's ominous invocation that "a specter is haunting Europe" or Jacques Derrida's notion of hauntology in his text *Specters of Marx* (1993). What is more, there is much important work that engages hauntology and haunted futures—particularly in postcolonial contexts (see, for instance, Piot 2010, and Goldstone and Obarrio 2016)—however for my engagement with the EDC program, Lim's notion of spectral time is key. My use of "spectral" is intended to call to mind the continuities between contemporary capital accumulation and the region's history of quasi-regulated accumulation through, for instance, practices such as piracy and privateering. These earlier instances in which pirates/privateers plundered their way across the region, sometimes under the protection of a European flag, and sometimes not, is echoed in contemporary neoliberal development. Then, as now, context is everything in this system that wavers between licit and illicit. The concept of spectral time is an attempt to capture this persistent yet elusive element, and instead of weighing the merits and faults of one moment against another, this rendering engages with the fact that people can be—and have been—killed, disappeared, relocated, dispossessed, and transfigured in the name of capital accumulation.[14]

The "US" in "USVI"

As a contribution to literature on the "anthropology of finance," *Virgin Capital* focuses on the effects of economic development on quotidian life (Appel 2019; Bear et al. 2015; Elyachar 2005; Marcus 1998; Maurer 1997, 2005; Roitman 2005), examining the ways in which new financial schemes are coming to redefine social spaces and polities throughout the world.

Given that this program operates in an unincorporated American territory, *Virgin Capital* addresses the significance of sovereignty—and non-sovereignty—in global circulations (Bonilla 2015; Hansen 2006; Hardt and Negri 2000; Kelly and Shah 2006; Ong 1999, 2006; Sassen 2003; Shah 2006; Singer 2003; Slocum 2006). The status of the USVI as a territory of the United States has long made the islands particularly attractive to, and penetrable by, American capital.

There is also much to be said regarding the continuing significance of empire broadly, and American rule in particular, although the operation of this neoliberal program provides insight into issues of cultural, political, and economic sovereignty that are applicable far beyond this quasi-American space. In today's global marketplace, there seem to be few development options for small states, especially those that are not independent but maintain significant political and economic relations with former metropolitan centers. In the Caribbean, for example, countries like Puerto Rico; the US and British Virgin Islands; the Dutch administered territories of Bonaire, Saba, and St. Eustatius; and the French overseas departments of Martinique and Guadeloupe all confront current processes according to the particular terms set by their dependent relationships to the United States, Britain, the Netherlands, and France.[15]

Through the EDC program, St. Croix has become a "node" in global financial circuits, although its position continues to be informed by its relationship to the US, as the island is primarily linked to *American* investment firms. For colonies such as the USVI and neighboring Puerto Rico, issues of dependency and empire remain deeply embedded in conversations about economic advancement. As in Puerto Rico, the centrality of this relationship of coloniality in the USVI has largely meant that the US experiences the financial benefits of the EDC program, while the USVI bears the weight of its operation. Following the devastation of hurricanes Irma and Maria in 2017, for instance, Puerto Rico witnessed the proliferation of what Naomi Klein (2007) has called "disaster capitalism," including widespread calls for the privatization of services such as the island's electrical provider (Morales 2019; Bonilla and LeBron 2019). As did the EDC before them, the fallout from these storms laid bare questions around economic advancement, sovereignty, and belonging, bringing to the fore what Klein (2018) has called "a very simple question: Who is Puerto Rico for? Is it for Puerto Ricans, or is it for outsiders? And after a collective trauma like Hurricane Maria, who has a right to decide?" (2018: 11). These questions, which Klein poses in regard to Puerto Rico, similarly animate my engagement with the EDC program as Crucians grapple with these issues of belonging and wealth in the face of crisis. What is more, the ostensibly environmental disasters of hurricanes Irma and Maria shed renewed light on the political and economic crises of both

Puerto Rico and the USVI, as the haphazard response of the United States to the devastation experienced in its colonies demonstrated the expendability of life in these spaces. As I have written elsewhere in relation to these historic storms, "The conditions on the ground in the USVI were appalling: the islands were barely inhabitable post hurricanes Irma and Maria with food shortages, a widespread, months long blackout, and daily competitions for necessary commodities like water and gasoline to power generators, which were in extremely short supply in the months following the storms. In addition, the extensive damage on the ground—roofs in the middle of once busy intersections, trees leaning precariously over pedestrian walkways—speaks volumes about the exclusion of these islands from the US national imagination and the willingness of American elected officials to turn a blind eye to the daily struggle for survival taking place under the American flag" (Navarro 2018: 175). In the familiar "rights and responsibilities" discourse of the US state, the United States has continually shunned the responsibilities of ensuring the survival of its pseudo-citizens in the USVI and Puerto Rico, while exercising its "right" of fiscal authority in these spaces.

In its marketing of the EDC program, the US Virgin Islands makes much of its status as an American possession in promoting its banking sector. For instance, on the program's website, designed to inform potential investors about its specifics, the "US" in USVI has long figured prominently. In his message to the imagined future beneficiaries of the program, the then-governor of the territory noted, "We are unique and our beloved Territory offers many benefits. We use US Currency and have the protection of the US flag and US courts. Manufacturers have duty-free, quota-free access to the US mainland with 'Made in the USA' labels on many types. Our Economic Development Commission benefits help qualifying companies reduce their taxes and increase their profits and rivals any benefits package across the globe" (Economic Development Authority n.d.). Governor deJongh's assessment of the territory as "unique" vis-à-vis development has much to do with the territory's status as an English-speaking possession of the US that is only a short trip from the East Coast of the United States. The fact that English is the primary language in the USVI makes it a more attractive relocation option for American investors with school-aged children (as is the case for many EDC families) than nearby Puerto Rico, where the task of transitioning themselves and their children to Spanish would constitute an additional challenge. Further, the status of the territory as a US possession lends it—and the program—an air of legitimacy, of being in compliance with the laws of the United States (whether this is the case generally remains in doubt on the island, as a not-insignificant number of EDC companies have been raided and/or investigated by federal authorities in recent years). This balancing act of leveraging one's coloniality in the service of economic advancement is one that has been undertaken elsewhere in the Caribbean, including, for instance, Barbados' promotion of itself as "Little England" (Reilly 2019) and the British Virgin Islands' depiction of itself as a place still in touch with its British roots as a "law and order society" (Maurer 1997).

   In addition to naming the continuing importance of American empire, this book engages with scholarship that addresses how contemporary processes of globalization are profoundly and intrinsically both racialized and gendered in ways that draw from older ideological and institutional constructions of race and gender in the region, but that also produce new dynamics of subject formation (Clarke and Thomas 2006; Freeman 2000; Hall 1997; Holt 2000; Khan 2004; Thomas 2004; Yelvington 1995). Gender has long been one of the primary units of analysis in Caribbeanist research, and scholarship on women and labor in the region has been particularly rich (Abraham-Van der Mark 1983; Anderson 1986; Barrow 1995; Barrow 1998; Bolles 1983; Ellis 2003; Kempadoo 2004; Leo-Rhynie 1997; Mohammed 2002; Mohammed and Shepherd 1988; Momsen 1993; Yelvington 1995). In this text, I explore how young, US-educated female EDC employees are both beneficiaries and victims of the current neoliberal moment, what this has meant for socioeconomic and political organization in St. Croix, and how these women navigate these new realities. A carefully painted portrait of the lives of EDC girls demonstrates the significance of preexisting hierarchies (of class, color, and gender) and the possibilities that have been created by the inception of programs like the EDC. These workers, I argue, negotiate their (relative) wealth and power in ways that reference both their membership in the wider community of St. Croix and their precarious position vis-à-vis global capital.[16]

   The Caribbean is a productive context through which to investigate these issues of capital and dependency, given the region's centrality to modern capitalism and the transatlantic slave trade, plantation development, circuitous systems of finance and insurance to keep plantation slavery afloat, and the massive debt burden on these small economies that remain in the shadow of the United States. It is also a space that has borne the full weight of capital's freewheeling jaunt through the region. The general distrust of this particular iteration of capital accumulation I capture in the book's title; *Virgin Capital* evokes both the ostensible "newness" of contemporary circuits of capital and points to the long history of the islands now known as the US Virgin Islands (formerly the Danish West Indies). Through an analysis of the EDC program, *Virgin Capital* undertakes the project of making clear the links between empire, capital, and neoliberalism.

As an ethnographic engagement with an economic *development* project, my analysis of the EDC program is informed by poststructuralist critiques (Escobar 1994; Ferguson 1990a; Pigg 1991; Sachs 1992), wherein development is seen as a field of discourse that is both informed by and productive of relations of power. However, I seek to go beyond their singular focus on the texts and language of development to also explore the effects of such discourse on the everyday lives of Crucians, an emphasis that is in concert with critiques of this literature (Babbington 2000; Berger 1995; Kiely 1999; Little and Painter 1995; Pieterse 1998; Peet and Hartwick 1999). By focusing on financial industries rather than, for example, structural adjustment policies or offshore factory production as has been done in earlier scholarship,[17] my work examines the extent to which new development initiatives might generate different challenges as well as opportunities for various sectors of Caribbean populations. This project, then, is designed to explore the myriad, cross-cutting effects of the EDC on St. Croix while taking seriously the claims of both EDC advocates and detractors.

On Belonging

In order to obtain the attractive benefits offered by the EDC program, applicant companies must fulfill certain program requirements, including a minimum investment of capital in the territory, annual donations ranging from $25,000 to $100,000 to local charitable organizations, residency in the US Virgin Islands for 183 days per

year, and a workforce consisting of a significant number of Virgin
Islands residents. On this final point, the statute governing the
program insists, "One of the basic purposes and objectives of the
Economic Development Program is the establishment and preser-
vation of opportunities of gainful employment for residents of the
United States Virgin Islands."[18] This statute in particular, and the
divergent, varying ways it has been interpreted, has been the site
of much consternation in the territory and is a site in which many
Virgin Islanders claim the disingenuousness of the EDC community
is on full display. This is because many EDC companies have chosen
to interpret the term "resident of the Virgin Islands" in its loosest
sense, relocating existing workers from the US mainland in order
to allow them to legally qualify as residents. Strictly speaking, they
are within their legal right to do so,[19] as the law defines a Virgin
Islands resident as either: "(1) Any United States citizen currently
domiciled in the U.S. Virgin Islands for one year or more; (2) Any
person who has attended a school in the U.S. Virgin Islands for at
least (6) years or is a high school or University of the U.S. Virgin
Islands graduate and who is registered to vote in the Virgin Islands"
(Section 703-1(r)).

Perhaps unsurprisingly one of the criticisms levied against the
program by residents of St. Croix is that companies simply relocate
their mid- and upper-level "Stateside" employees and then begin the
process of applying for EDC benefits. The effect of this is that the
original mainland staff of many EDCs remains largely intact, while
the companies are legally able to claim employment of the required
number of Virgin Islands residents. Advocates of the EDC program,
however, point to an alternate "resident" definition, one that refers to
those schooled in the territory, and argue that the program counters
"brain drain" by making it possible for Virgin Islanders living outside
of the territory to return. The option to earn a competitive salary,
in concert with an ability to overcome the "dull ache of lifelong
homesickness" (Glick-Schiller and Fouron 2001) experienced by many
Virgin Islanders living abroad, makes employment in the EDC sector
particularly appealing, despite its illicit elements.

Many Crucians return to the EDC community's generous interpretation of "resident" to make a larger claim regarding the lack of
interest on the part of beneficiaries to either materially improve the
lives of Virgin Islanders or integrate themselves into this commu-

nity. This latter point is one rooted in a notion of belonging. The economic and political reality of the USVI is such that mainland Americans and Virgin Islands–born residents possess the same United States passport (a document that is itself the focus of simultaneous desire and critique in the wider Caribbean region) and therefore have equal right to live and work in the territory. This notion of shared citizenship, indeed *sameness*, pushes up against a notion of community integration and belonging on St. Croix, a sense that each resident ought to be—indeed, is expected to be—invested in community in ways that go beyond individual economic well-being.

Claims about EDC people's lack of interest in belonging are also made through objections to their real estate purchases and a rejection of local—that is, public—uses of land. This shift in land use toward the privatization of formerly public space decenters community and privileges the market as the arbiter of appropriate use. On this point, the 2009 purchase of a well-loved local oceanfront landmark formerly known as "Grassy Point" particularly angered those who argued that EDC wealth was displacing Crucians seeking to purchase land, distorting the local real estate market, and disturbing public land use on the island. This bluff overlooking the ocean was purchased by an EDC businessman who built a luxury cottage there, closing off entry to the property and renaming the area. In a 2009 newspaper editorial, an academic and community leader on St. Croix suggested that many on the island were especially upset about the purchase of Grassy Point because it sought to make private a site long understood as belonging to the community:

> Why are so many callers [to my office] upset? The site is one of the few ocean areas on St. Croix where people, especially locals, communicate with nature. This oneness with nature started during colonial times when enslaved Africans rested from their labor on the surrounding cotton and sugar estates of Grassy Point.
>
> The shorelines of the Virgin Islands have been a place of physical therapy, recreation, meditation and rest to Virgin Islanders past and present. Our shores have been used freely for "donkey years" by all residents and visitors alike. To our fishermen, the sea and its shores are a way of life. (Davis 2009)

Anger over large land purchases by EDC people and the privatization of space contributed to tensions between Crucians and EDC people and reflects the broader neoliberal project of privatizing space (for example, Peterson 2006). Again, this was the subject of Karen's debate with her interlocutor in the post office. In both formal and informal interviews, Crucians with whom I spoke claimed that the greatest social cost of the success of tourism on its sister islands of St. Thomas and St. John has been the phenomenon of white mainland Americans "taking over." This view applied particularly to the tiny island of St. John, where real estate prices for the few acres of this eight-mile island not protected by the US federal government as part of a national reserve are prohibitively expensive[20]—a situation that has resulted in the displacement of St. Johnians to the larger island of St. Thomas. The morning and evening ferry boat transporting the day laborers working at St. John's various high-end resorts is an image cited by Crucians as evidence of the displacement of locals resulting from "economic success." Concerns over dramatic changes in the real estate market in the USVI are borne out by quantitative data: the average cost of a home on St. Croix doubled from 2001 to 2008[21]—yet the ways this statistic is interpreted vary widely. While a PricewaterhouseCoopers report found that "in tandem with the rapid growth of designated service businesses promotions under the EDC program, the USVI real estate market has revived since 2001, with strong increases in construction, renovation, and sale of existing homes,"[22] many Virgin Islanders take exception to such "revival," arguing that it has effectively priced them out of real estate and home ownership on the island.

Reworking Time

My research on the EDC program, an attempt to stimulate the economy of St. Croix by situating it as a node in global financial circuits, points to the ways in which this initiative—and global circulations more broadly—continues to be shaped by processes and hierarchies of gender and racialization.[23] As finance capital circles the globe in novel ways—seeking new profits, creating tax shelters (Maurer 1997), developing "enclaves" beyond state control (Ferguson 2006)—it is often implicated in a dramatic remaking of social landscapes. While such processes are hardly new for the region,[24] this text examines how the EDC program contributes to a "recharting" of the Caribbean in relation to capital (Maurer 1997), especially to the mutually constituting hierarchies of class, status, race, gender, and generation—hierarchies that are long-standing but nevertheless dynamic.

Beyond the objection to the practice of transplanting existing staff to the island in an attempt to circumvent local hiring requirements, the program also faces critiques regarding the selective engagement of EDC businesspeople with the larger community of St. Croix, and what critics argue is the repositioning of *some* Crucians through this program. Pointing to the fact that many EDC workers are middle and upper middle class, and very often attended private grammar and high schools together, EDC detractors claim that there is an inside network from which these companies select their "local" employees. These practices are the cause of resentment for many Crucians outside of these networks, who charge that EDC companies are "racist," a gloss for the class, race, and color discrimination they see at work in EDC hiring. This charge is the stuff of madness to EDC advocates, who understand and present the program as the salvation of St. Croix's long-struggling economy. These opposing views are not, I argue, simply a matter of miscommunication. Rather, they arise from radically different expectations of capitalism and time. The latter interpretation of the program, that it will not just improve but save St. Croix, is rooted in an argument about this program's novelty, the idea that this instance of neoliberal development marks a radical break with not just the *operations* of capital but also its intentions. The notion that the cure to what ails St. Croix is foreign (that is, mainland) capital and its representatives is rooted in the assumption that the handlers of global capital desire it to be distributed more evenly, and that removing protections (or "freeing markets") will only hasten this process. Critics of the program have a different set of experiences with—and expectations of—capitalism. Given the exploitation of the Caribbean through slavery and colonialism, political and economic systems justified by racist ideology, Crucians are wary of this program and expect—often rightly—that the mainland Americans brought by the EDC program will benefit economically by trading on the region's history of racialized oppression and its current dependent political status vis-à-vis the United States.

Managers of EDC companies, required by the local government to hire Crucian workers, do often employ a kind of shorthand in their hiring practices, scouting local private high schools for promising interns and hiring graduates of these schools who have gone on to attend college in the mainland US. Through their selective hiring practices that favor Crucians who have spent time in the US and speak generally unaccented English (cultural familiarities for EDC people and their clients that ostensibly allow for communication with greater ease, thus facilitating the flow of capital), EDC managers often unwittingly engage with and build upon the tripartite system of race/color classification and hierarchy—white, brown, Black—long at work in the region.

For Crucians who are critical of the program, the well-paying positions in air-conditioned offices offered to middle- and upper-middle-class Crucian women are an extension of the division of labor between indoor "house" work and labor performed outdoors in sugarcane fields during slavery. Here again, a framing of the EDC as an attempt to return to "slave days" reemerges. For proponents of the EDC program, this charge is anathema, as they claim to simply hire the most qualified candidates. My point here is to outline what this claim of "qualified" masks vis-à-vis capital's preferred engagement with the Caribbean and its subjects. In addition to desiring the most "qualified" candidates, handlers of global capital prefer people and places to be law-abiding and "orderly," an assurance that on some level their bodies and their money will remain safe.[25] This conflation of the past and present, of using the region's history of racialized economic domination to assuage the fears of today's global elites, is at the heart of *Virgin Capital*'s concern with temporality and spectral time. Here, the region's past doesn't innocuously inform the present. Rather, it haunts, lurking in the shadows, only showing itself with startling clarity to some, while leaving others entirely unaware of the apparition.

Particularly for the Caribbean, with its long history of international trade, commerce, and communities, it is crucial to point to the ways in which the current moment is *not* a radical break with world history but is in many ways a continuation of long-standing global communication and interconnection. This is not to say there is nothing new about contemporary circulations. Technological advances, for instance, have facilitated new circuits of people, things, ideas. More than this, the current moment finds formerly discrete spaces in unexpected conversation with one another, such as international banking programs linking small islands like Tortola to financial centers like Hong Kong, a sea change Bill Maurer (1997) has theorized in his work. The existence of these novel connections is a development I recognize and even selectively applaud, while remaining insistent that seemingly "global" circulations remain unevenly distributed, strengthening some "transnational connectivities" but not others, as Inderpal Grewal has argued (2005). What is more, these newer connections are not synonymous with foundational change in the terms of relationships between (former) metropoles and peripheries, as James Ferguson (2006) has noted. Thus, despite the particularities of contemporary circulations, *Virgin Capital* holds on to the elements of the past at work in current processes, as it focuses on the material *conditions* as well as local and global histories that facilitate these connections. This orientation creates a space for me to engage with both the on-the-ground conditions as well as the variously positioned actors that make these circulations possible. As scholars have pointed out in recent years, actual people in actual places make global circulations—and particularly financial circulations—possible (see, for instance, Ho 2009; Bear 2015; Yanagisako 2002).

In the introduction to *Globalization and Race*, Kamari Clarke and Deborah Thomas argue for the existence of what they term "racialized circulations." That is, they point to the need to ask "who travels, what travels, and how transnational alliances are tied to particular knowledge economies" (9). In the same vein, I dwell here on the particular histories that facilitate one instantiation of neoliberal development, exploring the continued salience of race, color, and gender, asking, "How do contemporary circulations of capital and people alternately build upon and complicate hierarchies long-present in the Caribbean?" That is, I take up the continuing centrality—in many cases, the increasing salience—of raced and gendered identities today. To this end, my research engages with the relatively privileged Crucian workers sitting at EDC desks. My focus is on the *support* positions that enable capital to circulate through the USVI, the people—mostly young women—who answer the phones and prepare the reports at EDC companies—local employees who allow these American financial entities to qualify for EDC benefits. This engagement enables me to explore the degree to which their positions are influenced by racialized histories as well as how their labor facilitates the US Virgin Islands becoming a node in global financial routes. For the Caribbean—with its long history of slavery and colonialism and particularly a present-day territory such as the USVI—emergent relationships between states and markets are often to the disadvantage or the complete theoretical elision of island residents while simultaneously relying on their labor.

The EDC program is a reflection of the current moment in the long history of economic development initiatives in the Caribbean. Following the collapse of plantation agriculture, attempts at economic revitalization in the region have focused on homesteading, tourism, industrialization—and now virtual transfers of wealth and information. While it may seem a linear trajectory, it is perhaps more productive to understand these models as existing in relation to one another, furtively smuggling in preexisting hierarchies, divisions, and expectations while creating new avenues through which they are confronted, affirmed—and *sometimes* subverted. The story of present-day circulations of capital in the Caribbean is neither wholly determined by the region's past nor entirely new. Rather, it is a hybrid of these—steeped in centuries-long processes of accumulation, while taking advantage of new pathways created by the current moment.[26] This development initiative, the EDC, is particular to St. Croix, but it is hardly unique in the current neoliberal moment. Rather, I use this program in an attempt to tell a larger story about contemporary capital accumulation and the political and cultural continuities of colonialism. Beyond St. Croix, or even the Caribbean region, mine is an analysis that situates the current moment in dialectal relation with past processes and points to the ways in which contemporary processes continue to be influenced by and draw from their predecessors while simultaneously adding new layers of complexity to these historical relations. Rather than being a tale focused on St. Croix, or even the wider Caribbean, *Virgin Capital* dwells upon the history that informs the operation of global capital today.

Methodology

The ethnographic grounding of this book is sixteen months of fieldwork I conducted in the USVI, primarily on St. Croix, during which I asked questions, hung around, and worked as an unpaid "intern" in order to explore the social, cultural, and political effects of the

EDC program. During this time, I gained insight into the public- and private-sector perspectives of this program by working with both the local government and two financial management companies receiving EDC benefits. My work with the government took the form of a five-month internship with the local agency responsible for overseeing the program, the Economic Development Authority (EDA). During this internship, I assisted with reviewing the EDC application process, attended public and private hearings relating to the program, and met with EDC beneficiaries. My primary ethnographic engagement with the private sector of this program took place through two internships I performed at EDC companies simultaneously over the course of eleven weeks.

Like the EDC girls I studied, my ability to secure these affiliations was informed by my access to privilege: I had been born and raised on St. Croix, and while I had attended public school for much of my primary education, I had—importantly—attended the parochial high school on the island, an experience that brought me into regular contact with high school students attending private school, given our largely shared social networks. Given this local educational background and my later experience attending both college and graduate school off-island (these were periods during which I lived on the US mainland, further undercutting any trace of a Crucian accent I may have had), I was squarely middle class and had preexisting friendships and acquaintances with several of the people who would go on to find employment in the EDC sector—and who would, later, become my informants. In addition to my class and gender, my race and *color* were vital to the way I was received by both EDC workers and EDC people. As a mixed-race daughter of a white German mother and Black father, I presented with the lighter complexion prized by the pigmentocracy at work across the Caribbean, and this color privilege worked to my benefit as I reached out to various EDC companies and ultimately secured "internships" at St. Croix Fund and Stanford.

One rendering of this reflection upon, and disclosure of, my own class, racial, and gendered subjectivity is that it is too inward-looking and self-indulgent. After all, the intervention of *Virgin Capital* is to situate and theorize an economic development initiative. Yet, the work of feminist anthropologists including Dana-Ain Davis and Christa Craven (2016) and Irma McClaurin (2001) has argued for the importance of autoethnography as a methodological and writing practice, particularly for anthropologists of color. In *Feminist Ethnography: Thinking through Methodologies, Challenges, and Possibilities*, Davis and Craven note that in response to critiques of autoethnography (such as those outlined earlier), feminist ethnographers have responded by, for instance, pointing to the "value of reflecting on one's own position to give context and nuance to ethnographic work" (Davis and Craven 2016: 134). Seen in this light, the disclosure of my positioning is an attempt to complicate the researcher/informant binary and reflect upon the ways in which my background and presentation informed my access to the EDC sector.

Chapter Summaries

In order to explore the central issues of the EDC program, this text is divided into five remaining chapters:

Chapter 2 outlines my methodology and introduces the two companies with which I interned during fieldwork. This chapter also provides me an opportunity to reflect upon my positionality in the field as a native anthropologist returning to the USVI in order to conduct this research. Rooted in my ethnographic engagement with my fellow workers, this chapter details my experience of becoming viewed as a quasi-EDC girl—an ambivalent position occupied by Crucian women working at EDCs.

Chapter 3 offers a history of the islands now known as the USVI and traces the economic and political history of St. Croix, St. Thomas, and St. John, while situating this history in the larger context of the region. Here I engage with development attempts in the Caribbean over time, addressing the successes and shortfalls that contributed to the turn toward finance-as-development programs, such as the EDC.

Chapter 4 traces the implosion of Stanford Financial and connects this spectacular failure to the larger shortcomings of the program and the longer history of development across the region.

Chapter 5 examines the relationship between EDC people and the broader community of St. Croix. This chapter is an analysis of the ever-shifting us/them binary between EDC people and Crucians, as well as Crucians and migrants from neighboring Caribbean islands.

A central focus of this chapter is the attempt to answer the question, "How do Crucians understand the presence of these 'Others'?" This question necessitates a discussion of the escalation of racially charged violence on the island and addresses the multiple and shifting race- and class-based antagonisms that were reinvigorated in the US Virgin Islands with the introduction of the EDC program.

Chapter 6 is an explicit engagement with the central issue of gender vis-à-vis the EDC program. This chapter examines the position of female EDC employees (EDC girls) and takes up the gendered expectations governing their behavior, connecting these to the larger discourse of respectability both within and outside of the Caribbean. "EDC girls," a group of local women who have contributed to the creation of a new social category on St. Croix, navigate the expectations of their employers in the EDC sector and those of the broader community around issues of spending, behavior, and belonging. This chapter traces this new ambivalent identity and its groundings in both long-standing local expectations surrounding women and emergent expectations concerning their levels of consumption. This engagement with the EDC program centers on middle-class women hired and trained by EDC companies to do a different—but related—kind of service.

Taken together, these chapters situate St. Croix in the long history of Caribbean development and contextualize the EDC program in the current moment. Bridging the positions of disenfranchised Crucians, who object to the EDC as a return to white domination in the model of slavery, and program supporters, who understand it as a radical break with the past and a step toward "progress," *Virgin Capital* argues that the EDC program on St. Croix contains elements of both: it is a program made possible by contemporary circulations, yet one that is rooted in historically informed hierarchies and circuits and the ongoing project of American empire. It is this ability of the EDC program to simultaneously conjure up the past and the future that I explore in the chapters that follow.

Chapter 2

Into the Field

Navigating Self-Reflexivity at "Home"

As I was driving my very-used car around St. Croix one day, I turned to a local radio station and heard an announcement about an upcoming event, an economic summit that would focus on ways to stimulate the island's lagging economy. The summit was scheduled to be held on the St. Croix campus of the University of the Virgin Islands in September 2007. After a few phone calls, I was registered as a volunteer for this public economic forum.

The economic summit boasted a deep roster of invitees and speakers, including local government officials and representatives from many of the island's private-sector businesses. The keynote speakers at this two-day conference were particularly impressive and included the then governor of the USVI, the senior editor of *Fortune* magazine, and a billionaire who was the topic of much discussion on the island as a result of his recent decision to relocate his substantial business enterprise to St. Croix. The words of this final speaker, Allen Stanford, were met with rapt attention as he talked about his commitment to the Caribbean, the importance of investing in the region, the necessity of overhauling the EDC legislation to compete more aggressively in the global market, and the importance of routing what he termed "pirates in the Caribbean." An article appearing in the *VI Source* immediately following the summit outlined Stanford's position:

The U.S. should jump start a wave of investment in the
Virgin Islands and the wider Caribbean Basin with changes
to the tax code, Texas and Antigua billionaire Allen
Stanford told St. Croix Economic Summit participants
Friday. Stanford heads the Stanford Financial Group, a
private, family-owned group of companies founded by his
grandfather in 1932. He was listed at no. 239 on Forbes
Magazine's latest list of the 400 wealthiest Americans.

Stanford shared his personal vision for a more prosperous Caribbean Basin, and the role the U.S. government,
the Virgin Islands and St. Croix in particular can play in
bringing about that vision. "On St. Croix, I believe a
big part of attracting the right kind of serious investors,
is if . . . the outdated EDC tax-incentive legislation was
rewritten as a new law," he said. "One that absolutely
eliminated tax cheating, that is simple to understand and
unambiguous." (Kossler 2007)

While at the St. Croix Economic Summit, I approached representatives
from several EDC companies, including a small hedge fund called
St. Croix Fund, as well as Stanford Financial, informing them of my
research and asking about the possibility of spending time at their
companies. Employment in this sector is highly sought-after, and
after encountering early resistance from EDC businessmen unwill-
ing to talk with me about the program, I was pleasantly surprised
when managers from both companies agreed to talk with me the
following week.

Becoming a "Nontraditional" Intern

On my first visit to St. Croix Fund, I was greeted by the sight of
employees gathered in the company's kitchen, eating roti and chatting, some leaning on cabinets and others sitting on the countertop.
Dressed casually in linen pants or jeans with T-shirts, these workers
were in the middle of lunch when I asked where I could find the
head of the company, Peter Davies. Being directed to a glass-paneled
conference room overlooking the Caribbean Sea, I found Davies,
dressed in khakis, a polo shirt, and sandals, surrounded by piles of

paper on a mahogany table that filled the room. Standing to greet me, Davies jokingly apologized for the state of the office. He went on to explain the nature of his business and asked me about my research and interest in the EDC program. A gregarious man in his early thirties, Davies had been described to me by friends familiar with the EDC sector as someone who took seriously his commitment to his adopted home of St. Croix and "got it"—that is, he was described as a wealthy white man who had relocated his business to St. Croix from the US mainland, but one who understood the social, cultural, and political impact moves such as his had caused on the island. Moving to St. Croix from the Northeast in 2003, Davies came with his wife and three young children to benefit from the tax relief offered by the EDC program and had quickly begun partnering with local nonprofit organizations and politicians. While Davies became active in assisting several causes, including education and animal welfare, he refused to displace local leaders and activists— many of whom were notoriously outspoken and remained quick to remind Davies of his status as an "outsider," despite his donations.

As our conversation went on, I explained my research and interest in working with his company, one of the EDC's with the longest presence on the island. Telling me of his own interest in anthropology, Davies agreed to "hire" me as an unpaid intern for the summer of 2008. During the eleven-week period, I was to serve as something of an office assistant, helping the receptionist, Xio, with daily tasks and working to organize Davies's office during the slow summer months. Excited about the prospect of gaining firsthand experience as an EDC employee, I left the relaxed atmosphere of St. Croix Fund and went home to prepare for my interview at Stanford Financial, scheduled for the following day.

Walking into the office of Stanford Financial the next day was a radically different experience from my interview at St. Croix Fund. Having been repeatedly warned about the strict dress code at Stanford by friends and informants, as well as being chastised for having the audacity to interview at this company at all, I walked into the office—more than a little nervous—dressed in a pencil skirt, long-sleeved blouse, and stockings. As my high heels clacked on the marble tiles in the office and echoed in the silent lobby, I was greeted by a petite white woman in her twenties whom I had long known through mutual friends. The receptionist—a position called a "concierge" in the parlance of Stanford—was named Melody. When I walked into the office that first day, Melody had her hair pulled into a chignon and was dressed in a slightly personalized version of the company's uniform of slacks, a dress shirt and blazer, and closed-toe pumps—along with the company's signature lapel pin. I waited in one of the several leather armchairs in the lobby while she phoned the manager scheduled to interview me. After a few moments, she directed me to a large conference room, which had an enormous wooden table surrounded by matching leather office chairs as its focal point. Not long after I sat down, Martin Matthews, the man I had met at the economic summit and who was currently on island for a few days to attend meetings, walked into the room, talking with another man. Accompanying him was a second man, whom I had not met before, a manager named Joseph Conners. When we all sat down, Matthews explained that—if given the position—I would be working closely with Conners.

As I explained my project once more, both men expressed an interest in "cultivating local talent" and having me come on board as an intern. I was assured of the position but was told I would be unable to start until a month later. The trouble, Matthews explained, had to do with space—having recently relocated to St. Croix, the company already had more employees (both hired locally and brought from the mainland) than it could accommodate. This problem was being addressed, however, as Stanford had already opened four offices and an executive suite in downtown Christiansted as well as an office in Frederiksted. In addition to these, the island was abuzz with news of Stanford's plans to build a 105,000-square-foot megacomplex. Talk of this development was everywhere that summer, and when groundbreaking took place in 2008, news sources both on island and on the mainland covered the event. An article on Reuters. com noted that "the Stanford Financial Group global management complex will be located on a 37-acre site at the southwest corner of the Henry E. Rohlsen International Airport and will house the Stanford companies' worldwide management functions and serve as the head office for Stanford's operations in the Caribbean. The new, state-of-the-art facility will serve as the base for the corporate support functions of Stanford's global network of financial services companies, including the Chairman's office and the business technology, compliance, finance, human resources, investment strategy and legal departments. Stanford will also establish in St. Croix the management offices for the Stanford 20/20 Cricket Tournament and Stanford Caribbean Investments" (Guyton 2008).

In addition to Stanford's financial management ventures, his stake in the cricket market—an arena he entered during his time in Antigua—was substantial. At the groundbreaking of his St. Croix complex, he told attendees that his Stanford 20/20 cricket tournament would be broadcast the following weekend to "150 million viewers, [and] the grand championship will have up to 500 million viewers" (Kossler 2008a). In fact, newspaper, television, and radio advertisements for the Stanford 20/20 cricket tournament were difficult to avoid on St. Croix during the period of my fieldwork, despite the lack of perceptible interest in the sport. While cricket is hugely popular in Antigua, and in many former British colonies, the short period of time during which St. Croix was ruled by the British (compared with the lasting influences of the Danish and the Americans) has resulted in a lack of familiarity with or perceptible interest in cricket on St. Croix compared to sports such as baseball and basketball. The notable exception to this is that the sport is played and followed by members of communities of Antiguans and British Virgin Islanders on St. Croix (so-called "down-islanders" or "garrotes").[1] Throughout my childhood, I would often walk past an auto repair shop near the center of the island that employed a number of immigrants from surrounding islands, such as Antigua and Dominica. As I walked past this shop in the late afternoons, I would watch in fascination as the employees set up the field with what appeared to be small hammers to play a sport I did not recognize. While conducting fieldwork, I found myself walking past this same makeshift cricket pitch, reflecting on the continued implications of differing colonial histories that had resulted in a child on St. Croix being entirely unfamiliar with the sport of cricket, as well as the fact that such varying experiences were glossed over by Stanford in his plan to expand his empire. Such historical differences between islands and their residents continue to be significant in the current moment and have become even more so with the addition of EDC people to St. Croix, as long-simmering tensions between Virgin Islanders and "down-islanders" have been reignited in recent years as a result of the racial and ethnic tensions brought to the fore by the arrival of this community of wealthy whites (a development I discuss in detail in chapter 5).

While acknowledged by the mainland press, news coverage of Stanford's megacomplex was much more effusive in the local media. Invitations to the groundbreaking ceremony were coveted and seemed to signal one's status on the island, as noted by the *St. Croix Source*:

> It was a glamorous affair. Guests walked a walkway lined with potted plants into a carpeted, air-conditioned tent the size of a hotel conference center on the spot where the complex is to be. Inside the tent, well-dressed, smiling Stanford representatives directed arrivals to their spots, filling their hands with glossy materials in smartly embossed folders.
>
> Several wall-sized photographic prints were arrayed along the back of the transitory conference center, forming a single, house-sized graphic advertising display reminiscent of a travel magazine ad.
>
> The glossy commemorative ceremony program clutched in most hands had copies of letters from various notables, topped by a note from President George W. Bush.
>
> "I send greetings to those gathered in St. Croix, Virgin Islands to celebrate the expansion of Stanford Financial Group," the brief letter opens, above Bush's signature in wide, felt-marker strokes.
>
> [Governor] deJongh said Stanford's arrival is a boon to St. Croix. "I think today, Sir Allen, you have given the push over the tipping point for St. Croix to take off," he said. "We used to say to people coming back looking for careers on St. Croix, 'Have you tried the private sector?' " Now we say, 'Have you gone to Stanford?' " (Kossler 2008a)

Indeed, it is difficult to overstate the excitement and feverish anticipation of Stanford's expansion on St. Croix. The newspaper *St. Croix Avis* noted that in addition to the office complex, Stanford was also in the process of "building a $38 million estate in Christiansted [which he said would] be one of the nicest houses in the world" (Editorial 2008). While Stanford's cricket interests and the construction of his personal homes were topics of discussion on the island, the enormity of the airport-adjacent complex, located "so he will be able to bring in people from all over the world [on] his private jets," dominated much conversation—and the news cycle—on St. Croix in late 2007 and 2008 (Editorial 2008). An article in the *St. Croix Avis* gives a sense of the atmosphere surrounding the groundbreaking ceremony:

> Executive Director of the Virgin Islands Port Authority Darlan Brin, whom Stanford selected as the ceremony's guest speaker [said], "This venture is the most significant since Leon Hess constructed Hess Oil on St. Croix. Any person can plan, but not everyone can implement or execute and the implementation process must be organized during the planning stages. This development is an impetus to attracting new business on St. Croix; this is our gateway to the Caribbean in the financial world." (Wiltshire 2008)

In response to this adulation, Stanford expressed his own excitement at relocating his enterprise, summing up his feelings about St. Croix with the statement, "For me, personally I am home" (Wiltshire 2008). This feeling of being at "home," demonstrated through Stanford's large land purchases, was largely experienced by Crucians as a grab at *ownership* of the island, rather than any attempt at community integration; many on St. Croix chafed at his move, seeing this home-coming-by-way-of-dispossession as a microcosm of the larger dynamic between the USVI and United States in light of ongoing concerns about land availability and affordability in the USVI, particularly on the island of St. John.

Stanford Financial was a global financial enterprise consisting of a commercial bank, an insurance company, and wealth management services that relocated to St. Croix in 2007. St. Croix Fund, in contrast, relocated to St. Croix from the continental United States in 2003 and was an informal company, headed by two relatively young business partners. These two beneficiary companies were both financial entities, yet they were—in terms of structure, organization, and operation—at opposite ends of the EDC spectrum: while St. Croix Fund was a hedge fund with ten employees, Stanford Financial employed approximately fifty people across its five expanding offices on St. Croix and was the subject of much discussion, and rumor, on the island. While both of these EDC companies were well known on the island—and employment at either was coveted—working for Stanford afforded a particularly high social status on St. Croix, a point raised by many of my fellow Stanford employees—by way of both complaint and celebration. During our conversations at work, many female employees at Stanford expressed concern about the fact that employment at this company carried with it both behavioral expectations and assumptions about one's financial position and decision-making ability within the company. For example, one frequent grievance had to do with the fact that they often received unsolicited résumés from friends, family, and in many cases strangers on the street. My engagement with the position of these workers forms the basis of chapter 6.

In addition to Stanford Financial and St. Croix Fund, I interned for five months with the Virgin Islands agency responsible for overseeing the program, the Economic Development Authority (EDA). During this internship, I assisted with reviewing the EDC application process, attended public and private hearings relating to the program, and met with EDC beneficiaries. Working with the local government in this way allowed me access to legislators and stakeholders on St. Croix as well as provided insight into their understanding of the role of the EDC program.

While I knew at the outset of fieldwork that working with EDC companies would be crucial to the project, it was not until I began the process of interviewing at these companies and hearing businessmen recount their often-onerous experiences of becoming beneficiaries that I realized it would be equally important to work with the agency responsible for making this process so "frustrating" for them. Charged with monitoring existing beneficiaries as well as processing new applicants, the EDA ultimately served as my first unpaid internship during fieldwork, a role that allowed me to glimpse into the inner workings of the program as a whole, providing me with familiarity with companies receiving EDC benefits, and, equally importantly, those with applications in process.

Beyond spending time with local officials and EDC companies, I also conducted research with residents of St. Croix not affiliated with the EDC program, including local elected officials, small business owners, and community organizers, in order to get at broader perceptions of the initiative and its effects on daily life. During these conversations, several issues of concern arose regularly, including hiring preferences on the part of many EDC companies that worked to benefit applicants from backgrounds of relative privilege in relation to color, class, and gender. In addition, the presumed insularity on the part of much of the EDC community, including their cultivation of increasingly "exclusive" residential and social spaces, contributed to the distrust with which many residents of St. Croix viewed the program and its participants. The formation of these new spaces translated into a discourse of "us/them" or "belongers/non-belongers" on St. Croix, a particularly contentious topic of conversation that featured prominently in this region characterized by long-standing and intense inter-island migration patterns. While beginning as a separation between EDC people and the larger community of St. Croix, this division sparked broader concerns about belonging and homeland, resulting in renewed demands for the rights of "native Virgin Islanders" (an extremely fraught category), clashes between longtime residents over the primacy of birthplace, and the displacement of long-term white residents as "gatekeepers" on St. Croix. What is more, the notion of "belonging" on St. Croix was necessarily informed by the fact that the island remains a possession of the United States, giving recently arrived EDC people as much claim to belong as those with generations-long presence on the island. All of these tensions swirled as I attempted to navigate a balance between homecoming and fieldwork.

"You Is One of We": Positionality in the Field

While in the field, I also grappled with what I often thought of as competing identities, as both a Crucian and an ostensibly objective anthropologist. In addition to this, the multiple, cross-cutting identities that I inhabited as a Crucian impacted both my access to informants and the lenses through which I viewed the information they shared with me. As spectral time is central to my analysis of the EDC program, it also impacted the way I conducted fieldwork, as contemporary events connected to the program (particularly those connected to "racist" behavior or events) would resonate with long-ago happenings I either grew up hearing about or directly remembered from my childhood, such that the past and present would seemingly merge in uncanny ways. For instance, the whispers of a long-ago "bad event" that I heard about throughout my childhood came clearly into view as the Fountain Valley massacre, a racially charged act of violence that divided St. Croix deeply along lines of black and white in the 1970s and one that was invoked by my informants by way of warning the EDC and its "people" of the dangers of classed/raced insularity and overt acts of racism.

At the time I conducted the fieldwork for this project, I was a woman my midtwenties, unmarried, and without children. Like ethnographers before me who conducted research in their home communities, I was often pushed to reflect on my positionality as a "native anthropologist" and consider the ways this positioning both allowed for increased access to my informants and complicated my ability to gather information. While Zora Neale Hurston famously described the discipline of anthropology as a tool—in her words, a "spy glass"[2]—with which she was better able to apprehend quotidian life in her home community, John Gwaltney took a different tack; the infamous epigraph to his text *Drylongso* reads: "I think this anthropology is just another way to call me a nigger." My approach to fieldwork was neither as utilitarian as Hurston's nor as cynical as that of Gwaltney's informant. Rather, the experience of conducting research in the place of my birth and childhood existed somewhere between these two poles; viewing anthropology neither as a tool that reliably provides much-needed distance nor as a discipline that exists solely for race-baiting, I situate my experience of working as a native anthropologist as an instance of belonging complexly—a positioning that necessitated working through allegiances, misunderstandings, and lingering notions of objectivity daily.

As it was meant to do, my anthropological training taught me the necessity of self-reflexivity on the part of the researcher if there is to be any hope of presenting a comprehensive ethnographic account (this same training demonstrated that a complete reproduction or telling of one's experience in "the field" is, by definition, impossible). And yet, it would be impossible for me to tell this story of the EDC program without telling the story of St. Croix. That is, I could not present an analysis of this initiative without inserting myself first as a girl, and then a woman, whose memories and worldview are completely tethered to that island and its changing fortunes. In order to tell any version of St. Croix's history of development, it is vital that I recognize the crucial "back door" access I had to informants on the island as a Crucian, born and raised on St. Croix. This admission of my positioning is meant as a gesture toward disclosure and honesty—yet it obscures nearly as much as it reveals: What does it mean to label a lifelong friend as an "informant"? How seriously, despite my most earnest efforts, did such friends, acquaintances, and neighbors take my "new" role as researcher—did I always remain "one of we"? Did these "subjects" remain "informants" on joint family vacations? During late-night phone calls? Or, when they were completely unable to understand me as anything other than a "native Crucian," necessarily opposed to the "others" brought to "our" island by a development program?

The divisions between "self" and "other," "researcher" and "informant," and even—with the combination of newer technologies like social networking websites with long-standing anthropological realities like the determination of some informants to demand favors long after the conclusion of formal fieldwork—"then" and "now" become, if not completely indistinct, increasingly faint. Certainly, these questions are not new. Anthropologists have grappled with them since the birth of the discipline—but perhaps no amount of training, of reading the accounts of others, is sufficient preparation for the mix of calculatedly professional and intensely personal experiences that characterize fieldwork. As the EDC is both old and new (it is a dynamic and "new" program—yet for some on the island it seems merely the most recent iteration of long-operating processes), so too are these struggles with fieldwork.

Here, I must make one final disclosure about the relationship between researcher and research by way of explaining the origins of this project. In 2003, shortly after graduating from a liberal arts college on the mainland US (or in "the States," as it is commonly known on the island), I returned home to St. Croix and, after a while, began looking for a job. Having recently earned a bachelor's degree in cultural anthropology, I found my search for work difficult at first. However, after a few weeks, a friend whom I knew from my high school network of house parties and varsity volleyball matches suggested I apply for "an EDC job." When I explained that I knew nearly nothing about economics or finance, he told me that my lack of experience was irrelevant, as companies were simply looking for "the right kind of local" to meet their hiring requirements. Building on the connections he provided, I prepared my résumé, and in the space of one week was offered two EDC jobs. Feeling unease about my clear underqualification for any job in finance and a lack of clarity about what work, exactly, I would be doing at these companies (the job descriptions I was given centered around vague comments about "office maintenance"), I declined these positions. Eventually, I would go on to graduate study and years later, during the period of my fieldwork, I was to bear witness to the inability of many of my friends and neighbors to even secure interviews in this well-paying sector. Unable to capitalize on the privileges of mobility, accent, color, and class as I had during my EDC interview process, they—presumably—were not "the right kind of local."

Becoming an "EDC Girl"

At the outset of my internships, I was unsure what, exactly, my days would entail. While my interviews at both St. Croix Fund and Stanford Financial had gone well, I was left wondering what role I would perform. Deciding it would be most productive to split my workweek between the two companies, I ultimately settled on working Monday through Wednesday at Stanford and spending Thursdays and Fridays at St. Croix Fund. From the outset, the scope, newness, and excitement surrounding Stanford compared with the size and comparatively long-term presence of St. Croix Fund told me that the environments in these companies would be vastly different.

During my first week at Stanford, my time was largely spent going through orientation, a process that mostly involved watching informational videos on the company and its history and getting introduced around the office. As was decided during my interview, I would be working closely with Joseph Conners, a likeable forty-some-thing man from the US South who worked as a senior investment analyst. While the Stanford office I was assigned to had many local employees of color, primarily in administrative and support positions, Joe was the only mainland Black employee with whom I worked. During my internship, I was to be a junior analyst under the super-vision of Joe. My tasks included researching possible investments and evaluating financial trends in order to assess the likely success of various investment strategies. Along with Joe and me, the particular Stanford office at which I worked housed eleven other employees, seven of whom were local women of color. Of these, six fit the standard profile of EDC girls: relatively young (in their twenties or thirties) and educated on the US mainland.[3] What was unique about this company and its employees vis-à-vis the EDC program as a whole was the styling of these workers—a difference that was a matter of degree, rather than of type. If EDC girls were seen on the island as set apart and somehow "different" from their fellow Virgin Islanders (an issue that is the focus of chapter 5), the local women employed at Stanford were seen as the epitome of that difference. Stanford's great wealth, the excitement surrounding his arrival on St. Croix, and the company's strict dress code that made no concessions to the unforgiving Caribbean heat—an issue that was particularly relevant during summer, the period of my internship—made Stanford and his employees central topics of discussion on the island among both supporters and critics. In addition to the workplace dress of slacks or skirts, blazers, closed-toe shoes, and stockings for women (a requirement that was unspoken, yet strictly observed in the office), other aesthetics surrounding the women working at Stanford marked them as different, not the least of which was the much-commented-upon golden lapel pin that employees received shortly after beginning their employment. Perhaps as a marker of my liminal inclusion in the Stanford enterprise, I received a keycard granting me access to the building in which I worked but was never awarded this singular status marker, although a woman who began at the company on the same day I did was invited to dinner with several managers a few weeks into her employment and ceremoniously presented with her golden brooch. This lapel pin, an embossed gold rendering of the company's trademark eagle, was often noticed and commented upon by island residents. While having lunch with friends near the office in Christiansted, I frequently noticed the ways in which the staff at various restaurants catered and were particularly attentive to Stanford workers, a group that was marked apart from the lawyers and even other EDC girls in the area by this pin.

In comparison to Stanford, the environment at St. Croix Fund was very casual. This small company that employed approximately ten workers at any given time was one of the EDC businesses that encouraged employees to "dress down." During fieldwork, I often heard objections to the casual dress code at EDCs. For many Crucians, the notion of arriving to work wearing flip flops was anathema and flew in the face of local notions of appropriate dress, a cultural construction common throughout much of the formerly colonized

Caribbean. Writing on the nearby British Virgin Islands, Bill Maurer (1997) notes, "BVIslanders complain that white people and many American blacks are sloppy and lack 'style.' People often comment on how they dress, especially how women dress. The worst thing for a woman to do in the BVI is to wear a 'shapeless' or 'unstructured' dress. People are expected to be neat and pressed. BVIslanders like sharp lines and shoulder pads, not flowing waves of loose fabric Cleanliness, manners, and even morality are judged on the basis of the style and fit of one's clothes" (Maurer 1997: 69). Although the dress code at St. Croix Fund was not the most lax I encountered during fieldwork (that distinction went to the company at which the CEO met with me wearing board shorts and no shoes), the difference between dress expectations of St. Croix Fund and Stanford was significant. Moreover, behavioral expectations were vastly different at these companies: employees at Stanford rarely talked about personal matters during work hours and cultivated an air of formality when addressing each other in the office, while workers at the much-smaller St. Croix Fund frequently joked with each other and relayed stories in a mix of business English and Crucian—a dialect with which I was familiar and one I never heard employees using at Stanford. In fact, it is difficult to even imagine Crucian being spoken at Stanford, given the solemnity of the office.

Read alongside one another, my early experience interviewing for employment at EDC companies and my later fieldwork encounters with this sector demonstrate the deep impact that access to privilege has vis-à-vis this initiative. As access to informal networks (where news of internships and jobs are often shared), relative wealth, and lighter skin—all, that is to say, coming from the "right" background—are often precursors to well-paying EDC employment, privilege begets privilege. Here, history in the form of preexisting hierarchies is the ground upon which contemporary stratification is not only maintained—but magnified. Throughout the remaining chapters, I examine how Crucians engage with the benefits and costs of the newfound forms of privilege made possible through the EDC program.

Chapter 3

Spectral Time

Tracing Racial Capitalism in the USVI
from Plantation Slavery to the
Economic Development Commission

The racialized anxiety brought to the fore by the EDC program did not begin with this initiative. Rather, flashes of these tensions in the USVI can be traced alongside paradigm shifts in economic development: as new waves of migration have occurred to fill labor shortages, anxieties around belonging and displacement have also emerged. That Crucians ground their critique of neoliberal development (of which the EDC is but an instance) in the framework of *slavery* demonstrates the long history of racial capitalism that has engendered these anxieties.

Moments of racially dependent capital accumulation in the USVI have included slavery, yes, but also a circuitous history of colonialism, with these islands having been ruled by seven different colonial powers to date: Spain, England, French, Dutch, the Knights of Malta, Denmark, and the United States. In this chapter, I outline much of this history as a way of providing necessary background that informs Crucians' critiques of the EDC. On its face, the claim that a banking program has as its aim a return to enslavement is patently ridiculous, as EDC proponents are eager to point out. However, through a detailed engagement with the history of these islands, centering their role in projects that were predicated on the exploitation of Black people, the logic—and fear—that undergirds this critique begins to emerge.

The islands today known as the US Virgin Islands were "discovered" in 1493 for Spain by Christopher Columbus, who named St. Croix "Santa Cruz." Spain would long maintain a nominal presence on these islands, while devoting much of its attention to the nearby, and far more profitable, possession of Puerto Rico. With the waning of Spanish influence, a number of European countries briefly occupied St. Croix, jockeying for position and attempting to extract value from the island. Today, the Virgin Islands engages with this past with a mix of pride and reverence, notably in the realms of politics and tourism: the flags of the United States, Denmark, and the USVI fly over Government House on St. Croix, and the flags of all seven powers that have ruled the island remain hoisted on flagpoles in Sunny Isle, the island's central shopping district. In December 1970, in advance of the first gubernatorial election in the territory (the previous governors having been externally appointed), the Virgin Islands legislature passed Bill 4705, which outlined the adornment that would identify the territory's leader during official events. This symbol, a livery collar, was created as a symbol of office that would "link the long history and culture of the Virgin Islands to an historic election of the First Elected Chief Executive Officer of the Virgin Islands" (Bill 4705, Eighth Legislature of the Virgin Islands). The rendering of this collar, a symbol still in use today, included medallions for each of the countries that had ruled the islands, presumably the "long history" to which the bill alludes.

While the territory remains invested in its long colonial past, it is the presence of the Danes and Americans that have the most significance for life in the US Virgin Islands today: Given the length of Danish rule (1671–1917), their presence on these islands remains strongly felt, particularly in relation to the built environment, as much of the architecture is quintessentially Danish (built largely from Danish brick), and the street names in the historic towns continue to include the Danish word *gade* (or street)—for instance Dronningens Gade (Queen Street) and Kongens Gade (King Street). Even the names of the two historic towns on St. Croix—Christiansted and Frederiksted—come from Danish sovereigns, kings Christian VI and Frederik V, respectively. Coupled with the long shadow cast by the Danish presence, the contemporary reality of American ownership of these islands shapes daily life. It is this status of dependency, shared by neighboring Puerto Rico, that is the ground upon which the EDC program is built.

Plantation Slavery

Before becoming the US Virgin Islands, St. Croix, St. Thomas, and St. John were the Danish West Indies (DWI), occupied by Denmark from 1671 to 1917. While St. Thomas was claimed by Danish colonists in 1672, neighboring St. Croix, some forty miles away, was not purchased from the French until 1733. During their rule, the Danish were actively engaged in the transatlantic slave trade, a global set of processes connecting Africa, Europe, and the Americas through the capture, sale, and purchase of human beings within a brutal system designed to erase their humanity and transform them into property. This trade in human beings was a defining feature of life in the Caribbean in particular, and Denmark participated in this system through its chartered company, the Danish West India and Guinea Company, from 1671 until 1754, when the islands were converted to crown colony rule under the Danish monarch. During the period of Company rule, its charter allowed for extensive inter-ventions by Company directors, including "all powers of colonial government, except the conduct of foreign relations reserved to the Danish crown . . . a monopoly of all trade with the West Indies, and its colonies could import duty-free all goods from Denmark" (Boyer 1983: 7). Expanding upon the jurisdiction of this Company, Arnold Highfield has noted the broad powers it enjoyed to "take the island of [St. Thomas] into its possession, [its] authorization to build forts, to render justice [and] to employ forced labor" (High-field 2018: 169). On the point of enslaved labor in the Danish West Indies, estimates vary on the number of slaves imported, but the number is quite certainly over one hundred thousand.[1] Given this volume, African slaves consistently outnumbered the population of white settlers on these islands,[2] and the importation of enslaved Africans to the Danish West Indies led to a wholesale transformation of life. In terms of the economy, it was the unpaid labor of slaves that allowed for the emergence of a planter class and the wealth of plantations that processed sugar, as well as smaller production levels of molasses, rum, and cotton.

It is difficult to overstate the impact of the slave trade across the Caribbean; in addition to its qualitative impact—the social and ideological orientations originating under this system that have left as their legacy societies that continue to be largely organized around race, class, and color hierarchies originated during slavery—the sheer

volume of human cargo that circulated through the region is staggering. Carmen Deere (1990) writes, "It is estimated that the Caribbean
received 47% of the 10 million African slaves brought to the Americas" (8). In addition to being necessary to any understanding of the
transatlantic slave trade, the overwhelming number of slaves in the
Caribbean also had an enormous impact in the region, as slaves greatly
outnumbered whites on many islands. On St. John, for example, the
"establishment of plantations [began] in 1717, by which time there
were eight times as many blacks as whites in a population of over
4,000" (Harrigan and Varlack 1977: 388), while on St. Thomas
slaves "comprised one-third of the total population, outnumbering
whites 336 to 225 in 1733" (388)—a ratio that contributed to a
high degree of tension, and often fear, on the part of planters and
their families. In the Danish West Indies, the ratio was of particular concern for white residents, and the colonial population briefly
attempted to shore up their numbers with indentured servants. As
was the case on many Caribbean islands, however, this system failed.[3]

Despite this imbalance in the ratio between white and Black
inhabitants of the island, the dominance of whites was established
by the dehumanization of enslaved workers and the enforced separation of whites and Blacks. On St. John, for instance, this social
order resulted in the ostracizing of members of the plantocracy who
attempted to disrupt this division: Karen Fog Olwig (1985), for
instance, recounts the charges against one Lieutenant Stürup who
had "been seen dancing in one of the slave houses" on a plantation
(20). While enslaved persons suffered extreme bodily punishments,
including those that led to death, this policing of white behavior—
particularly their near-complete separation from the enslaved workers,
while living in close proximity—is a residential and societal division
that has echoes in contemporary patterns on St. Croix today.

If white slave owners living in the Caribbean were concerned
about slave rebellions, uprisings that would have been very possible given the numerical imbalance, these fears did not dissuade
them from profiting from slave labor and trading. The production
of sugar through plantation agriculture was a particularly lucrative
endeavor, and there was much interest on the part of European
powers in entering this market. Of the countries that participated
in the trading of slaves and plantation agriculture in the Caribbean,
the most numerically significant were the British, Dutch, French,

and Spanish. The Danes entered these markets rather late and on a much smaller scale: the Danish "empire," consisting of St. Croix, St. Thomas, and St. John, has been described as "Lilliputian."[4] Beyond the small scale of these holdings, their very value to Denmark was in question: early St. Croix governor Jens Hansen pointed to the inadequacy of the Company directors he was given, noting that he had access to "twenty living men, of whom one is sixty years old, and the others such drunkards that they are hardly able to stand, much less post the watch."

As Denmark's colonial ambitions were not as far-reaching as those of its peers, its role in the history of slavery and colonization has long been understudied. Nevertheless, the dehumanizing conditions faced by enslaved persons bound for Danish territories were the same as those found on slave ships traveling under other European flags. The passage from the African continent to these islands was incredibly arduous, with enslaved Africans regularly dying during the Middle Passage from the African continent to the Americas, with living and dead remaining shackled together.[5]

Upon arrival in the Danish West Indies, slaves were purchased and distributed among the islands' plantations to cultivate crops, primarily sugar and cotton. St. Croix featured hundreds of plantation estates—with names such as La Grange and La Grande Princesse—units into which the island remains carved today. Work on the plantations was arduous, with sugar being the chief crop cultivated in the fields. Slaves worked from sunup to sundown, whether in good health or ill, and were miserably treated, with beatings and mutilations featuring prominently under Danish rule: limbs—or entire bodies—could be trapped in the grinding mills. The economic system of plantation slavery was made possible in the Caribbean, as elsewhere across the New World, by a worldview that centered whiteness as the culmination of humanity and conversely positioned Black Africans as animal-like and subhuman. This racism shaped daily life on plantations in the Danish West Indies, with Black women being singled out for a particular brand of discursive abuse, being labeled promiscuous, hypersexual, and deviant—a process of dehumanizing and "ungendering" (Spillers 1987) used to justify the systemic rape of enslaved Black women. The particular sexual and physical violence to which Black women were subject demonstrates the ways in which both race and gender were central to the operation of slavery.

What is more, this everyday inhumane treatment received by slaves in the Danish West Indies was compounded by torturous punishments. Records in the Danish colonial archives detail the penalty for enslaved Africans found to be part of a planned rebellion on St. Croix in 1759. The suspected architects of this uprising were found by Danish authorities and suffered punishments that included being burned alive and hung by the legs until suffocating to death.[6] The penalty for crimes both large and small included public whippings at Fort Christiansvaern: slaves could receive between twenty-five and five hundred lashes at the public whipping post, a hated sign of Danish slave rule. This torture device has continued to impact life on St. Croix many years after the end of slavery, as its remnants were inadvertently unearthed in the year 2000 during construction at the site of the fort,[7] a waterfront military outpost that sits only a few hundred feet away from the Stanford office where I conducted my research.

Despite all evidence to the contrary, Denmark's method of rule receives mention in literature on colonialism in the Caribbean due to its ostensible "leniency." For instance, Jens Larsen has written that "cruelty toward slaves in the Danish West Indies was not at all common except in the case of rebellions and, even then, was similar to that inflicted in Europe upon offenders against criminal laws" (Larsen 1950: 59–60). This depiction of Denmark as somehow perpetrating a benevolent form of enslavement is widespread, and thus an explicit engagement with the history of Danish slave trading and colonialism is vital to both academic literature and the daily lives of the descendants of enslaved Africans in the US Virgin Islands today.

Beyond a Narrative of Danes as "Progressive" Slaveholders

Two historical developments frequently factor into the rendering of Danish rule as benign: (1) the early date at which Denmark abolished the slave trade under its flag—1802—making it the first European flag to do so; and (2) the royal edict of 1831, permitting free Blacks to be registered as "white" on census rolls. About the first point, it must be said that abolition of the slave *trade* was not synonymous with the abolition of slavery in the Danish West Indies, as the Danes announced the decision to end their participation in this market in 1792 and allowed a ten-year "grace period," a decade during which the slave population increased upward through what have been described as "feverish importations" (Hall 1992: 3). Further, while Denmark may have been the first European nation to abolish the trading of slaves, other European powers followed suit shortly thereafter: the British Caribbean in 1807, the Dutch Caribbean in 1814, the French Caribbean in 1817. Denmark's decision to end its participation in the transatlantic slave trade did not spell the end of slavery in the Danish West Indies, as this system continued through 1848: on July 3 of that year a major slave rebellion occurred on St. Croix, led by a slave named Moses Gottlieb, better known locally as General Buddhoe. Frustrated with having the date of their emancipation pushed further and further back, enslaved Africans marched to Fort Frederik, the Danish fort on the western end of the island, and demanded that then-governor Peter von Scholten grant them their freedom. This event ultimately forced von Scholten to declare an end to slavery in the Danish West Indies, although there is much scholarly debate over the extent to which his longtime mistress, a free colored woman named Anna Heegard, influenced this decision to end the barbaric practice of enslavement in these islands.

Following this successful uprising and the abolition of slavery, workers who had been formerly enslaved remained tied by annual contracts to work on plantations for pitiably small sums of money and, as a result, rebelled against the Danish once more in 1878 during the "Fireburn" (or "Contract Day") rebellion on October 1, in which workers burned down plantations across the island and demanded fair pay for their labor. These miserable conditions are remembered in song throughout the Virgin Islands. For instance, the song "LaBega Carousel," still performed in these islands by local musicians, outlines the paltry sums and undesirable conditions under which Black workers labored to run a carousel ride on St. Croix:

> I rather walk and drink rum whole night
> Before me go ride on LaBega Carousel
> You no hear what LaBega say,
> "The people no worth more than fifteen cent a day"
> I am walking, I am looking, I am begging
> Before me go ride on LaBega Carousel.

Of the women who led the revolt, known as the "Queens" of Fireburn,[8] "Queen" Mary was the most renowned: "Queen" Mary Thomas is noted in the history of St. Croix as one of the great advocates of parity for Black residents and has been memorialized in textbooks, statues, and song. What is more, this historical memory of Queen Mary echoes the rich history of female-led slave resistance in the Caribbean, including for instance Nanny of the Maroons in Jamaica, Betto Douglas in St. Kitts and Nevis, and Adelaide Disson in Trinidad and Tobago.[9] The folksong "Queen Mary" is sung by schoolchildren, and its lyrics read in part, "Queen Mary, oh where you gon' go burn? Queen Mary oh where you gon' go burn? Don't ask me nothin' at all. Just give me the match and oil," referencing the inferno that consumed over fifty plantations and much of the town of Frederiksted (see Highfield 2014). Elsewhere, I have argued that the commands of this call and response "posit a situation in which Queen Mary and the hearers of this song engage in a joint enterprise for Black freedom over space and time,"[10] once again bringing the framework of complex time into view.

The second piece of evidence often cited in an attempt to situate Danes as benevolent slaveholders, an 1831 pronouncement by King Frederick VI that further solidified the hierarchy between enslaved Africans and those who were free, must be looked at more closely because of its direct impact on the operation of the EDC program. A contingent of free Blacks left the Danish West Indies for Copenhagen in that year, to air their grievances against Danish colonial society, including charges of frequent and illegal punishments, and put forth a request to have their rights and property respected by white planters. In response, the king issued a decree stating that certain members of the "free colored class" should not only be recognized by white Danes, but could be counted among their number:

> Where free persons of color, of both sexes, assimilate in color to the whites, and they otherwise, by a cultivated mind and good conduct render themselves deserving to stand, according to their rank and station in life, on an equal footing with the white inhabitants, all the difference which the color now causes ought to cease. The right of deciding thereon, must be left with the Governor General, *who also will direct the names of such persons to be struck off*

the protocols for the registry of the free colored population, and to be entered, as white inhabitants, in the congregation to which they belong. (Campbell 1943: 15–16; emphasis mine)

This formalization of a pigmentocracy in the Danish West Indies built upon the long-standing practice of oppression rooted in both race and color. Fundamentally grounded in the dehumanization of Black bodies, the economic system of slavery was particularly attuned to gradations of color. For instance, slave societies were contexts in which ostensibly quantifiable percentages of Blackness were marked in categories such as "mulatto" (of mixed Black and white parentage), "quadroon" (one-quarter Black), and "octoroon" (one-eighth Black). This system of racial classification had life-and-death implications for enslaved Africans, as those with lighter skin were often tasked with lighter labor and granted a reprieve from the unforgiving elements by working inside of plantation houses. Anna Heegard, for instance, was an "octoroon" as her mother was classified as a mulatto and her father white. This classification translated to lighter skin and European features, providing Heegard the ability to move more freely in society and granting her greater access to power and privilege, as seen in her public partnership with Danish governor von Scholten. Pointing to this link between color and labor, William Boyer has aptly written that working in the fields was "held in contempt by those with lighter skins, who usually had better jobs or worked less but earned more" (1983: 61).

This relationship between work and color is central to my analysis of the EDC, as the related issues of class and "social color"[11] still inform life and livelihoods today. The importance of race and color to social standing and economic possibilities into the present moment of neoliberal development on these islands, as seen in EDC hiring—a process that residents frequently point to as favoring young women with lighter complexions who, relatedly, come from backgrounds of relative class privilege. The present-day existence of a pigmentocracy in the Caribbean informs EDC hiring such that the air-conditioned office positions on offer in this sector are often occupied by lighter-skinned Crucian women. This link between color and privilege is nuanced insofar as one cannot draw a neat line from lighter skin color to relative wealth and privilege—and yet, this historic connection carries into the present moment in significant ways, particularly in relation to the EDC program. The reality that there are many dark-skinned Crucians who are middle class and have access to forms of privilege does not diminish the deep-seated color privilege at work in the Caribbean in general and in the USVI in particular. This link between color and class is demonstrated, for instance, in Jamaica through the category of "brown" (Henriques 1953) and the social capital of lighter-skinned women known as "brownings" (Mohammed 2000).[12] Conducting undergraduate fieldwork for an unrelated project in Jamaica a number of years ago, I myself was regularly hailed on the streets of Kingston as a "browning" by way of cat-calling and general identification. The color benefits that accrue in the Caribbean affect nearly every facet of life, including assumptions of wealth, propriety (Ulysse 2007), and access to services, including health care and social services.[13]

Beyond the Caribbean, other formerly colonized spaces, notably Latin America, also continue to grapple with the legacies of "social color." Contemporary analyses have produced reports with titles such as "Pigmentocracy in the Americas: How Is Educational Attainment Related to Skin Color?"[14] and "Is Mexico a Post-Racial Country? Inequality and Skin Tone across the Americas."[15] The latter, produced by USAID and Vanderbilt University, builds on data collection undertaken by the Mexican government in which a "color palette [was used] to measure individuals' skin tone" and found that "Mexicans who were classified by the interviewers as having darker skin tones tend[ed] to have lower levels of education and [be] worse off economically than their lighter skinned counterparts."[16] All that is to say that while it is crucial to apprehend the nuance of color privilege, it is not just race—but color—that matters in Latin America and the Caribbean. Unwittingly or not, color influences EDC hiring, as perceptions of a candidate's desirability for employment is assessed through a number of factors, including education and network—aspects of one's background that, in the USVI, are influenced by the historical and contemporary reality of "social color."

Toward Agricultural Development and Tourism

While slave revolts on St. Croix and, to a lesser extent, St. John[17] would eventually lead to emancipation from slavery in the Danish

West Indies, technological advances also played a role in the move away from plantation agriculture as the economic driver of these islands. On St. Thomas, the advent of maritime technology, including the development of modernized processes that reduced the geographic significance of the long-important harbor on that island, had far-reaching economic implications. On St. Croix and St. John, the international drop in the price of their primary crop, sugarcane, came largely as a result of the introduction of beet sugar. This decline was precipitous, as the 114 sugar mills to be found on St. Croix in 1796 dwindled to a single one by 1908. In addition, the economic turmoil in the DWI and throughout the Caribbean came as a result of financial shortfalls in Europe, caused by decreased production across the region following the success of the Haitian Revolution. As was the case in many societies that relied heavily on enslaved labor, the economy of the Danish West Indies went into steep decline following Emancipation (France's demand that Haiti pay compensation for loss of "property" was perhaps the most damning demonstration of this economic downturn, but plantation owners in the Danish West Indies were also compensated, by the Danish government, for their losses). However, the lack of economic profitability that befell the islands cannot be blamed solely on the loss of uncompensated labor. Rather, a series of developments, including weather events[18] and technological advances in sugar production, marked a downward turn in the economy. As a result of these factors, then, the economies of all three islands in the DWI were in peril in the nineteenth century.[19] It is under these conditions that the United States became involved: after unsuccessfully attempting to divest them through a treaty with the United States in 1902, the Danish sold St. Croix, St. Thomas, and St. John to the United States in 1917.[20]

The purchase of these islands occurred within the broader history of US domination, as the country sought to expand its holdings, given the prosperity it experienced in Puerto Rico, the Dominican Republic, and Cuba at the end of the nineteenth century. With the purchase of the former DWI, the United States owned what has been accurately termed its "first black colony," a space to which it would import the racist Jim Crow mainland policies.[21] The implications of this sale on race relations on the islands were made even more marked by the oft-cited "progressive" attitudes and policies instituted by the Danes, including the 1831 royal edict that enabled "well-behaved" free Blacks to register as white in official rolls. The complexity of race was further increased by the fact that the directors of the Danish West India Company had long delegated many tasks related to the administration of these islands to free Black and mixed-race islanders. The new owners of the islands now known as the United States Virgin Islands (USVI) entered this tangled classification system that took into account class/color/behavior[22] while firmly In the midst of its Jim Crow era.

Upon purchasing St. Croix, St. Thomas, and St. John, the Americans sought to improve both the economy and the standard of living in the USVI through such measures as social welfare programs and the introduction of American-style schools.[23] Unfortunately, many of these social improvement measures were short-lived and ultimately unsuccessful as a result of the Great Depression that began in 1929. The combination of new shipping and agricultural technology led the economies of St. Croix, St. Thomas, and St. John into such decline that US president Herbert Hoover bemoaned their purchase and infamously described these islands as the "effective poorhouse" of the United States after touring them in 1931.[24] Hoover placed much of the blame for this state of affairs squarely on the shoulders of local residents who "had made no effort to find employment in other directions when their old-time industries had declined." He was, in fact, " 'disgusted' at the way the people had ignored the gospel of self-help, and he entertained little hope that they would react favorably to that principle in the future (Evans 1945: 289). This reaction to the economic misfortunes of the territory foreshadows the salvific doctrine of neoliberalism, that financial security is first and foremost a matter of individual effort.

Given the continually depressed economies on these islands—particularly on St. Croix—as well as their varied natural resources, the Americans employed a two-pronged approach in the 1930s and 1940s: tourism on St. Thomas and agriculture on St. Croix. Regarding the latter, the Americans focused on homesteading through the Virgin Islands Company, an entity chartered in 1934 that encouraged the purchase of vacant land to be used for peasant farming and the continued cultivation of sugar. Sugarcane cultivation remained an area of economic emphasis in the newly christened US Virgin Islands in the early twentieth century, with sugar being processed at three facilities across the island of St. Croix: the Bethlehem sugar factory, the Estate Richmond factory, and the La Grange factory. Of these, the Bethlehem facility remained in operation the longest, processing sugar for the last time in 1966 (Thurland 2014). In order to find the required additional labor post-Emancipation, workers were largely drawn from surrounding Caribbean islands, including St. Kitts and Nevis, Puerto Rico, and Antigua and Barbuda (Lightfoot 2015).

As was the case during slavery, men and women continued to work alongside one another in the fields following its abolition. In her oral history collection recounting the life experiences of "cane cutters," Karen Thurland echoes this point about women's work in the sugar market, noting the labor performed by women including planting, weeding, and harvesting (2014: 145). Examining the contributions of one woman's work, Georgianna Clarke, Thurland notes that "seven days a week she got up at 4:30 or 5:00 a.m. to . . . cook breakfast, lunch, and dinner" for over two hundred cane cutters in the camp for which she was the cook (112).

While this focus on small-scale agricultural development as the route to economic prosperity is a recurring theme both in the Virgin Islands and throughout the Caribbean, the Americans broadened their approach on St. Thomas, spending their early presence on that island promoting tourism. Larger hotels were built, which were meant to house the hoped-for tourists that would shore up the nascent industry, a sector that would take off in earnest in the 1950s, after Americans lost access to their preferred Caribbean vacation destination of Havana following the Cuban Revolution. This focus on tourism—and away from agriculture—on St. Thomas included the promotion of a newly created Carnival that began in 1952. The development of a tourist sector was transformative for the small island of St. John, as well, with the establishment of Caneel Bay resort by Laurence Rockefeller. Rockefeller's donation of large tracts of land on St. John to the US government, and the subsequent establishment of much of the island as a national park in 1956, has long frustrated local residents who object to restrictions on hunting and accessibility placed by the US federal government both then and now. Crystal Fortwrangler (2007), for instance, has pointed to the racialized exclusions related to this park, including a critique of programming that marginalizes or excludes Black history on St. John. Fortwrangler's work also names power divisions tied to funding of the park, as this money largely comes from the white community on the island. Describing the independent group that pursues funding for the park, Fortwrangler writes that it is generally seen as "a 'lily-white organization' unconcerned with issues of importance to St. Johnians and disrespectful of St. Johnians' unique and historical relationship with the island" (2007: 512). In a different register, these concerns echo those of Virgin Islanders on St. Croix who fear cultural and physical displacement in the wake of the EDC program.

The transformation of St. John from a small farming island to a tourist destination in the 1950s was so complete in 1985 that Karen Fog Olwig wrote, "A large number of St. Johnians worked at Caneel Bay in the mid-fifties, and it is difficult to find many St. Johnians over forty-five years of age today who have not at some point in their lives worked at the resort" (1985: 165). With the advent of this new source of income, questions around labor and the benefit of this industry for Virgin Islanders arose, as workers from surrounding islands (particularly the neighboring British Virgin Islands) came to St. John to find work in the newly established tourist market. This importation of labor began largely as a result of the dissatisfaction of St. Johnians who complained about substandard pay, miserable working conditions, and no route to upward mobility within the industry. The arrival of workers to fill these employment slots contributed to simmering tensions and economic competition between Virgin Islanders and those who had their roots in other Caribbean islands who were often referred to with derogatory labels such as "garrot" (or garrote) and "gasso." That "garrote" is the word for a method of torture by strangulation sheds light on the ways in which Virgin Islanders viewed these labor migrants. These divisions spilled over into the realms of both law and education, with a segregated education system that barred "alien" children from attending public schools in the territory as well as mass deportations (Gore 2009). Both these tensions around labor and the centrality of the tourist market continue in the current moment, as employment in this industry—which has historically been found on St. John at Caneel Bay Resort[25] and the few other hotels that dot the tiny island, by taxi driving, or by selling handicrafts to vacationers—remains a vital source of income for St. Johnians today. This reliance on tourism raises questions of access and mobility (as North Americans and Europeans frequently visit the territory for leisure, but not the reverse), but also of race and gender, as Black people in the region continue to find low-wage work within this industry.

Much work has been done on the gendered implications of tourism, particularly on sex work in the Caribbean (see, for instance, Kempadoo 1999 and Roland 2011). Beyond this, however, there is the gendered framework at the very heart of the tourist industry in which ostensibly virginal islands and their servile inhabitants (including, frequently, island women working as chambermaids in hotels) are sold to monied visitors. Scholars have written powerfully on this sale of the feminized region (see Nixon 2015 and Sheller 2014) and the complex responses of Caribbean residents to this set of exchanges. Yet, while there are aspects of gender and race at work in this industry that build on the history of Black bodies at work in the region, it is vital to note the ambivalence with which many in the Caribbean regard tourism, as island residents and their families are often entirely dependent on the income they earn in this sector for their survival.

The two-pronged approach of the US in cultivating a tourist market on St. Thomas and St. John rather than supporting agriculture, St. Croix's longtime economic driver, stoked still-simmering tensions around economic competition, visibility, and quality of life between the islands.[26] When the development of a tourist industry began to pay dividends in the 1950s and resulted in a tenfold increase in visitors (Dookhan 1974: 273), the dynamic of color-as-social-capital of the previous era continued to play an important role in shaping life in the territory. For instance, the celebration of Carnival was buttressed by events, notably "queen shows" (or beauty pageants) in which beauty was quantified such that lighter skin and European features were prized above all else (Oliver 2009). The continuing benefits of color shore up Crucians' analysis that connects ostensibly distinct moments of economic development to the longer history of racial capitalism, positioning the EDC as but the most recent iteration of this unfolding project.

Industrial Development

With the advent of tourism and the decline of agricultural production, land that had formerly been used for sugar production was sold off to developers. On St. Croix, the most significant of these purchases were made by Harvey Aluminum Corporation and Hess Oil in the 1960s, marking the shift toward industrial development in the USVI.

Pointing to the significance of the change from agriculture to industry, one "cane cutter," Sam "Old Timer" Garnett, recalls:

> And then, there was this big hoopla when the government decided to bring Hess Oil here. Well, all hell break loose. Some people even pay big money to go to court to stop it. Some people didn't want industry, but you had to find something because sugar production was being phased out. Plus, it was getting expensive to deal with the sugar, and you had no workers because [of stricter immigration laws] and then you won't have any workers to deal with the sugar. (Thurland 2014: 137)

The establishment of Hess Oil on St. Croix by Leon Hess in 1966 was the beginning of large-scale industry on St. Croix, as this facility for refining crude oil was a major employer on the island as well as one of the largest oil refineries in the world, occupying over two thousand acres (Highfield 2014). Hess Oil would, in the late 1990s, partner with Petroleos de Venezuela and transform into the entity HOVENSA. While the purpose of introducing heavy industry to the USVI was to stimulate the local economy and alleviate unemployment, there were deep tensions and local frustrations, as the refinery faced charges of racial discrimination in both hiring and offers of housing to its senior employees. Writing in the 1970s, Gordon Lewis (1972) has argued that within the refinery "at the middle and upper employment levels there is a decided preference for expatriate personnel; thus, the Hess and Harvey compounds begin to look like examples of North American company towns, characterized by varying degrees of racial segregationist patterns, they have sprung up all over the Caribbean after the model of the bauxite company town of MacKenzie in Guyana" (Lewis 1972: 125). The other large industry that came to the USVI in the 1960s was the alumina processing plant Harvey Aluminum, which was used to process imported bauxite into alumina. While some Caribbean countries, notably Jamaica and Guyana, have large deposits of bauxite, this is not the case on St. Croix and much of the material was to be imported—as was the labor that would process the red dust of bauxite into aluminum. As with Hess Oil, the local community on St. Croix again complained of being largely excluded from employment within this sector: in 1970, 20

out of 471 employees at Harvey Aluminum were Virgin Islanders
(Boyer 1983: 261), with the bulk of employees being Caribbean
migrants (derisively termed "garrotes") for lower-level labor and
white Americans for more specialized roles. What is more, much of
the land on which Harvey Aluminum operated had been taken from
local farmers. David Bond (2017) has written that "in a particularly
nasty turn of events, colonial authorities seized the most fertile swathe
of land on the island from small farmers and handed it over to the
industrial coalition, claiming, 'St. Croix has had a sugar economy for
long enough'" (608). Beyond racism in hiring, land extraction, and
increases in racial tensions, this industry did massive environmental
damage to St. Croix: as bauxite is itself a dustlike consistency, it is
prone to being swirled about by Caribbean winds, coating vehicles,
homes—and being ingested by residents unfortunate enough to live
near a processing facility.[27] During its operation, Harvey Aluminum
was situated toward the center of the island near the working-class,
and primarily Black and Puerto Rican, neighborhood of Machuchal
rather than the exclusive, and largely white, East End of the island.
This location speaks to the presumed expendability of some communities and the power that exists at the nexus of class, color, and
race in relation to not just economic well-being but health and,
indeed, survival.

The move to industrial development also relied heavily on
preexisting racial hierarchies that pitted "modernized" countries
(modernity determined by access to machinery largely constructed
of aluminum, including airplanes and military weapons) against "pre-
modern" Caribbean—largely Black—countries that provided the raw
material for these innovations.[28] What is more, Mimi Sheller (2014)
names the racialized histories and practices that bring these extractive
industries[29] to the Caribbean (including reliance on migrant labor made
to be cheap and a long-standing colonial relationship of extraction
from the region) as well as the displacement of local and indigenous
communities as a result of environmental harm, including flooding
indigenous communities to power the infrastructure necessary for
aluminum production.

Despite these negative effects, a dual focus on industry and
tourism as the drivers of the Virgin Islands economy was representative of the larger moment in development thinking in the region
post–World War II. Deere (1990), for instance, has written on this

paradigm shift, the harbinger of which was Puerto Rico's industrial development through the landmark program Operation Bootstrap:

> Following the consolidation of a US-centered world order after WWII, and also as a consequence of the national-ist upheavals which swept the region in the 1930's and 1940's, a new framework for economic development became generalized during the 1950's. The essential goal of the new strategies in the various territories was the creation of a modern industrial sector through a process of import substitution. Influenced considerably by the Puerto Rican "Operation Bootstrap" strategy to lure US capital, "industrialization by invitation" became the main strategy for economic change. Foreign investors were invited to exploit the reservoir of cheap labor in the region by means of generous tax exemptions and other incentives. (Deere et al. 1990: 4)

A development program in Puerto Rico that offered generous tax exemptions to American companies willing to relocate to this American-owned island, Operation Bootstrap was a watershed, but it was not the first time that tax incentives had been used by a Caribbean island to lure investors. In fact, in an attempt to increase the number of white inhabitants in the then DWI, the Danish West India Company offered both access to farmland and tax forgiveness to planters who would come to these islands from across the region beginning in 1735 (Hall 1992: 13).

The seeming-success of Operation Bootstrap, including an increasing Gross National Product (GNP),[30] was so great that it was heralded by its chief architect, Teodoro Moscoso, as "produc[ing] one century of economic development in a decade" in his testimony to the US Finance Committee. Operation Bootstrap inspired many Caribbean island–nations to center their economic development around similar industrialization programs, including Trinidad's Aid to Pioneer Industries Ordinance (1950) and Jamaica's Industrial Development Corporation (1952).[31] In 1965, Mexico implemented a slightly different version of industrial development with its maqui-ladora program, which focused on assembly-line work for larger transnational corporations.

Given the ostensible success of industrialization throughout the region, the US Virgin Islands, and St. Croix in particular, invested heavily in the creation of similar programs: they focused primarily on Hess Oil and Harvey Aluminum, as well as a watch-manufacturing sector, administered through the Industrial Development Commission (IDC). Although the government of the US Virgin Islands attempted to stimulate industrialization through tax exemption in the late 1940s, it was not until 1967 that these companies began relocating to the US Virgin Islands in earnest.[32] Noting the substantial impact of this initiative, Gordon Lewis has written that "the importance of these [tax privileges] can be readily appreciated from the fact that in 1964 approximately 9% of 2,400,000 watch movements consumed in the USA were assembled by 11 watch manufacturing plants in the [USVI]" (1972: 148). As was the case in Puerto Rico, the economy of the US Virgin Islands seemed to be benefiting greatly from this focus on industry.

However, given the popularity of industrialization programs in the Caribbean through the 1960s, their outcomes must be assessed in context. While a cursory glance suggests industrialization was a success, a more nuanced reading reveals its serious shortcomings—including those of Operation Bootstrap, the initiative on which many such programs were based, as their success largely relied on outmigration and the decimation of local industries in favor of benefiting North American corporations.[33] Among the major shortcomings of this program and similar versions across the Caribbean from the perspective of the island nations that hosted these corporations, was that they favored US companies by allowing them to relocate in low-wage areas[34] (an arrangement that was particularly the case under Operation Bootstrap, as advocates of the program traveled from Puerto Rico to the mainland to successfully lobby for exemption from federal minimum wage guidelines). Also vital to any assessment of this moment of development is a consideration of the reliance on foreign capital—and foreign control—that characterized these industrialization-by-invitation programs.

While the Operation Bootstrap program was aided tremendously by Puerto Rico's status as a US possession, enabling its advocates[35] to market the program as a "safe" and pseudo-domestic move,[36] it is exactly this political relationship that made it difficult for Puerto Rico to protect its local agricultural sector, the industry on which it had previously relied most heavily. A. W. Maldonado (1997) has described Puerto Rico's inability to impose regulations on its ruling power, the United States, as well as the wave of imports from the mainland that suffocated the local industry. This relationship of competition engendered by Operation Bootstrap foreshadowed the dismantling of trade preferences and creation of programs such as export-processes zones, marking the beginning of Caribbean islands competing against subsidized US products.[37]

The questionable economic benefits of industrialization-by-invitation are also inflected by issues of gender. For instance, the Mexican maquiladora program was understood as a primarily female sector (Prieto 1997; Benería and Roldán 1987; Elson and Pearson 1986; Fernández-Kelly 1983; Fuentes and Ehrenreich 1983). This identification of industry with women has been widely noted, and there has been much research on the impact of this dynamic, including on the overwhelming preference for young women in factory work (see especially Safa 1995; Ellis 1995; Yelvington 1995), as they were understood by managers to be more docile, nimble, and submissive to authority than their male counterparts. There are also analyses that focus on the displacement of women's economic agency in agriculture and handicrafts with the advent of industrialization (see, for instance, Nash and Fernandez-Kelly 1983). The ideology surrounding women as "ideal" workers has shifted over time, as female factory workers during industrialization were preferred as laborers who could be paid less, given the assumption that they were supported by men and merely earning extra, or "pin," money (Enloe 1989). Following the shift away from industry and toward finance and information management, women have remained preferred laborers, as employers rely on the prevalence of female-headed households in the Caribbean as evidence that women are more "stable" and reliable than their male counterparts.

Beyond these critiques, other analyses point clearly to systematic failures of the industrialization model to achieve economic stability throughout the Caribbean region as well as the "hidden costs" of such programs, including rising unemployment, forced migration, and deepening social inequalities. In fact, Puerto Rico's unemployment rate increased from 12 to 20 percent in a decade, and the island became largely reliant on subsidies in the same period.[38] Outside of the Puerto Rican example, this trend of rising unemployment as a result of industrialization continued throughout the Caribbean. James Ferguson notes that "the industrial promotion effort largely failed to accomplish its goal of creating enough jobs to absorb the region's growing labor force. . . . In the first place, the little foreign investment that did come to the region was largely confined to Jamaica and Trinidad and Tobago.[39] . . . There were too few projects and the projects that were undertaken were too capital intensive to prevent unemployment from rising in a context of rapid population and labor force growth" (Ferguson 1990b: 67). Adding to the issue of growing unemployment was the fact that most islands shifted from a primary focus on agriculture to industry—a move that often economically displaced more people than it benefited.[40] As a result, Caribbean residents migrated elsewhere in large numbers in the 1960s[41] (often to the mainland US and Britain). In fact, the large numbers of Caribbean migrants who relocated to the US and UK were an integral part of the "success" of industrialization programs in the region as "it is estimated that between 1940 and 1969, 700,000 Puerto Ricans migrated to the US, accounting for 48% of those working age in 1970" (Deere et al. 1990: 129).[42] Elsewhere in the region, this pattern held true as well: "In Jamaica, as in Puerto Rico . . . migration to the US, Britain, and other Caribbean islands became . . . virtually institutionalized" (Maldonado 1997: 143). In Britain, devastated after World War II, Caribbean migrants such as those aboard the *Empire Windrush* (see, for instance, Fryer 1984) were encouraged to relocate and assist in the rebuilding of Britain. Moreover, circuits of Caribbean laborers have been in motion since the late nineteenth century, serving as a substantial source of labor for projects such as the Panama Canal and building railroads in Costa Rica (see Lefever 1992; Putnam 2002; Greene 2009). However, this is not to suggest that the various destinations targeted by Caribbean migrants have been pleased with their arrival. In fact, many countries have adopted racist measures to halt the flow of Caribbean migrant laborers.[43] While it is necessary for capital to have a malleable labor force that will perform tasks others will not, or what Tadiar (2013) has called "surplus" or "disposable" populations, the response from many receiving countries has been "not in my backyard."

Largely as a combined result of the optimism with which industrialization programs were adopted and the widespread disappointment at their failure to produce economic stability (while often increasing social inequalities), there was a clear shift to left-leaning political and social agendas across the region in the late 1970s.[44] Given the critiques leveled at many industrialization-by-invitation programs, including charges that the benefits to foreign corporations far outweighed those received by the islands that hosted them, this period saw "a steady expansion in the economic role of the state, a deepened commitment to and reevaluation of the role of Caribbean regionalism . . . and a general diversification of international relations" (Deere et al. 1990: 5). Further, this turn toward more liberal policies across much of the region reflected frustration with the raced and classed outcomes of the previous decade of development—a moment in which representatives of foreign business, who were most often white and male, relocated to the Caribbean and reaped substantial economic benefits. Despite political and social campaigns to make development work for Caribbean islands (that is, to increase the economic benefit to the region, rather than solely to the foreign corporations), the state of affairs across the region remained largely the same, as islands continued to depend on foreign capital and demand to stimulate their economies.

Deepening these divisions even further was the fact that the sector of the "local" population with which these businessmen generally interacted both socially and professionally was the mixed-race or "Creole" elite. As relates to the US Virgin Islands, it has been argued that "the complex interrelationships among the various segments of the three-tiered group [white, "Creole," and Black] have changed over the years only to the degree that a European-oriented class system has become an American-oriented class system" (Lewis 1972: 162). Here, as in earlier scholarship on the region, Creole is used to indicate mixed race—for instance, in the Danish West Indies, the offspring of Danes and enslaved Africans (Campbell 1944). However, both the term Creole and the amalgamating process of creolization have played a large role in anthropology of the Caribbean. For instance, Slocum and Thomas (2003) have noted that the "creolization paradigm redirects our attention from the elaboration of binary societal models toward a *process* that embodies a particular power struggle and that works through the dynamic articulation of gender, color, class, status, and culture" (2003: 557; emphasis mine). However, despite even this corrective, scholars have warned against the overreliance on "creolization" as the lens through which the Caribbean region is best apprehended (see Khan 2001; Munasinghe 2001). This emphasis on the processual nature of creolization speaks to its slow unfolding and draws necessary attention to the power dynamics that shape this process-of-becoming. That is, in the Caribbean (as elsewhere) people and things (including languages and cultural forms) do not simply meld together uniformly. Instead, an emphasis on, for instance, the positioned actors within a society (with attention to their class, race, color, and gender) provides a far more useful lens through which to view the region.

Neoliberal Development

The failures of industrialization in the Caribbean combined with the frustration that arose during the 1970s in attempting to move beyond this model led to a paradigm shift in development thinking, beginning in the 1980s and continuing today, under the heading of neoliberal development. This has been a move centered around virtuality that has largely produced programs focused on data/information management ("informatics") and finance (see especially Freeman 2000 and Maurer 1997). This approach to development is one rooted in an assumption of the salvific nature of the financial market to intervene in crises both economic and social. Often attempting to incorporate new markets into global circulations, initiatives rooted in a notion of neoliberal development have had particular significance for the smaller islands in the Caribbean. Bill Maurer's (1997) text on financial transformations in the region, for instance, is entitled *Recharting the Caribbean*, a nod to the refiguring of islands in the region into functioning points in global transfers of wealth and information. This paradigmatic shift toward virtuality has also demonstrated the continued salience not just of state power but of Empire broadly (Hardt and Negri 2000). Both Bonilla (2015) and Ong (2006) have pointed to the complexity of sovereignty, with Ong introducing the notion of "overlapping sovereignties" to describe the intricacies of territoriality, citizenship, and administration in the current moment (Ong 2006: 19).

This incorporation of markets into a global economic system rests heavily on previous moments of racial capitalism, as the spaces identified as particularly attractive for capital investment often earn this dubious distinction as a result of previous racialized domination, such as slavery and colonialism. This connection between previous and contemporary conditions of vulnerability, particularly in the realm of economic policy, can be observed across the region. Working on Puerto Rico, legal scholar Diane Lourdes Dick has introduced the term "tax imperialism," a framing that links projects of American empire building and consolidation with economic policy. Lourdes Dick argues that "modern tax havens may signal the longstanding domination of more developed nations, territories, and possessions" (2015: 83). This lens centers the ways in which the project of empire has been furthered through economic policy—specifically, initiatives aimed at "economic development" that more often than not rely on American capital in order to function and benefit the economic interests of the United States. For instance, scholars such as Lourdes Dick (2015) and Morales (2019) have pointed to the ways in which the removal of a tax credit meant to attract US capital to Puerto Rico resulted in the steep decline of the Puerto Rican economy, which had become largely dependent on this quasi-foreign capital. The exodus of this capital, largely in the pharmaceutical industry, that was the result of the loss of this tax benefit, resulted in Puerto Rico turning increasingly to borrowing—which has produced the staggering debt crisis in which the territory has found itself in recent years. Toward the end of the article in which she outlines her theory of tax imperialism, Lourdes Dick (2015) includes a quote from an essay "How to Know the Puerto Ricans" that reads:

> The first thing we must realize is that the Puerto Ricans have been exploited for hundreds of years. That strangers have been knocking at the door of the Puerto Rican nation for centuries[,] always in search of something, to get something[,] or to take away something from Puerto Ricans. Because of this, "when you come to knock at the door of a Puerto Rican home you will be encountered by this feeling in the Puerto Rican—sometimes unconscious in himself—of having been taken for a ride for centuries." (2015: 84)

This perspective of serving as the ground upon which wealth has accumulated over time, or having "been taken for a ride for centuries" echoes the sentiments on St. Croix, where the EDC exists in a long line of projects. Spectral time creates space for the aspect of this repetition that is not simply monotonous—it is terrifying. If, it stands to reason, slavery and its racial order once ruled these islands, why could it not happen again?

Engaging with these transformations through the framework of neoliberalism produces different outcomes than would apprehending them through the lens of globalization, which lacks an emphasis on the singular, apprehensible project of consolidating class power (Harvey 2005). Neoliberal development is rooted in the assumption that rather than turning to national governments to improve the lives of its citizens, we should look to multinational corporations and the capital they bring with them to improve lives and livelihoods. At the heart of contemporary transformations across the Caribbean, neoliberal development emphasizes privatization (away from the nationalizing of industries across the Caribbean in the post-independence moment of the 1970s),[45] political stability and individual exceptionalism despite material lack across entire communities, while privileging the needs of the market and transnational capital through supranational entities. For instance, the structural adjustment programs meted out by the International Monetary Fund (IMF) across the region have largely gutted social safety nets through austerity packages and downgraded currencies across the region, leading to the prohibitively high cost of needed goods[46] and ruinous debt servicing. It is in this context of the shift from the heavy industry of the 1970s to the light, flexible, virtual transfers of the 1980s and beyond that many Caribbean nations implemented new development strategies. In the USVI, this shift took the form of the EDC program, while Barbados turned to "informatics" (Freeman 2000) and the British Virgin Islands deepened its commitment to its offshore banking sector (Maurer 1997).

In the Caribbean, the move toward lighter industry characterized by virtuality was seen, at least initially, as an attractive alternative to the service-sector jobs provided by tourism. This was because the local population anticipated training in new skills, and because the financial services companies were to have less of an environmental impact across the region. These expectations, however, have not been realized in the Virgin Islands, largely because the EDCs have led to employment for some Crucians, but certainly not all. What is more, the continuing influence of gendered ideology surrounding desirable laborers and the persistence of "social color" alongside the continued dependence on foreign capital have meant that Virgin Islanders largely view the EDC program as more of the terrifying same; they critique both hiring in the EDC sector (which is inflected by gender, color, and class) and the residential enclaves populated by wealthy, white members of the EDC community as racist. What is more, the very foundation of the program builds on racialized histories of global capital and its handlers circuiting through the Caribbean to increase their wealth while ruining the lives and livelihoods of Black residents. Thus, Crucians who, like many people of color, have continued to find themselves at the bottom of the global economic pile in the wake of neoliberal policies and programs, find fault with both the execution and structure of the EDC program as an iteration of racial capitalism that has long made their lives, and those of their forebears, far worse.

As the US Virgin Islands exist today as a possession of the United States, the geopolitical reality of continuing coloniality is linked to the neoliberal ethos of market centrality, particularly through an emphasis on "stability" (specifically, political stability to ensure the safety of capital) and privatization. For example, a 2002 issue of the *Virgin Islands Investment Analysis*, an investment newsletter printed on the mainland for Americans interested in relocating to the USVI, makes clear the importance of this stability afforded by the USVI's status as a US territory, warning:

> Do Not Invest Outside the United States. Even seemingly stable island governments, such as those associated with Great Britain, for example, have established a history of turning possessions over to completely new forms of governments as short-term expediencies take precedence. In addition, investing outside the United States endows one with a whole new set of legal and cultural barriers that are often discovered only by painful first-hand exposure. (*Virgin Islands Investment Analysis* 2002: 1)

More than simply a framework for thinking, neoliberalism now exists as an ethos—an ethic in which market exchange will ensure the greatest good. The degree to which this logic is internalized (which, in the case of the EDC, amounts to the widespread failure of market rationality to convince Crucians of its veracity), marks its success, what Derek Hook (2007) and Gill and Scharff (2011) have noted is the necessary "mentality" element of Foucault's governmentality. Drawing on the work of David Harvey, Gill and Scharff (2011) write, neoliberalism "sees market exchange as an ethic in itself, capable of acting as a guide to all human action, and it holds that the social good will be maximized by maximizing the reach and frequency of market transactions" (5). This logic has manifested in seemingly disparate realities across the globe, including socialization through drug courts in the US (Kaye 2019), migratory circuits linking Nigeria and Europe (Plambech 2014), the production of a market of "narratives of abjection" that enable African asylum-seekers to gain the attention of government officials (George 2013), and the astronomical rise of adjunct labor in the American academy (Navarro 2017). However, what links these disparate new realities is the centering of the market and corporate interests over and against an analysis of community benefit.

The quintessential examples of neoliberalism are found during the "lost decade" in Latin America—the 1980s, when a number of countries in the region (but especially Argentina, Mexico, and Chile) found themselves in a series of severe debt crises largely as a result of borrowing from supranational organizations like the World Bank and International Monetary Fund (see, for example, Corbridge 1993; Dello Buono and Bell Lara 2007). These events serve not as the beginning of neoliberalism but rather as clear examples of its dangers and ability to shape-shift in different contexts. What is more, they demonstrate the hallmarks of this system, including privatization of land (away from a notion of "the commons" and toward private property) and an emphasis on entrepreneurship (such that there is a transformation from citizens who can expect services to entrepreneurs who earn capital and must consume). These examples demonstrate the neoliberal privileging of the individual (those who possess and maximize their human capital) away from the community. At work in the EDC, these shifts form the basis of Crucians' objections.

The EDC program and those like it emerge out of this neoliberal logic and rest on earlier moments of racialized capital accumulation. For instance, EDC hiring preferences that favor middle- and upper-class Crucians who have attended college in the States speak to the continued centrality of class, color, and mobility. This example also demonstrates the interrelationship of states, state functions, and markets, as corporations are largely able to name their price vis-à-vis wages, taxes, and regulatory oversight. Finally, the advent of neoliberalism has brought with it a general misdirection of attention away from structural forces of disempowerment and toward the importance of serendipity, or individual "luck" (see, for instance, Comaroff and Comaroff 2000; Piot 2010 and 2019).

This history makes clear that while initiatives such as the EDC are emergent—and indeed "new"—they do not constitute a radical break with the past in which the Caribbean region is steeped. Rather, these initiatives are rooted in—and, in many ways, made possible by—the history of plantation agriculture and colonialism in the region as well as continued (often pseudo-colonial) political relationships. This is particularly the case in the US Virgin Islands, which relies heavily on its status as a US territory in the marketing of its EDC program. Further, such programs often reinvigorate dynamics of race in novel ways: the twenty-something, female descendants of historically well-to-do Creole families in the US Virgin Islands at work in the EDC sector are a contemporary embodiment of the continuing importance of the tripartite system of color long at work in the region—white, Black, colored/Creole—as well as long-standing gender dynamics.[47]

The EDC program, then, is a reflection of the current moment in the long history of economic development initiatives in the Caribbean. Following the collapse of plantation agriculture, attempts at economic revitalization in the region have focused on homesteading, tourism, industrialization—and now virtual transfers of wealth and information. While it may seem a linear trajectory, it is perhaps more productive to understand these models as existing in dialectal relation to one another, furtively smuggling in preexisting hierarchies, divisions, and expectations while creating new avenues through which they are confronted, affirmed—and sometimes subverted. The story of present-day circulations of capital in the Caribbean is neither wholly determined by the region's past, nor entirely new. Rather, it is a hybrid of these—steeped in centuries-long processes of accumulation, while taking advantage of new pathways created by the current moment of neoliberal development. As ever, the suffering of the past is never far from the minds, and worldview, of Crucians and thus spectral time serves as a framing that names both the alternate temporality and the fear that informs Crucians' responses to the EDC program.

Chapter 4

The End of an Era

The Shuttering of Stanford Financial

Just seventeen months after the St. Croix Economic Summit, the irony of Allen Stanford's words about ending financial plunder in the Caribbean would hit St. Croix as his assets sat frozen, his employees summarily dismissed, and the already-low level of local support for the EDC program took a perilous dip as a result of his indictment by the US Securities and Exchange Commission (SEC) for fraud. Alleging his entire operation to be a house of cards, a "Ponzi scheme," the SEC arrested Stanford and his chief officers in early 2009.

Many of the objections to the EDC program, including exclusionary hiring practices and fears about real estate scarcity, concern the behavior of particular "EDC people"—and thus tacitly accept the validity of the program as a means of economic development. Yet beyond these individual concerns, there is much discussion on St. Croix about its very legality. On the whole, Virgin Islanders are largely wary of the EDC as an ill-defined and suspicious—yet potentially lucrative—program. These suspicions, often dismissed by program advocates as being merely "backward, anti-development propaganda," have some of their roots in rumor—but they have also been shored up by continued federal investigation of beneficiary companies on the island.

During fieldwork, my exploration of federal raids on EDC companies began by way of gossip. As I rifled through my bag in the women's locker room at a gym after exercising one afternoon, I overheard two women discussing the start of "the case." Listening more intently, and perhaps blurring the line between anthropological data-gathering and unqualified eavesdropping, I realized they were discussing the start of preliminary legal proceedings against an EDC company that had been the talk of the island for months, as a result of its offices being raided by the Internal Revenue Service (IRS). Quickly gathering up my things, I left the health club and drove to the nearby courthouse to see what I could learn about this case.

In one of the more notorious instances in collective Crucian memory, the IRS employed undercover agents in its investigation to determine whether the partners in Company X were complying with EDC requirements, including spending the required number of days (183) in the territory. The federal government charged that the business of this company was "primarily the solicitation of partners and the marketing of Virgin Islands tax benefits to taxpayers, not the business described at the initial public hearing, or its application for an EDC certificate, nor the business authorized in the certificate as eligible for tax benefits."[1] Or, as the government argued more bluntly later in that legal motion, "the business of [Company X] was not the sale of business services, but the sale of tax evasion." The investigation of this company further blemished the reputation of the EDC program as a whole, adding fuel to the already-raging public debate about its legitimacy. Having found sufficient evidence, the IRS carried out a raid on the company's office, terrifying employees and confiscating all manner of documents. At an EDC get-together a few months after these events, I found myself talking with an accountant who was working in the office next door to Company X in the industrial park on the day of the raid. She described nervously peeping through a slit in the window blinds in her office as federal officials in SWAT gear and bulletproof vests swarmed the office next door and carted out boxes of documents. This instance was, perhaps, a spectacular implosion, but for many Crucians wary of the EDC program and the racialized circulations of capital on which it was built, it shored up deep-seated suspicions about the legitimacy of the program and its beneficiaries.

Near the beginning of my internship with the EDA, I was able to tour the William D. Roebuck Industrial Park,[2] a site whose name and warehouse structure are holdovers from the program's roots in industrialization. Once filled with manufacturing tenants, including seamstresses and watchmakers, the Park now sat largely uninhabited and in general disrepair,[3] standing as a visual reminder of the shift from manufacturing to finance that enabled the creation of the EDC. A physical remnant of the past, with gaping bays where formerly thriving manufacturing businesses once stood, the Park became a space that housed a very few EDC companies, primarily technology and financial management companies that were better suited to small offices than the enormous hangars offered by the Park. The space of this nearly empty Park, the juxtaposition of old and new, past and future, is an embodiment of my analysis of the EDC program as an instance of cutting-edge global financial circulations that contains elements of class, color, race, and gender hierarchies all too familiar on St. Croix and in the Caribbean more generally.

While the investigation against Company X was ongoing and was often regarded as epitomizing the problems of the EDC program, it is hardly the only one of its kind; of the seven EDC companies with which I interviewed or attempted to interview, four had been investigated in some manner by federal authorities. These semi-regular, and often armed, raids by federal government agencies understandably contributed to the suspicion with which the program was viewed on the island. When Stanford Financial quickly pulled out of St. Croix after the indictment of its CEO by the US Securities and Exchange Commission (SEC) in early 2009, it was an echo of what had come before.

183 Days

As a result of continued infractions that many beneficiary companies attributed to a lack of clarity in the law governing the program, the US Congress passed legislation in 2004 to enforce stricter regulations on the program and its beneficiaries. Chief among the issues addressed by this bill, the American Jobs Creation Act of 2004 (Jobs Act), were changes to residency requirements that mandated that beneficiaries spend 183 days each year in the USVI and specified the kinds of income that would qualify for the program's tax break. EDC supporters viewed this bill and these changes as the death knell of the program, a set of strict rules that would drive capital—and its handlers—to a friendlier environment. An article published in the local newspaper, the *St. Croix Avis*, in 2004, outlined the changes included in the Jobs Act:

> These changes will negatively impact the V.I. treasury because it changes the requirements for more than 100 companies that enjoy tax breaks as part of the EDC program. The new rules would require VI taxpayers to be physically present in the Virgin Islands at least 183 days in any tax year to be a bona fide resident for tax purposes under the U.S. Internal Revenue Code. The new provision would only allow VI source-income to qualify as EDC benefits. It eliminates the possibility that some of an EDC beneficiary's U.S. source income connected with a VI trade or business, could qualify for tax reduction under the EDC program. [Then-] Gov. Charles Turnbull . . . said that his administration was "not standing still" on the issue and continuing to lobby against the changes in Washington D.C." (Lett 2004)

The aftermath of these federal interventions—both the raids and the legislation—was an escalation in the ongoing debate on St. Croix between supporters of the program (a community that largely consisted of EDC people, some local EDC employees, and local legislators) and its detractors. The coalition of EDC supporters included members of the local government, including former governor Turnbull and the territory's then-congressional representative Donna Christensen, whose response to the stricter regulations was, "This is not what we wanted or what we needed."[4] These advocates, including employees of the EDA and "local political and business leaders . . . traveled to Washington to educate U.S. Treasury officials and other government leaders about the potential negative impact of the proposed new rules and regulations on the economy of the U.S. Virgin Islands" (Economic Development Authority 2007: 2). On this journey, program supporters had a project similar to that of Puerto Rican Industrial Representatives (or IRs) during Operation Bootstrap. Describing these IRs as "mostly young Puerto Ricans with educational and practical experience in business and attracted to public service," A. W. Maldonado writes that they were tasked with "gain[ing] entry into the offices of investors and executives in order to 'sell' Puerto Rico" (1997: 81). Decades later, despite the manifold failings of industrialization in the region and beyond, the "sale" of these islands to the US remained under way

In addition to local media, mainland news sources also covered the changes brought about by the Jobs Act. Centering around one of the more successful and locally recognizable EDC businessmen on St. Croix, an article written for the business website Bloomberg. com addressed the impact of this legislation on the EDC program:

> Warren Mosler, who opened a hedge fund firm in St. Croix five years ago, is having what's become the usual conversation with people who were lured to the U.S. Virgin Islands in 2001 by the prospect of legally cutting their tax bill by 90 percent. Almost half of the 49 funds that set up shop in the islands have fled in the past two years. Mosler complains that hedge funds were chased away by federal tax law changes and an Internal Revenue Service that says it suspects rampant fraud by those that signed up for the tax incentive. . . . He's surveying the sparse happy hour crowd [at a beach bar frequented by EDC people]. "Unfortunately, the fear is causing a case of running away from the police when you're not guilty," he says. (Donmoyer 2007)

This piece ultimately concludes with a reiteration of the continued centrality of relationship between the United States and the USVI, as one local official complained to the reporter that the US federal government "think[s] of us like we're outside the United States.'" "Still," the author concludes, "islanders know Washington holds the key to their salvation" (Donmoyer 2007).

In response to the Jobs Act, the government of the USVI hired the firm PricewaterhouseCoopers to gauge the effects of this legislation. That study found that the restrictions on residency and source-income put in place by the Jobs Act did, indeed, have a striking effect on the program and, as a result, it would become "more difficult for the USVI to retain and attract investment" (PricewaterhouseCoopers 2004: 1). Echoing this finding, the EDA itself outlined the ongoing negative consequences of the Jobs Act, as the program "continued to experience reductions in applications as well as business shrinkage and closures. The promulgation of residency rules, the ongoing audit of EDC beneficiaries by IRS/Treasury, its negative national media coverage . . . contributed heavily to the downturn being experienced by the agency" (Economic Development Authority 2007: 6). Anecdotal evidence bore out this scenario of a downturn in the program, yet whether these difficulties were the result of investors "running away from the police when [they] are not guilty," as Mosler would have it, remained a matter of contention on St. Croix. While the business community and local government officials supported the EDC program and critiqued the Jobs Act as unfairly targeting the program and its beneficiaries, many of the island's residents outside these sectors viewed these regulations as much-needed interventions into a program structured to unfairly benefit wealthy white investors at the expense—both financial and what many on the island termed "cultural"—of Crucians. The debate between these two camps—those in favor in the program and those who found fault with it—had long been raging but was made clearer during the galvanizing moment of the Jobs Act in 2004.

Two articles published in the *Virgin Islands Daily News* days apart demonstrate these widely varying assessments of the EDC program. On June 8, 2004, a resident of St. Thomas submitted an editorial entitled "While the Rich Gets [*sic*] Richer," in which he claimed that the EDC program was "giving away" much more than it was receiving:

> As our senators sharpen their pencils trying to "fix" years of overspending and corruption, the excuse for not preserving one of our last remaining public beaches and controlling rampant development will be, "but we can't afford to buy Vessup beach." This is ridiculous when you look at what we are giving away with the "EDC"/IDC benefits. . . . We are taxing the poor and allowing the rich to come here and live without making just contributions. Our schools need computers and books but these extremely wealthy people don't feel connected to their "home" in the U.S. Virgin Islands to give where they really live. We are giving away the cow and milk! (Brent 2004)

In response to these claims, a supporter of the program submitted an equally polemic article entitled "EDC Program a Godsend" two days later:

> EDC companies employ more than 3 percent of the population, contribute millions of dollars per year to local charities, schools and other social benefit organizations. They have invested hundreds of millions of dollars of capital improvements to establish EDC businesses in the territory. Tens of millions of dollars in wages are paid annually. Tens of millions are spent locally on goods and services. The list goes on but you get the idea. The EDC program is and continues to be a bright light attracting capital and people to create a diverse and stable V.I. economy. The EDC program is one of the greatest economic stimulus plans to ever grace the shores of the Virgin Islands. Our ability to *understand and engage the opportunity will determine the future of the people of the Virgin Islands.* (Difede 2004; emphasis mine)

The author of this article suggests that "understand[ing] the opportunity" offered by the EDC holds the key to approving of the program. However, this argument is belied by the Virgin Islanders I interviewed, including EDC employees, whose critique was rooted not in misapprehension but rather in the connection they posit between the program and previous forms of racial capitalism that have damaged the region. It is central that this critique is not principally a quibble over the amount of capital brought into the territory. For instance, PricewaterhouseCoopers has estimated that the "total direct and indirect jobs attributable to DSB's represent[ed] 8.4% of total USVI employment in 2004" (PricewaterhouseCoopers 2004: 8). Echoing this assessment, the EDA noted that "the addition of the designated services category as a product of the Economic Development Commission has resulted in the expansion and growth in the financial services industry in the Territory" (Economic Development Authority 2004). However, critics of the program point to the need to nuance these figures: *Who* are the people hired for these jobs? What definition of "Virgin Islander" is being used to make these claims of employment? What are the costs (in terms of land/property, cultural sovereignty, and belonging) of an expanding financial services sector?

This chapter explores the positioning of the EDC program and its participants on St. Croix through the rise and dramatic fall of the program's most prominent beneficiary, Stanford Financial. The meteoric rise of this company on St. Croix and its eventual decimation—a development described by program supporters as an anomaly not reflective of the program and by its critics as hard proof that EDC people are indisputably corrupt—serve as bookends to this chapter. The example of Stanford shores up my argument for understanding the EDC program as neither a dazzling program that incorporates St. Croix into global financial circuits in wholly new ways nor as a perfect replica of historical processes of inequality on the island. Rather, the way in which the government and many residents of St. Croix clamored for the attention of Stanford and his billions is reflective of the desperation of the Crucian economy—a continued consequence of economic stagnation on the island that has its roots in St. Croix's inability to successfully diversify its economy beyond a historic reliance on agriculture as its primary economic driver. These are troubles that have persisted through attempts at industrialization and economic diversification (see chapter 3)—and the fierce hope that this billionaire and his capital would save the island. The significance of Stanford as a paternal figure, a "great white hope," was not lost on Crucians; however, while many residents tried desperately to gain employment in his company, others vocally criticized Stanford from the moment he arrived. Rumors of Stanford's megalomaniacal intention to purchase the entire island were widespread and as evidence for these claims his detractors pointed to Stanford's insistence on being called "Sir Allen," in reference to his knighthood conferred by Antigua. Long before his indictment, many on St. Croix were suspicious of Stanford's company, describing it as a "cult," an assessment that was fueled by the widespread clamor to apply for employment, the company's unusually strict—and formal—dress code, and seemingly circumscribed opportunities for local employees to participate in community events.

Rather than tracing the implosion of Stanford Financial for sport, this chapter takes seriously the hope many on St. Croix invested in this company, the positioning of its employees, and the crushing blow dealt to St. Croix when this business became but the most recent and sensational in a long line to leave the island quickly amid suspicion. While supporters of the EDC program long heralded the initiative as categorically different from the territory's past attempts at economic stimulation, the continuing hasty retreat of EDC companies results in a vacuum on St. Croix much like that left by "runaway shops" (Safa 1981) and failed tourism initiatives across the region. While the financial services market on St. Croix attempts to position itself as entirely different from tourism, it results in many of the same long-term effects and is but a new way of doing service rather than a radical break with such attempts at economic stimulation. Financial services and tourism are two ends of a spectrum that remains informed by the historical legacy and continued implications of processes such as slavery, colonialism, and neoliberal development on islands that are still dependent on foreign dollars.

Despite the excitement surrounding Stanford's arrival on St. Croix, there were those who objected to this relocation. Among these critics, reactions ranged from skeptical to hostile. From residents who were merely hesitant, the explanation I received most frequently was that Stanford was "just another EDC man," albeit an extraordinarily wealthy one. These were, in part, objections to the patron model in which Stanford's vast wealth was seen as a boon to the island and the expectation that he would donate widely to charities and handsomely pay his local employees. What is more, in the fervor surrounding Stanford's arrival, fears about members of the EDC community hoping for a return to "slave days" on St. Croix were reignited.

Throughout this text, a central aim of my project is to historicize and contextualize the responses of those who opposed Stanford's arrival on St. Croix as something other than "anti-development" or "against progress," as advocates of the EDC program often have.[5] Rather, I argue that the accusations levied at the EDC program in general, and at Stanford in particular, are indictments of the unevenness of global processes, both historical and contemporary. That is, Crucians who describe EDC people as separate and Other and decry the program as a return to slavery are making an argument concerning the ways in which processes in the region—including the global financial exchanges of the current moment—result in already-wealthy white people being made wealthier by the resources of the island. That this indictment of unequal processes included the current moment of globalized capital and an actor such as Stanford was anathema to supporters of this man and the program that brought him to St. Croix, and these supporters dismissed objections as merely "backwardness" or a lack of understanding. This claim was embedded in the pro-EDC newspaper editorial in which the author argued that "our ability to understand and engage the opportunity will determine the future of the people of the Virgin Islands" (Difede 2004). Indeed, at the time of his arrival, Stanford seemed, to many, to represent the very future of the Virgin Islands.

While employment at Stanford was highly coveted, the women working at this company were subject to particular challenges both within and outside of the office. Given their recent employment and the widespread assumption of their newfound wealth as Stanford employees, these women were alternately bombarded with requests for financial assistance and pleas for help in "getting in" (that is, landing a job) at Stanford and lectured about their poor choice in going to work for "he"—so foremost in the minds of Virgin Islanders had this businessman become that he was often referred to simply as "he." During conversations with friends, for instance, I was repeatedly asked, "You hear what he do now?"—a question that invariably had to do with Stanford's most recent land purchase or a development in the building of his megacomplex. During my interview with then-chairman of the EDA Board of Directors Albert Bryan,[6] shortly after Stanford's groundbreaking ceremony, I raised the issue of Stanford and the Virgin Islanders who had recently begun to work for his company:

TAMI NAVARRO: About the groundbreaking that happened yesterday: I don't know if you got a chance to look at the *Avis* yet, but [I'm thinking of] the Stanford thing, and one of the quotes was, you know, "now we're 'home' and gonna set up shop here, but one of the biggest roadblocks is the EDC statute as it stands today and it basically needs to be revisited because it's 'outdated.'" [What are] your thoughts on that?

ALBERT BRYAN: If we look at the total impact of the Economic Development program . . . I mean, yesterday. Yesterday, at the groundbreaking, they had three very bright young Virgin Islanders—two who had, well I should say one who has been here for a while. One who moved home, from a very firm financial background, and finally slid herself in down there [at Stanford], and one who moved home *to* work for that company. And three of them hold very prestigious positions in that company. That's what [the EDC] is about. I'll tell you, this Allen Stanford deal I think is going to do a lot to help. I think because a lot of the Designated Service Businesses are so small it's hard to notice the impact [on the island]. There are a lot of talented Virgin Islanders who live here, who are underutilized, or underemployed that will seek out employment and find employment, too.

Bryan's comment that Stanford's arrival would do much to address the unemployment on St. Croix reflected the groundswell of hope that accompanied the billionaire's arrival on the island. However, his optimism about correcting underemployment on the island was at odds with the experiences of many would-be EDC employees who often found themselves in support positions without much work to do or saw positions filled by transplanted mainland staff who had only recently achieved the designation of "Virgin Islanders."

The tensions between Crucians and EDC people were often framed as racialized, specifically through frequent invocations of St. Croix's history (particularly the Fountain Valley attacks). For instance, during an interview with Lakisha, a twenty-eight-year-old Black woman employed as an administrative assistant at Stanford Financial, she pointed to the simmering long-standing tensions that had been reignited by the arrival of the EDC program. Lakisha had long been aware of Stanford and his wealth and had, in fact, thought of him as something like the "king of Antigua," as both of her parents immigrated to St. Croix from that island and described his many successful business ventures there. During my conversation with Lakisha, I asked her if she was happy with her decision to work at Stanford. At the time I asked the question, I had in mind the rumors surrounding the company and the restrictive dress and behavioral codes in the office. However, in response, Lakisha talked about some of the challenges she faced from within the company:

LAKISHA: I'm happy with the opportunity I have to grow, but I have had some personality conflicts with superiors because of some prejudiced comments. Like, one person [within the company] asked me, "You have a movie theater here? Does it have air conditioning?" As if we watch movies in a shack! This isn't the States. Things aren't as big, but we have stuff! Anyway, sooner or later they will realize they are living in the Caribbean, and St. Croix don't play.

Lakisha's comment that "sooner or later they"—that is, EDC people, and specifically higher-ups at Stanford—"will realize they are living in the Caribbean, and St. Croix don't play" hints at the racial tensions that have increased on St. Croix with the arrival of EDC businessmen and their families, an issue that is the focus of chapter 5.

This specter of racial violence that hovered over St. Croix during my fieldwork was attributed by my friends and interviewees to the arrival of EDC people. Charges of racism against them were so common that I could expect to hear at least one such complaint each day. As evidence, residents cited examples as disparate as their inability to secure work in this sector, impolite exchanges with EDC people at restaurants, and their presumed desire for segregation on St. Croix. In talking with Lakisha, I mentioned my own experiences with preconceptions—expectations she immediately saw as racialized—in my research when I mentioned that white CEOs and managers were often visibly surprised that I was born and raised on the island when I went to conduct interviews at EDC companies. I went on to tell Lakisha that I was frequently asked, "You're from here?" or "Where in the States did you move from?" As I recounted these experiences, in which my (lack of) local accent and status as a graduate student at a mainland university came together for my EDC interlocutors in ways that positioned me as outside of Virgin Islands identity, a light of recognition lit up her face, and she began nodding knowingly. "Yeah," Lakisha said, "they think you have to be a dumb, Black local."

Beyond blanket objections to Stanford as yet another unscrupulous EDC businessman, there were those who adamantly opposed Stanford and his business in particular. One such resident was Karen, the woman I met in the post office arguing about Stanford and the rising cost of real estate on St. Croix. During our early meetings, held around the time of the much-discussed groundbreaking ceremony, the grounds of Karen's objections to this man and his enterprise were less than clear to me, given her penchant for frequently venturing into conspiracy theories and indemonstrable claims concerning Stanford's never-ending desire for real estate and political power on the island. However, as John Jackson (2008) notes, conspiracy theories and seemingly paranoid fantasies can be productive pathways for anthropological insights. In his work, Jackson puts forth the term "racial paranoia" to describe these worldviews vis-à-vis racially based suspicions and antagonisms, writing, "We can't begin to understand race today without taking [paranoid] beliefs (as wild as they may seem) quite seriously—not as points of fact but as organizing principles for how people make sense of their everyday lives and forces potentially allied against them" (Jackson 2008: 7). While trying to bear this insight in mind, I remained skeptical of Karen's pronouncements concerning Stanford's nature and plans, including her claims that he was "just an evil man" and that he would soon be purchasing the entire historic town of Christiansted in order to convert it into a Key West–style tourist mecca. One evening after returning home from my internship at Stanford Financial, I received an email from Karen—a short message—that said simply, "Did I tell you that Stanford bought the home from [a wealthy longtime island resident]—was to be a polo field with a 200 acres + for 25 million? He also closed on the Christiansted marina." Exhausted from a day of attempting to decode financial statements, I went to bed. When I returned to this email months later, I was unable to find out how much truth there was to Karen's claims, as Stanford's personal and business assets had been seized by the US federal government when he was charged with operating a multibillion-dollar international fraud. What had seemed like groundless speculation about Stanford's nefarious intentions for St. Croix a few months before had become reality.

While Stanford Financial dominated much conversation on St. Croix during my fieldwork and internships, the same was not true of St. Croix Fund. As a small hedge fund, the stirrings of economic unrest on the US mainland began to affect this company in the summer of 2008. With much of their attention drawn to calming skittish investors and attracting new clients, I was unable to talk much with the few members of management at this company. In their absence, I was able to spend time with the support staff, the three local women working at the company—however, when I began to talk about the EDC sector, the conversation inevitably turned toward my internship at Stanford. I was asked, "What is it like?" and "Have you met *him*?" "What do you do there?" One day, near the end of my simultaneous internships at Stanford and St. Croix Fund before the former was shuttered, I told Peter Davies I had to leave the office early, as I was expected at a Stanford employee appreciation mixer. On my way out, I was surprised when an assistant, who had remained suspicious of my ethnographic motives and rarely spoke to me, stopped me near the door. Eyeing the silk dress and blazer I had changed into for the event, she said to me, "You know, *I* was invited to interview at Stanford, but I said no." While I was never able to get her to explain this statement—or her reasons for declining the Stanford interview—the implication seemed to be that while she worked at an EDC company, employment at Stanford was a line she simply would not cross. Her reading of me, then, as an "employee" at Stanford Financial, a company at the very epicenter of local debate during my fieldwork, seemed to be that I had somehow been co-opted by the corporation and betrayed the local community—one of the competing understandings of the often-envied local women working at Stanford.

As if to encapsulate the distance between most island residents and the rarified group chosen as Stanford employees, the staff appreciation mixer was held at Sir Allen's private office, housed in a mansion in Christiansted overlooking the historic town. As I glanced around the room that evening at the Stanford employees, my attention was drawn to the local workers, Virgin Islanders who were simultaneously admired, envied, and resented on the island. That evening, as we were surrounded by crystal, teak, and marble, we were offered appetizers passed not by servers but rather by the owner of one the island's tony restaurants. This evening, it seemed, encapsulated both the hopes of EDC advocates and the fears program critics expressed about the initiative further enriching the already privileged.

Quarterly Meetings

A few weeks into my internship at Stanford, Joe buzzed me on the intercom to come upstairs to his office. As I sat down, he explained that the company held quarterly meetings throughout the year, meetings that would now be held in the USVI in order to fulfill EDC mandates requiring business be conducted in the territory. As a result, Joe said, he and I, along with his fellow investment analysts, would be working from a nearby resort. The next morning, promptly at 8:30 a.m., I arrived at the conference room of The Ocean hotel, a nondescript, airless room with gray walls where I would be meeting, along with Stanford analysts from around the US, for the next two weeks. After pouring a cup of coffee and finding Joe, I sat down and listened as he named the people in the room and explained their roles. The twenty Stanford employees at these quarterly meetings had all traveled from the mainland to the island to review the investment strategies they employed on behalf of their investors. Besides Joe, myself, and a third Stanford employee from the St. Croix office (a woman who began her employment at the company at the same time I did), all the analysts in attendance were white, although two had brought their assistants, resulting in the presence of two Hispanic women in the room. Over two-thirds of the group was male, and they were generally in their midthirties to early forties. The leader of this group was a white woman named Laura Pendergest, a manager who regularly corralled the group, keeping the attendees focused and on topic. On that first day of the meetings, I wondered what the women back at the office were doing while I spent these two weeks at The Ocean, listening in as the analysts argued over investment possibilities around the globe. As I silently bemoaned my bad luck at being taken to these two-week meetings, I realized the group was breaking for lunch, a meal that we would all eat together at the hotel. While I suspected this would be a very different experience from the lunches I had recently been having with the female Stanford employees in the office, I was nevertheless excited to leave the conference room and escape the talk of stock ticker symbols that had dominated the morning session.

Over lunch on the patio of the hotel's main restaurant, I chatted with Joe and Laura, suggesting local sights she might enjoy. Unfortunately, she would not have much time for sightseeing, Laura explained, as she and her husband were leaving on a ferry for the British Virgin Islands the next afternoon, heading to a private island they had rented for a long weekend. As my shock about the wealth of these employees subsided, Joe caught my eye and changed the subject, telling me that during the quarterly meetings, attendees regularly went out to dinner together and would be dining at restaurants around the island nearly every night of the two-week period. Excited about the prospect of gauging Virgin Islanders' responses to me as a part of this group (that is, would I be viewed or treated differently when people saw me as part of a group of Stanford employees?), I asked Joe to let me know which restaurants were chosen. One Friday evening near the end of the meetings, I excitedly got ready to go to dinner with the group at Coral Point. This Friday evening dinner was something of an event, a tourist-display complete with steel pans and colorfully dressed stilt walkers that was always well attended. As our group of ten settled into our seats, I was disappointed to realize that I did not recognize anyone in the dining room outside of my group. Given their short stay in the territory and lack of corporate attire at this dinner, this group of diners, wealthy men and women brought to the island by the EDC program, went unrecognized. The amount of power and money they wielded also went unrecognized that evening, as stilt walkers posed for pictures and the crowd swayed to the sounds of calypso music and crashing waves. Would this group of analysts realize the impact of the program in which they were participating, I wondered? This scene once again brought to mind the centrality of *mobility* to this program—that is, the ability of these US-based Stanford employees to move nimbly between the mainland US and St. Croix, capitalizing on opportunities and remaining privileged across boundaries that are economically insurmountable for many Crucians. Once the Stanford megacomplex was built, they would be able to conduct business on St. Croix without ever setting foot on the island beyond the company gates, much like the state of affairs in that other source of Caribbean economic development, the export-processing zones that allow international companies privileged access to the region and its labor (see Black 2001). Long after these analysts returned to the US mainland, residents of the Virgin Islands would be dealing with the social, cultural, economic implications of the EDC program and its beneficiaries. As I took in the crowd, my mind returned to Laura and her husband, away on the private island they had rented. "Could the EDC program, through companies like Stanford Financial, create such mobility for Virgin Islanders?" I wondered. That question went unanswered, as the next time I saw Laura was a Saturday morning in February 2009 when I opened the business section of the *New York Times* and saw her in handcuffs being escorted to court to address the charges of fraud brought against Stanford Financial.

More of the Same: Stanford Indictment

After returning to the mainland at the end of my fieldwork, I received an early-morning phone call from a friend living on St. Croix: "Can you believe it?!" she shrieked. Having no idea what she was talking about, I was stunned when she told me that Allen Stanford had been charged with fraud and his assets frozen by the federal government. In disbelief, I called several friends on St. Croix, all of whom told the same story: they woke up one morning and Stanford, merely the largest and most conspicuous in a long line of disreputable companies lured to the island by an economic development initiative offering enormous savings, had closed its doors amid as many rumors as had surrounded its opening. In early 2009, the tone in the local media concerning Stanford seemed to be one of muted surprise. Given all the excitement surrounding the company's move to the island and the vocal endorsement of the local government, it was a huge blow to St. Croix when Stanford Financial was alleged to be a pyramid scheme, and Sir Allen was charged with perpetrating massive fraud. Yet Crucians had experienced this betrayal—and from within this sector—before. The ongoing criminal case against Company X had also dealt to a blow to the EDC program and the island as a whole, but even that notorious case was far from the first of its kind. Nor was this unique to St. Croix. All across the Caribbean this is a familiar story as factories and export-processing zone (EPZ) industries lock out workers without warning.[7] The shuttering of Stanford Financial, the pinnacle of the EDC program and source of hope for St. Croix, reinforced the suspicion with which many Crucians had long viewed the program. The fact of Stanford's assets being frozen by the federal government left the previously much-envied employees of the company "locked out of their offices and without paychecks" or access to their retirement funds (Baur 2009).

While this turn of events was humbling, no one I spoke with— even the most outspoken critic of Stanford and his company—expressed any pleasure at the comeuppance of these formerly envied Virgin

Islanders. Rather, they bemoaned the jobs lost and the further—that is, recurring—economic decline of the island. That Crucians did not relish the fall of Stanford's local employees suggests a recognition of the precarity of their EDC privilege and the possibility of their reintegration into the community. The frequent federal investigations of EDC companies and their subsequent closings had perhaps prepared Crucians for such an eventuality at Stanford, as well as armed them with the knowledge that while new social and class arrangements are created on St. Croix by the EDC program, these emergent hierarchies are far from fixed and fall away when companies leave. In addition to recognizing the fleeting nature of local EDC privilege, the local reaction to Stanford's closing also points to the ambivalence with which these workers had long been viewed: while the privileges and status garnered by their employment at Stanford were envied, these women were never viewed as occupying the same position as global elites, EDC people who had the power to interview, hire, and dismiss Virgin Islanders at will. Rather, the privilege of EDC girls was relative and grounded in local networks as they negotiated their positioning as both Crucians and EDC employees.

In order to assist the newly unemployed Stanford workers, the Department of Labor held an emergency information session, a seminar whose events were outlined in a *St. Croix Source* article:

> With dozens of St. Croix employees of Stanford Financial Group suddenly left jobless in the wake of allegations of massive fraud, court orders appointing a receiver and freezing the assets of financier Allen Stanford, the V.I. Labor Department held a rapid-response workshop to help them sign up for unemployment benefits.
>
> The Securities and Exchange Commission filed a complaint against Stanford in February, alleging fraud at the Antigua-based Stanford International Bank, triggering the freezing of assets and closures on St. Croix and elsewhere.
>
> The department's Rapid Response Workshops are designed for mass layoffs or plant closings, to provide workers who were severed from their places of employment with vital information about the various services available to them to help in the transition.

About 38 former employees came out for the work-shop Wednesday.

The newly unemployed run the gamut from information-technology professionals to investment analysts to electricians. What they all share is a sudden employment crisis and financial uncertainty. "I sold my house and moved here with my family to take this job," said [one attendee], an IT professional who join[ed] Stanford a year and a half ago. "Now my family is here, my house is here. I've been looking off-island for work. I will probably have to leave my family here and let my kids finish school while I look for work. It's been a struggle." [A Department of Labor official] had good and bad news for the workers. The amount of unemployment benefits depends on both the employee and employer contributions to unemployment insurance. "For you to get the employer share of the contributions, the employer would have to have deposited their contribution," he said. But not all Stanford's employer contributions had been made, and with all the assets frozen by the receiver for now, it is not clear when or if those employer contributions will be made. (Kossler 2009b)

The local response to the closing was anger directed at Stanford himself—and at the local government for its unquestioning embrace of his investment in the island. An article entitled "Pipe Dreams and Ponzi Schemes: Is This the Promise of the EDA?" posted on VirginIslandsWatch.com in March 2009 captures the sense of betrayal in the territory:

Why is it that the Virgin Islands keeps popping up in scandal after scandal? In addition to engaging in its own share of corruption the Virgin Islands seems to invite corrupt (or, at least questionable) individuals. What's next?

Pipe dreams & Ponzi schemes: is this the promise of the EDA?

Allen Stanford has been accused of owing more than $226 million in back taxes and of running an $8 billion Ponzi scheme. In the article posted on Bloomberg news, all Governor deJongh could say was: *"I'm disappointed,"* *deJongh said in an interview at Government House in Christiansted, St. Croix's largest town. "Clearly he was a large player within the Caribbean, but also I'm very disappointed from the standpoint of the number of Virgin Islands families that are affected."*

Pipe dreams & Ponzi schemes: is this the promise of the EDA?

What about disappointment that his vetters missed some glaring discrepancies—namely multi-millions in disputed taxes. Did this not raise a red flag? Then again, after the Rodney Miller debacle we know that ethical discrepancies mean nothing when welcoming non-Virgin Islanders to rape our community.

Thankfully, the economic collapse exposed Stanford. Yet, the Governor is disappointed that the promised billions Stanford was to invest would not be forthcoming. Stanford's demise is a blessing in disguise. Right now, Antigua and Barbuda had to undertake emergency measures to seize Allen Stanford's property in hopes of preserving the jobs he "brought to the community." Just think, Virgin Islanders—had Governor deJongh not been "disappointed," this could be our lot! Oh Joy!

How many schemers have we welcomed to the Virgin Islands that have yet to be exposed? How much snake oil has Governor deJongh sold us?

Pipe dreams & Ponzi schemes: is this the promise of the EDA?

It is coming to the point where we must question everything. It is coming to the point where all actions of the VI Government must be scrutinized with an air of distrust. It is coming to the point where we need to resurrect the Three Queens and "let fire burn!"

Answer the call: Virgin Islands for the Virgin Islanders . . . those at home and those abroad! (Ballentine 2009; emphasis mine)

The claim in this article that "non-Virgin Islanders" are welcome to "rape our community" relies on a binary of us/them that pits

"Virgin Islanders" (a fraught category that continues to be subdivided) against "non-Virgin Islanders" (that is, EDC people). What is more, the invocation of the "Three Queens" and Fireburn (the 1878 labor revolt on St. Croix) in relation to Stanford's indictment demonstrates the way in which, for many in the Virgin Islands, the EDC program does not represent a break with the past and move toward a new global integration but rather a revisiting of earlier processes of racialized inequality and oppression—a moment in which spectral time comes to the fore. Thus, the charge that the EDC program marks a return to "slave days" makes clear the logic behind the final line of the article, a call to action against the "non-Virgin Islanders" in the territory. This specter of racialized violence, the focus of chapter 5, is presented as the outcome of tensions between (Black) Virgin Islanders and the (white) EDC people attracted to the island by the promise of a tax holiday.

In the national press, the coverage of Stanford's indictment was equally damning. The economic crisis continuing to envelop the US in early 2009, a catastrophe that was attributed to greed on the part of many in the financial services industry, resulted in a backlash against investment bankers, traders, and financial managers in general. The impact of the recession on the American public was significant: unemployment rose to the highest numbers in decades, homeowners with rapidly escalating mortgages found themselves unable to pay and facing foreclosure, business owners reliant on consumer confidence saw their businesses wither. The effects of the US economic crisis were equally pronounced in the financial services sector, as several major investment banks closed, many others survived as a result of US government intervention, and countless smaller banks and hedge funds—including St. Croix Fund—shuttered their doors as a result of the contracting economy. The mainland arrest of Bernard Madoff on charges of carrying out a $50 billion Ponzi scheme further angered the American public, and news of the charges against Stanford only fanned these flames. An article in the *New York Times* in February 2009 describes the meteoric rise of Stanford in terms that echo Lakisha's comment that he was seen as the "King of Antigua":

When Robert Allen Stanford arrived [in Antigua] in the early 1990's, few locals had ever heard of the Texas financier. Today, he dominates so many aspects of life on this sun-drenched Caribbean island that some have taken to calling it "Stanford Land."

At one point or another, he has owned an airline that many locals and visitors fly on. A local newspaper that covers their goings-on. A vast residential complex where many live. Two restaurants where they eat. And the national stadium where they go to watch cricket, the island's favorite sport.

But the crown jewel of his domain has long been Stanford International Bank, an offshore institution that attracted billions of dollars of cash from clients around the world—and especially from Latin America—seeking a haven for their wealth.

Despite raised eyebrows and occasional investigations of Mr. Stanford—or Sir Allen, as he is called here since he was knighted by the Antiguan government in 2006—his sway has continued to grow. That is, until this week, when the Securities and Exchange Commission accused Stanford International of orchestrating a huge fraud that may have bilked investors of some $8 billion that regulators say cannot be accounted for. (Krauss, Creswell, and Savage 2009)

In the weeks following the initial allegations, Stanford's assets were frozen and he, along with several high-ranking officials within Stanford Financial, were arrested. As the charges mounted, the always-present criticisms of Stanford intensified, and long-skeptical observers seemed prescient. In a May 2009 article in the *New Yorker* focusing on the events surrounding Stanford's fall, the author recounts the ceremony at which both the Antiguan-born author Jamaica Kincaid and Allen Stanford were to be honored:

Some on the island have always thought of Stanford as a freebooter who has prospered magnificently on their shores. Jamaica Kincaid was born and grew up in Antigua, and wrote a fierce portrait of the island, "A Small Place." At the ceremony at which Stanford was knighted—with Prince Edward in attendance, and marching bands—Kincaid also received an award. When Stanford approached her, she refused to shake his hand.

"Your honor demeans my own," she told him.

[In speaking with the author, Kincaid said,] "He's always been a crook and everybody knows it. Stanford is a standing scandal in Antigua he's both a joke and a benefactor. In Antigua there's always a man, a person who comes in from the rest of the world—a pirate. Piracy is very close to Antiguan history. They've been coming and hiding money and stealing for hundreds of years. This man comes to Antigua and corrupts the place, and everybody's happy because they're making money.

"The ones who aren't benefitting from it, like me, are the opposition," she continued. "In the papers, after I refused to shake Stanford's hand, I was rebuked by Sir Vivian Richards, the great cricket player, who I had no idea was in with Stanford." She then brought up the airport, "the most holy place" in Antigua, she said. "What Stanford did was he bought land around the airport and transformed the airport. When you go into it now, there are those lovely gardens—he has great taste in gardens. When you came to it in the past, it was just sort of an airport in the tropics. People came to feel it was just a matter of time before Stanford called it the Stanford Airport. No longer, I suppose. I can't tell you how sweet it is." (Wilkinson 2009: 24)

Kincaid's choice of piracy as the metaphor with which to describe Stanford is particularly apt, and ironic, given his earlier professed desire to rid the region of "pirates in the Caribbean." In her work on Jamaica, Anita Waters (2003) finds that "the lawlessness of pirates is linked with the extraordinary liberties enjoyed by Europeans in the colonies" (172). Yet the activities in which pirates engaged were not *always* illegal. Rather, they operated in ways that often straddled the border between licit and illicit, depending on whether they were operating under a European flag. Anne Galvin (2002), for instance, outlines the position of colonial privateers, linking these figures to contemporary developments in Jamaica. What is more, broader processes continue to skirt the boundaries of legality and invoke questions of sovereignty, including the use of flags of convenience in which countries offer their maritime flag registrations to other nations for a fee. Ronen Palan (2003) writes that flags of convenience (FOC) "traditionally, offer 'easy' registration low or no taxes, and no practical restrictions on the nationality of crews. . . . By transferring a ship from a genuine national register to a flag of convenience, an owner runs away from taxation, safely regulations, and trade union organization" (Palan 2003: 52). Both the rise of offshore banking in the Caribbean (see also Vlcek 2017) and practices such as flags of convenience have particular relevance for islands in the Caribbean and their economic development, as they underscore contemporary attempts to navigate questions of sovereignty, mobility, and capital.[8]

After the End

The flood of salacious stories covering Stanford's fall in mainland media outlets like the *New York Times*,[9] *Newsweek*,[10] *Esquire*, ABC News,[11] MSNBC,[12] and more did little to alleviate the difficulties faced by Stanford's former employees. Attempts to help these victims were more difficult to come by and they were largely left to fend for themselves. On St. Croix, many of the Stanford employees who relocated to the island to work for the company could no longer afford to stay. For local workers, once the object of envy and suspicion as a result of their affiliation with the program and this celebrated company, the loss was substantial. Despite the excitement surrounding Stanford's arrival on St. Croix and the promises of newness and increased incorporation into global financial markets, the collapse of this company, yet another EDC to disappoint the island and its residents, was a familiar story for Crucians.

Chapter 5

Putting Race to Work

Racialization and Economic Opportunity

Processes of racialization have long undergirded capitalist interventions in the Caribbean. Enslaved plantation labor, sharecropping, tourism, and both heavy and light industry have been made possible by hierarchies of gender, race, and color as discussed in the previous chapter. This chapter provides ethnographic insight into the ways in which race—and racialized anxieties rooted in these earlier moments of racial capitalism—continue to not just inform but shape the financialization of the US Virgin Islands through the EDC program.

I tie together race-based tensions, instances of racist violence both predating and occurring during the EDC program, and fears of a return to formalized residential and economic segregation in the model of the plantation system together within the framework of spectral time. Racialized anxieties that emerged in relation to EDC people were slippery, as they sometimes elided and sometimes inflamed tensions about "native" USVI identity. These anxieties that often cropped up in the form of rumors about the EDC and its people point to the ways that the present, the current moment of neoliberal development, is shot through with fears of past encounters with global wealth and its handlers.

Local Reaction to the EDC Program

On St. Croix, there are two competing interpretations of the EDC program: the first is that it is a quintessentially modern project, an

97

attempt to situate this eighty-four-square-mile island as a new frontier in transnational financial processes. The second interpretation is that the initiative is a problematic refashioning of slavery, drawing on the politically dependent status of the USVI and preexisting race, color, gender, and class hierarchies. This second assessment challenges the claims of "newness" in the first but also points to the ways that long-standing hierarchies have become reinvigorated to influence and shape the trajectories of Crucians' lives. The critical reception of the EDC program reflects Crucians' critique of capital in multiple registers, as both a project of wealth consolidation (that is, a claim that the rich get richer through the program—pointing to an uneven playing field) and an insistence on engaging with the program through the lens of racial capitalism by centering the processes of racialization that facilitate these circuits.

Contrary to the claims of its advocates, the EDC is neither an entirely virtual financial program demonstrative of a clean break with the island's racialized past nor, as critics suggest, is it an exact replica of white domination of the island in the model of slavery or colonialism. Rather, the EDC program is representative of a new moment of *differently* global processes and is an initiative that incorporates a formerly omitted island into global financial circulations while maintaining elements of race, color, class, and gender that are reminiscent of earlier processes in the region. This rendering points to the ways that financial markets are grounded in particular realities that reflect sedimented histories. This is what has always characterized the region. Neither wholly old nor new, the EDC program is indicative of the current state of affairs in an international market in which financialization and neoliberal policies of freeing markets reign. While many new spaces *have* been opened, the relations on which these initiatives are based were established long ago, as they reproduce the race and color power dynamics seen since slavery and colonialism. This means that my work is an examination of St. Croix as an emerging space vis-à-vis global financial processes. However, it is also a grounded analysis of the implications of this development program on the women with whom I worked, as the Virgin Islanders whose lives have been affected by this initiative, a focus that recenters conversations about globalized capital on the workers who make these processes possible.

During my time in the field, the ambivalence with which many Virgin Islanders regarded the EDC program was strikingly clear: when telling friends and acquaintances I had returned to the island to study the EDC program, I became conditioned to expect one of two responses—either a request that I slip their resume to someone at an EDC company or derision that I was in any way affiliated with the program. Negative comments were so common that I was completely unsurprised by the reaction of an off-duty waiter I had come to know in passing. After a long day of attempting to decipher financial projections in my role as an EDC intern, I sat in a dimly lit restaurant, rehashing the events of the day with a friend who was filling in as the bartender that night. Overhearing our conversation, a Black waiter in his midfifties named Tyrone, who had not long ago finished his shift, shouted, "I hope you study how they discriminate against we!" In response, I mumbled something about "studying all aspects" and "remaining impartial." As I considered his reaction later, however, I realized that the "we" Tyrone invoked is entirely unsteady—as the binary between "us" and "them" was to be called into question during the entirety of my fieldwork. That is, to parse the ways "they" discriminate against "we" would necessitate a clear sense of who occupied each of these camps—a delineation that simply was not possible on St. Croix in 2008, as the island was in the midst of its Fifth Constitutional Convention that became a territory-wide debate around these very issues of discrimination and inclusion. What is more, the "discrimination" invoked by Tyrone was multilayered: It wasn't clear that Tyrone was, or would be, seeking employment in the EDC sector in the near future, leading him to be primarily concerned with exclusionary hiring preferences. So then, what did his concern about "discrimination" prefigure? Was it an indictment of patterns of residential segregation that saw EDC people clustered on the East End of the island? Perhaps, but it was just as likely that he was invoking the larger social segregation of EDC people, the ways in which they seemingly preferred to limit their interactions with Crucians to the extent possible.

The shifting binary of us/them sometimes referred to divisions between the largely white EDC community and Black residents of the Virgin Islands but was just as readily used to refer to long-standing tensions between so-called "native" Virgin Islanders and residents whose parents had immigrated to the territory or who had done so themselves. While the managers of EDCs are, on the whole, white mainland Americans, their employees are most often lighter-skinned Crucian women, a structure uncomfortably reminiscent of the tri-partite race/color hierarchy of white/brown/Black at work in the Caribbean during slavery and colonialism in which lighter-skin ranked above the despised level of "Black." This race- and color-inflected history is reflected in the assessment of the EDC as an attempt to return the island to "slave days" that often saw the division of labor organized along lines of color, with lighter-skinned slaves generally performing domestic work indoors as opposed to work in the fields.

Many EDC supporters, however, see the initiative in an entirely different light. Peter Davies of St. Croix Fund, for instance, argued that while EDC beneficiaries *are* getting tax breaks, they are also connecting the island to international financial markets and con-tributing to the local economy. "And besides," he went on, "the money we're saving isn't that much." This particular defense begs the question of whether Crucians' primary objection to the program is financial. It is not clear that this is the case. Rather, objections are largely couched in terms of its overall structure, critiques that emerge at the nexus of race, class, and exclusion. The invocation of "slave days" is not an indictment of inequitable wages being paid in the EDC sector, given the contextually high salaries they generally offer. It is not even, centrally, a critique of the tax holiday that undergirds this program. The question of whether Crucians would be angry about the program if beneficiaries were paying taxes is key—and the answer is a resounding "yes," for it is not simply circuitous financial practices to which they object, but it is these in combination with perceived slights and instances of racism together with increased stratification along lines of race, color, class, and gender. While money is an important part of how the EDC is received, it is not the only lens through which Crucians engage the program. Instead, they frame the EDC in a long line of projects that rely on foreign capital, benefit those who are wealthy and white, *and* allow those ostensible interlopers to "take over" their (Black) community. This constellation comes together in the form of spectral time. Seen in this light, Peter's comment that the money he is saving "isn't that much" (a statement that is very much open to debate, given the 90 percent tax waiver beneficiaries enjoy) does not attend to the central critique of the program: How did he—and his business—end up on St. Croix? What are the histories and contemporary realities of inequality that led to his presence on this American-owned island, his ownership of a large home on its East End, and his role as an EDC employer—that is, an arbiter of privilege? Rather than emphasizing how much money was or was not saved by individual EDC beneficiaries, these nonquantitative questions push in a different direction—toward more complicated conversations that center race, gender, class, and empire.

On St. Croix, the public perception of the EDC program is that it brings wealthy white capitalists to the island, where they are able to increase their wealth at the expense of Black residents, a situation they object to as both exploitative and familiar, drawing connections to the long history of racialized wealth accumulation in the region in general and in the USVI in particular. This narrative has traction on the island because it is, in part, true: EDC companies are able to save vast amounts of money by way of tax abatement (despite Peter's protestations) and, in order to do this, they are contractually required to hire local workers who are often lighter-skinned and drawn from backgrounds of relative privilege. However, this telling elides much, including the racial/ethnic composition of the island today, histories of migration and racialization that led to this contemporary reality, and nuance within the ranks of EDC people who are generally—but not uniformly—white (for instance, Joe Conners, my manager during my time at Stanford, was a Black man from the US mainland). Local resentment over the presence of EDC people, their selective engagement with the local community, and exclusionary hiring and residential practices have combined to result in escalating tensions between the local community of blacks and long-term whites against EDC people. However, beyond the tensions between white and Black, or even white and "EDC," the presence of these global elites and their assumed indifference toward St. Croix has resulted in a greater emphasis on race and (birth)place on the island, as would be demonstrated by an increasingly racialized hostility present in a territory-wide debate in 2008 at the Fifth Constitutional Convention over defining "native" Virgin Islanders.

St. Croix, like sugar islands across the Caribbean, was built on the labor of enslaved Africans, Black workers to whom Afro-Crucians today point as their forebears. While this Black/white relationship of oppression and violence is the primary narrative of labor history in the Virgin Islands today—and directly influences the ways the EDC program is received—the history of labor and migration in the territory exceeds this rendering. Noting the long history of ethnic diversity, and divisions, in the USVI, Robert Aldrich and John Connell (1998) have written:

> Few territories have been so characterized by immigration as the USVI. In the 1960s, the "Development Decade," the USVI gained from its strategic position as a regional growth pole based on its capacity to draw upon relatively unlimited supplies of United States capital and expertise, and on its ability to attract a highly elastic supply of West Indian labor, and the population doubled. Extensive immigration posed problems for infrastructure and service provision, and raised long-standing questions about identity and the role of aliens or "down-islanders." Between 1960 and 1976 the population density tripled, urban conditions worsened, and tensions between Virgin Islanders and others mounted. (Aldrich and Connell 1998: 106; see also Dookhan 1974)

The vast majority of the population in the US Virgin Islands identifies as Black. Data from the most recent (2010) census shows that 76 percent of the territory's population identifies as "Black or African-American" (USVI Population 2010). The second most numerically significant group in the territory is "Hispanic or Latino (of any race)," followed by those who identify as white (16.7%). This data only obliquely gestures to the long, complex history of migration to St. Thomas, St. John, and St. Croix, particularly as it is reflected in the capacious category of "Other"—statistically the smallest, it includes the Jewish community, as well as East Indians and Arabs. This elision is significant, as there are long-standing communities of Arabs and Jews in the USVI—the latter of which have had a presence on these islands since the 1600s (Cohen 2011). The subsumption of these groups into the category of "Other" in the process of data collection is telling, as they are often viewed as either peripheral to or entirely outside of what constitutes the local community on St.

Croix. The Arab community in particular is largely seen as set apart on St. Croix and is closely associated with business ownership (particularly of supermarkets and gas stations) and generally uninvolved in local politics (see Cohen 2011 and Roopnarine 2009). The erasure of this reality by my informants in their telling of their encounters with the EDC program results in beneficiaries cast into the slot of wealthy whites intent on oppressing Black community members, a framing that leaves no space for ethnic groups that fall outside of these ostensibly fixed poles of difference.

The history of migration to St. Croix, St. Thomas, and St. John is long and complex. In addition to Arab and Jewish communities, those characterized as "others" include those who have moved from elsewhere in the region (often derogatively termed "down-islanders" or "garrotes" in the USVI), East Indian migrants from India and Trinidad, and descendants of the single cohort of indentured laborers brought to the islands (then the Danish West Indies), as well as migrants from Puerto Rico. While planters in some Caribbean colonies, particularly Trinidad and Guyana, relied heavily on indentured Indian labor to maximize the profits to be made from sugarcane, the history of the Danish West Indies features only one ill-fated attempt to supplement enslaved African labor with workers brought from India: In 1863, the steamship *Mars* left Calcutta, bound for St. Croix. These workers were brought to the island after Emancipation, and planters hoped this imported labor would enable them to continue cultivating the plentiful cane that sprang up around them while alleviating their fears of a labor shortage. As it happened, good weather had made the year 1862 a boom year for sugarcane growth on St. Croix, which only increased planters' anxieties of labor shortages. Planters estimated "15,000 hogsheads of sugar and 10,000 puncheons of rum for the 1862 season,[1] an output larger than any [they could have hoped to have] for a long time to come" (Sircar 1971: 136). Thus, the arrival of the *Mars* and its passengers was much awaited. Yet, just eighteen months later, this group of indentured laborers began to fall ill and die as a result of disease combined with inadequate food and housing conditions—including one noted instance in which six Indian workers (both male and female) were housed crammed together in a single room (Sircar 1971). Given these conditions, over 200 of the original group of 316 indentured workers who arrived

on St. Croix in 1863 refused a second contract and were returned
to India in 1868. As K. K. Sircar has written, "Fortunately for the
Indians no second batch had embarked for St. Croix" (1971: 142).

Comparatively, the history of Puerto Rican migration to the
US Virgin Islands is more complicated. The geographical proximity
of Puerto Rico to the Virgin Islands, particularly St. Croix, from
which it is separated by just over one hundred miles (a trip that can
be completed by seaplane in forty-five minutes) has contributed to
much exchange between these American territories. The fact of their
shared positioning on the periphery of the United States as territories
in the Caribbean means they face many of the same hurdles vis-à-
vis expressions of autonomy (an issue I discuss later in this chapter
in relation to the Fifth Constitutional Convention in the USVI) or
inclusion in the American public imagination of itself, as was powerfully demonstrated by the US federal response to these territories
following hurricanes Irma and Maria. These factors, combined with
the need for labor in the Virgin Islands at various moments, have
resulted in a long and dynamic relationship between these territories.
For instance, a shortage of workers in the sugar industry on St.
Croix during the Great Depression, and the further decline of this
industry in Puerto Rico—especially in Vieques—as a result of American military interventions, contributed to large numbers of Puerto
Ricans relocating to St. Croix beginning in earnest in the 1920s
(Bermúdez-Ruiz 2010). The long-term use by the US of Vieques
as a site of its bombing exercises decimated both the area and labor
opportunities, and employment became concentrated within American
military bases, leading many to flee. In her collection of oral histories
related to the sugar industry on St. Croix, Karen Thurland (2014)
includes the life history of Agapito Ramos, a man who left Vieques
and came to St. Croix with his family as a child. Ramos recounts
his experience of the journey:

> The Navy took Vieques and Culebra, so all the people from
> Culebra went to Vieques to live. Then the Navy made a
> runway, so they took everybody out and also made a place
> to throw bombs. We traveled on a sailboat that didn't
> have any motor. My uncle Nilo de Jesus had a boat, and
> I think tis [sic] he who brought us here. My mother told

me that she got seasick, and I got so sick that I nearly died on the way to St. Croix. (Thurland 2014: 115)

This harrowing journey was but the first of many difficulties faced by Puerto Rican migrants seeking to improve their fortunes on St. Croix. As did migrants from elsewhere in the region, Puerto Ricans were met with racism, linguistic exclusion, and disdain for their connection to sugarcane cultivation, a form of labor that was viewed by many on St. Croix as outmoded and indelibly linked to slavery. This initial icy reception would transform dramatically over the years, given the growing numbers of this community and their eventual incorporation into political and cultural life on the island. This transformation was so complete that in 1964, the public holiday Virgin Islands–Puerto Rico Friendship Day was created to "honor Puerto Ricans residing in our midst and other Puerto Ricans who have made substantial contributions to the advancement and progress of the Virgin Islands." The legislation outlining this holiday articulates the extent to which Puerto Ricans had become integrated into the Virgin Islands community, reading in part "whereas the people of the Territory of the Virgin Islands and the people of the Commonwealth of Puerto Rico have a long, happy association as relatives, good neighbors, business partners, fellow Americans and warm friends . . . the Governor of the Virgin Islands . . . call[s] upon the citizens of the Virgin Islands to observe the occasion."[2] This holiday has grown over the years to include receptions, cultural performances, and a beauty pageant whose winner is crowned Miss VI/PR Friendship Queen.

These histories of racialization, particularly in relation to labor, are crucial for understanding the ways racism continues to inform life and opportunities, particularly in (post)colonial spaces. Lisa Lowe (2015) has outlined the historical and contemporary significance of "liberal ideas of human person, family, and society" (33). It matters very much how—and why—particular groups arrive. Yet, despite the significance of these histories of migration and the formalized depth of ties vis-à-vis the Puerto Rican community, this nuance all but disappears in the face of tensions that have resurfaced in the wake of the EDC program. That is, in the face of the seeming familiarity of the EDC program as an extension of racialized oppression, this complexity fades into the background, transforming the EDC program into a struggle exclusively between Black and white participants. This demonstrates the purchase of spectral time: in spite of the reality of ethnic diversity that Crucians encounter on the island every day, the experience of living through the moment of the EDC program is articulated in ways that elide these complex histories of movement, replacing them with a Black/white narrative of oppression in the model of slavery.

I had long been aware of the hesitance with which many on St. Croix regarded the EDC program—in fact, this was a large part of what drew me to this project initially. The suspicion with which many Virgin Islanders regarded the EDC program was strikingly apparent; as something of a "representative" of the agency—although I quickly made clear my actual position as an anthropologist *studying* the program rather than an employee or advocate—I received overwhelmingly negative reactions, ranging from curious stares to recitations of criminal charges brought against various EDC companies. What I had not, however, anticipated was the level of frustration I ultimately encountered from Virgin Islanders. One afternoon as I was shopping at a boutique in town[3] for a dress to wear to a friend's upcoming wedding, a woman whom I had come to know in passing came in and asked how long I had been back on island and where I was now working. As we entered separate dressing rooms, I offhandedly said that I was on St. Croix "studying the EDCs," to which she responded—over the divider that now separated us—"they're getting over on the Virgin Islands [and] we're not getting enough back for what the EDCs are getting." Here again, the question of "what they are getting" exceeds an exclusively quantitative analysis. This question of the inequality between program beneficiaries and Virgin Islanders was by now familiar to me and thus an issue I raised with the then chairman of the EDA Board, Albert Bryan:

> TAMI NAVARRO: I did an interview yesterday with somebody who's active in the, sort of, EDC world, and his take on it is that people who are not 100 percent for it, the reason for that, the main reason for that is that they don't *understand* it, and they don't understand the benefits they're getting. But I, I would say that it's pretty

clear that there are some people in the community who aren't, you know, gung ho about the program, and so, given how drastically it's changed our economy, what do you think that hesitance or suspicion or resentment, what do you think that's rooted in?

ALBERT BRYAN: I think as a people we have, the way we are as a Caribbean people and as a Virgin Islands people, we have enjoyed years and years of prosperity where other Caribbean nations . . . *have not.*

TN: Because of our relationship with the United States?

AB: Exactly. And, because of that I think we have been . . . and for the most part we've been insulated against a lot of things; we take care of one another in the V.I. When you introduce businesses that are . . . there seems to be a perception in the VI that businesses should be run as social institutions. Being more socialist, rather than capitalist . . . I think when you're doing business with anybody, you need to realize that "this person is in business . . ."

TN: . . . to make money.

AB: To make money! And if you negotiate from that position, your expectation level will be less, in terms of what that person will *give* you, and will rely more on what you can negotiate out of that person. And, here, I think that the way the program has been characterized by some of our leaders, not only this program, but business in general, big business in general in the V.I., as "they should be more" I . . . I can't even say, "they should be better" I shouldn't say "better," "super corporate citizens."

As I would soon realize, the vast difference between these views of the program had an enormous impact on the island as they represented differing experiences of capital, belonging, and time.

Becoming "Business-Friendly"

As the sun set early one evening over Crystal Bay, a seaside resort on the eastern side of St. Croix, I hurried over to the pool and was greeted by the sight of three enormous white canopy tents strung with lights covering the better part of the large deck surrounding the pool. Attempting to follow the directions of the office memo that brought me here, I was there, along with my EDA coworkers, dressed in my best estimate of "island elegant" clothing: white linen pants and a sky-blue top. We were there for a "meet-and-greet" cocktail reception between the agency and the beneficiaries it governed. While I had only recently begun "interning" with the EDA, I quickly realized this was an attempt not only to bridge two vastly different worlds but also to foster better communication across them, as the government's "anti-business attitude" was often noted by beneficiaries. As I walked over to the tents searching for a familiar face, I saw clusters of breezily dressed men wearing silk and cotton shirts dominated by pineapple and coconut themes and a few women in pastel-colored sundresses. Spotting someone I knew from the office, I rushed over and grabbed one of the few remaining seats at the EDA table and began chatting with my coworkers about the night ahead.

Although I had only been working at the EDA for a few short weeks before that night at Crystal Bay, I had already heard rumblings about beneficiaries' frustrated expectations of friendliness and service at the EDA office and witnessed firsthand some of the differences between daily life at the EDA and EDCs. Initially, the most glaring difference was that the government office consisted entirely of people of color, while the EDC offices I had visited were largely white. As time went on, however, I found other contrasts nearly as striking, including the frequent lapses into the dialect of Crucian at the EDA, compared to the strictly (self-)policed "proper"—or business—English spoken at EDCs. Beyond linguistic, or even racial, differences, the chasm between the EDA and EDCs was also demonstrated through ideological differences; while it is the job of government employees at this agency to work closely with EDC applicants and process their requests, they were steadfast in their view of these applicants as "dem deh"[4]—that is, distinctly different from "us." The unsteady "us" here refers to St. Croix–born Crucians and workers who had immigrated from surrounding islands, a shift in which Black workers were unified under the banner of "us." Given the frequent office tensions between these groups, rooted in decades-long tensions between "down-islanders" and self-identified Crucians, this coalition was unstable—yet these real and ever-present divisions often receded when faced with EDC people, only to be inflamed with all the more intensity on other occasions.

The vast majority of the businessmen—and they are generally men—whose companies benefit from the program arrive to the territory from the mainland US. Often, these program participants are white and have no ties to the island beyond the EDC program. In fact, they often have not spent *any* time in the territory before learning of the program—with the exception of a few who may have vacationed in the USVI previously. The racial politics of these recent arrivals are much discussed and bemoaned by Crucians and long-term island residents alike, with EDC beneficiaries cast in the role of racist newcomers interested only in financial gain while maintaining a critical distance from "locals." As evidence of this, many on St. Croix point to the fact that EDC people tend to live in an enclave, an area of the island known as East End. While this neighborhood has long been home to the well-to-do, including, historically, many white families, there is a new and particularly virulent resentment of EDC people as set apart and racist for choosing this exclusive neighborhood. This residential separation, combined with the social insularity and vast wealth of EDC people, serves as fodder for anxieties about race, wealth, and belonging.

The suspicion with which EDC people are regarded stems from a concern that they are intent on recolonizing the island in the model of plantation slavery and ushering out "Crucian culture" in the name of some version of professionalism. For instance, in order to secure internships within the EDC sector, I called on a number of friends and acquaintances who had some relationship to the program. After being turned down by a company in which I knew a number of employees well, I began to worry that EDC companies might not necessarily want an anthropologist in their office on a daily basis. This concern made the necessary cold-calling and cocktail-party networking with EDC people, tasks that already left me riddled with nervousness, that much more difficult. However, as the weeks wore on, I began to go on a number of EDC interviews, attempting to get internships approved and scheduled. In the midst of these pressure-filled visits,

I was often struck by the stark difference in office attire between EDC businesses and almost any other office environment on the island. Right before one interview, I was at a café telling a friend/ informant how nervous I was about my upcoming meeting when my cell phone rang. Not recognizing the number on my caller ID, I was concerned that it was someone from the company calling to cancel. When I answered, I realized it was indeed someone from this would-be employer, and they were calling to ask what I would like to have the office's personal chef make me for lunch following the interview. Still nervous, I responded quickly and raced to their office. Upon arriving, dressed in my best approximation of "businesswear" at the time, I realized my nerves were unwarranted, as the major partner of the firm (a multimillionaire from the Midwest), strolled into the mahogany-paneled conference room overlooking the ocean to meet with me dressed in board shorts, a threadbare polo shirt, and no shoes. While this was the most extreme version of "dressing down" I came across during my interviews, it is a vivid demonstration of differences between "EDC people" and "everyone else" on St. Croix. As such, it remains the case that many EDC offices—excluding, notably, Stanford Financial—are "casual" in a way that is unfamiliar to most Crucians. These differences in office norms, demonstrated here through dress, tie into what are seen as larger "cultural" divisions between Crucians and EDC people.

Yet another such difference is telephone etiquette. When calling an EDC company, an employee will likely answer: "Company X!" In contrast, telephones at most offices on St. Croix are answered: "Good afternoon, Company X, how can I help you?" This seemingly insignificant difference raised, if not the ire, then at least the thorough annoyance, of some Crucians who felt "brushed off" by the brusque way many EDC phones are answered. As I stood in the kitchen at St. Croix Fund one day, I spoke with Leslie, a woman who worked in the office, and asked her how she thought the EDC program and EDC people were received on St. Croix. In response, she acknowledged the existence of what she termed a "cultural gap" that was problematic—but wanted to maintain the possibility of benefit to some Crucians:

> LESLIE: For the locals that are working for the EDC com-
> panies, I think that it's very beneficial to us, you know, and
> it's hard because a lot of these, the heads of the companies

come down here, and there's a big cultural gap, you know. And I think that they're learning more and more, but it's very different. Like, our company per se, we had a staff meeting the other day and it's like we're talking about "how do we answer our phones?" And, Wall Street, they don't really care to say "good morning, good afternoon," they just want to know "what do you want?! Don't waste my time." Here, you have locals calling and they're like [in Crucian accent] "don't this person have any manners?" That kind of thing, and so, it's really . . . It's a weird situation, I guess. And it's hard for them to understand our culture.

This assessment that differences in phone etiquette are the result of EDC people finding it "hard . . . to understand [Crucian] culture" is a generous one, as it presumes a desire on their part to become familiar with ways of life on St. Croix. It matters very much if this divergence in practice around greeting is rooted in difficulty adhering to the politesse that characterizes exchanges on St. Croix or, alternatively, emerges from a deep inattentiveness (bordering on myopia) and a lack of interest in local cultural practices. Leslie herself leans toward the former, yet the practice of skipping pleasantries and getting right to the matter at hand was often cited by Crucians as evidence of EDC people's lack of interest in becoming part of the broader community. This frustration is not limited to St. Croix and is related to the Jamaican notion of "broughtupcy"—or being raised correctly—an assessment of "good manners" that recently arrived and ostentatiously wealthy EDC people are judged as lacking.

The fact that EDC people are viewed—both by disgruntled would-be employees and members of the white "old guard" on St. Croix—as having "new money" is central to these larger divisions, as EDC people are seen as failing to fulfill their duties in the patron/client relationship that has historically governed interactions between wealthy whites and local communities in the Caribbean. This chasm of behavioral expectations is noted both anecdotally and in formal advice to would-be beneficiaries:

There is a divergence of attitudes in the islands regarding the acceptance of mainlanders as neighbors. There are certainly native islanders who are against the influx of mainlanders. Additionally, there are small fringes who are racially motivated and concerned about the islands becoming a home for the elite. On the whole it should be noted, the islanders are gracious, warm, and sharing. It is very important to realize the slower lifestyle in the island and to adjust to this, as opposed to superimposing the "feverish stateside pace" on the island culture. This may only lead to conflict and frustration in building friendships and in getting things done. (*Virgin Islands Investment Analysis* 2002: 3)

In a surprising twist, Leslie's assessment of the difficulty EDC people experience in understanding Crucian cultural practices may lead to inefficiency—or "frustration in . . . getting things done." This potential consequence is in addition to the negative reaction garnered by the "feverish stateside" approach at work in the EDC sector.

The EDC program brings to the fore long-standing tensions and anxieties, and it also introduces much that is new—including employment opportunities, subject-positions, and indeed professions. As EDC people sought to transplant themselves to the USVI with relative ease, their arrival led to the creation of a cottage industry of self-described EDC "handlers." A capacious occupation, members of this group included freelance consultants who worked to minimize the inevitable red tape related to relocating a business and savvy lawyers who claimed to have the necessary contacts and inside information (ranging from EDA board members' preferred charitable organizations to the "back way to drive from the airport to the Ritz Carlton") to facilitate an EDC's admission into the program. I spoke with one such "handler" named Carol, a white woman in her midsixties who lived on St. Thomas and worked primarily on that island as well. While she was now employed in the government sector, Carol was brimming with anecdotes of the lengths to which EDC people had asked her to go in order to ameliorate their discomfort in her previous role as a consultant. One managing partner of a hedge fund, she told me as we spoke over the phone, had recently moved to St. Thomas from Pennsylvania, where he had served on the board of trustees of a university. He remained extremely invested in the well-being of this university, and particularly that of their athletic teams. As he'd had to leave Pennsylvania in the midst of that school's football season, he had planned to faithfully watch the games from St. Thomas—a plan that was unexpectedly derailed by faulty wiring in his new home. He'd called Carol, furious about the shoddy electrical work that he encountered, and demanded that she find an electrician who would upgrade his circuits. Impatient with the length of Carol's search, her client performed the work himself—a decision that would blow the feeder providing electricity to his entire neighborhood, leading to a blackout. As a result, Carol had to summon the island's electric provider as well as a licensed electrician. Still seething and now standing in the dark, Carol's client stressed to her that his primary concern was that he be able to watch his team's football game, regardless of what had to be done and seemingly unconcerned about the impact of the blackout on his neighbors. Listening intently, I shook my head at this tale of imperiousness-gone-wrong. Still, it wasn't immediately clear to me how this experience was meant to shed light on the often-tense relations between EDC people and members of the local community. "Don't you see?" Carol asked—"it's about making them as happy and comfortable as possible and that usually means with as little interaction with the community as possible." Expanding on this, she said that she'd had to call upon her professional network to get an electrician on site quickly—a network, she was quick to add, that included realtors, lawyers, accountants, and doctors, all of whom now specialized in attending to the needs and wants of EDC people. Her mantra in her work as an EDC handler, Carol said, was "how do we service these people?"

This issue of "servicing" the EDC program and its people was deeply concerning to many Virgin Islanders. Was the EDC an initiative meant to improve the economic fortune of these islands by training and employing Virgin Islanders, or was the upward mobility promised by the program's supporters only possible for some well-positioned residents? That the terms of the EDC's arrival were not set by Virgin Islanders was clear from the outset. What my conversation with Carol pointed to were the myriad ways in which local residents continued to experience and navigate its unfolding presence.

"We" versus "Dem Deh": Shifting Antagonisms

As a "nontraditional intern,"[5] my exact duties at the EDA fluctuated from day to day—for instance, during my first week, the office was in the midst of compiling its Annual Report, a situation that allowed me immediate access to files I otherwise would not have had quite so quickly. After the initial flurry of activity associated with preparing the EDA's Annual Report however, the pace of my office tasks slowed down. Adding to this slowdown was the fact that I had begun my internship in mid-November, during the lead-up to the winter holiday and Carnival season on St. Croix. On my drive to work one morning a few weeks into my new role at the EDA, I attempted to construct a mental to-do list, some office tasks that would keep me busy through the likely slow workday. My carefully constructed list disappeared, however, when I walked into the foyer of the EDA office and was greeted by the sounds of Christmas carols set to a calypso beat streaming through the office. Stopping at the receptionist's desk, I asked what was going on. She told me "we going liven up this place," and that the staff was decorating for the holidays by stringing garlands between doorways and hanging ornaments on a plastic Christmas tree.

From my first day at the EDA, I had realized that the experience of working there would be very different from the encounters that I had with the EDC community, as all of the employees were people of color, a noticeable difference from the largely white EDC offices I had visited. Even more striking, however, was that work at the EDA was often conducted in Crucian dialect, rather than the "business English" that was a prerequisite in EDC offices. Beneath the familiarity and seeming friendliness of these exchanges, however, I quickly noticed simmering tensions between workers who identified as Crucian and those who were labeled "down island."[6] During office disputes over matters such as workload, divisions between self-identified Crucians and "down-islanders" arose. When discussing EDC people and their applications, however, these divisions receded and employees spoke of themselves as a single group of Black residents of St. Croix in relation to wealthy white EDC people, marked off as "dem deh."

Tensions between Virgin Islanders and residents born on surrounding islands have long been present (see, for example, Dookhan 1974; Harrigan and Varlack 1977; Gore 2009). I grew up hearing a steady stream of taunts and insults hurled at classmates singled out for their "down island" accents or styles of dress. However, the office clashes I witnessed were inflamed by a heightened discourse of race and place on the island as a result of the EDC program.

With the coalescence of the EDC community, a group identified by both occupation and "racist" attitude, relations between Black and white residents on the island had become increasingly strained and elided histories of migration and contemporary realities of the multiethnic makeup on St. Croix: Trinidadians, Puerto Ricans, and Arabs were not named in this category of "dem deh," even though these communities were very much present—and had been for decades and, in some instances, centuries. Instead, these "others" labeled as "dem deh" were squarely EDC people—set apart with this identifier not solely, or even primarily, because of race. Rather, this distinction was a mark of these divisions along lines of race—alongside wealth, and social and cultural insularity.

Tensions of race, violence, and capital have come together before the arrival of the EDC program on St. Croix. In addition to the rebellions during and immediately after the period of slavery (most notably, in the Fireburn uprising), the period of rapid industrial—and population—growth on St. Croix also resulted in flashes of violence that continue to inform race relations on the island today. By 1972, St. Croix had been in the process of transforming into an industrial island for just over a decade. Hosting Harvey Aluminum and Hess Oil—as well as migrant Caribbean laborers and white American workers—the island saw rapid transformations in its population and increased anxieties around Virgin Islanders being displaced by "outsiders." While the population of white residents in the US Virgin Islands was 5,373 in 1960, it was dramatically higher by 1970—standing at 11,339 (Boyer 1983: 311). Boyer (1983) notes that in this period "for the first time, native Virgin Islanders were in the minority. . . . Tourist facilities and condominiums, heavy industry, the duty-free shops, the golf course, were all built with white capital and alien labor, and the difference between boss and worker increasingly became the difference between white and black'" (312).

These anxieties—about economic change and racialized displacement—came together in dramatic fashion in 1972. On September 6, five armed assailants attacked the Rockefeller-owned Fountain Valley golf course, killing seven white people and one Black person in an event that would come to be known as the "Fountain Valley Massacre." The events leading up to—and following—this massacre remain a topic of conversation and debate on the island, but it is

widely agreed that this attack on a luxury golf course was born out
of racial tensions. Arnold Highfield (2018) has noted the position
held by some that "the rapid commercial and industrial development
of the island in the 1960s brought such swift changes that the island
and its people could not cope with them" (229). During the ensuing
criminal trial, the five men charged in this attack frequently complained
that they were tortured by law enforcement (both local and federal)
and subjected to racist taunts. This massacre and its aftermath would
become increasingly sensationalized, after all five men were found
guilty at the end of a months-long trial marked by racist slurs and
wrangling between local and federal law enforcement. One of the
accused assailants, Ishmail LaBeet—the alleged mastermind of the
attack who has long maintained his innocence—highjacked a plane
bound for New York and has been living in Cuba since 1984 (see
Kastner 2017).

The Fountain Valley Massacre served as a tipping point for racialized anxieties on St. Croix, as this attack was followed by a period
of increased violent crime that saw twenty white people murdered
on the island in the mid-1970s. This violence—and the threat of
violence—continues to cast a shadow on life on St. Croix. In addition to the decades-long plummeting of tourism on St. Croix that
continues into the present moment, the specter of "Fountain Valley"
hangs over the racialized anxieties surrounding the EDC program.
For instance, I was taken aback when one particularly even-tempered
friend, Michael, a Black man in his late twenties who worked outside
of the EDC sector, ended his account of being slighted by a white
EDC businessman by saying, "They best remember Fountain Valley."
In the moment, I did not push him to say more about this exchange
or his meaning, but in the time since I have come to view his invocation of Fountain Valley as a warning of what can happen when
the community becomes factionalized and the scales of privilege tip
precipitously in favor of those demarcated as "outsiders"—or "dem
deh." Thus, while they have been seemingly ever-present, antagonisms between white and Black residents of St. Croix had been
escalating since the early 2000s, closely mapping onto the arrival of
large numbers of EDC beneficiaries. These tensions would concretize
around the attack of a Black woman by a white man on St. John in
2005.

A Black Majority: Violence and the EDC

In addition to the specter of violence inherent in comments such as "remember Fountain Valley" and reminders to white residents that they constitute the minority in the USVI, incidents of *actual* violence in the form of increased crime have marked this deterioration in Black/white relations on St. Croix. During conversations with EDC businessmen during my internship interviews, the topic of crime, and its abundance on St. Croix, would inevitably arise. "Was it always this bad?" many interviewers asked me when they learned I had been raised on the island. A large part of the reason that many EDC people have experienced unusually high incidents of crime on the island has to do with the fact that the enclaves in which they tend to live have been specifically targeted by burglars. While there are no crime statistics available by neighborhood, an online news service covering the Virgin Islands reported in 2005 that "crime in the territory [was] on the rise, going against the downward trend of violence in the rest of the United States. According to statistics from the Federal Bureau of Investigation, violent crime in the territory rose 13 percent in the first half of 2004. In the rest of the country, violent crime fell 2 percent."[7] In light of the fact that the EDC was established in 2001, and the Jobs Act occurred in 2004, this increase in crime matching the consolidation of the EDC community is of note. Further, my own experience renting an apartment "out East" that was burglarized, anecdotal evidence from talking with EDC people, the 2008 inception of a CrimeStoppers tip-line in the territory, and posts on the online listserv "STX Crime Watch" all point to the conclusion that whites have increasingly been the targets of crime, particularly robbery, on the island. In one scheme seemingly tailored to EDC people, a group required to be on island only 183 days per year, thieves would break into unoccupied homes and steal everything inside, including large appliances such as flat-screen televisions and expensive refrigerators.

In order to explore the issue of escalating crime, I arranged an interview with a woman closely involved with local law enforcement. I had met Victoria, a white woman in her forties who had moved to the island from the Midwest, five years before this interview. We had met before I began fieldwork or even graduate school: I was living and working at a nonprofit organization on St. Croix when the East End home in which I was renting an apartment was burglarized during a rash of break-ins in the neighborhood. At that time, Victoria and her husband had been in the process of organizing a neighborhood watch of East End residents. Since then, she had developed a relationship with the local police force and helped to increase local efforts to fight crime. On my way to our interview, to be held in an area of the island that signals the beginning of the East End and thus frequented by EDC people, I recalled our first meeting and looked forward to hearing about the developments in local crime fighting. When I arrived at the agreed-upon café, Victoria, dressed in madras pedal pushers and a pastel polo shirt, was on her cell phone, talking with a local police representative about an upcoming meeting. When she hung up, I reminded her of our earlier encounter, and asked why she had remained active in battling local crime. In response, she told me of entire houses being "cleaned out" with burglars stealing large flat-screen televisions, refrigerators, and stoves. Noting that burglars frequently targeted the homes of "snowbirds"[8] and EDC people for these crimes, she argued that something had to be done. Drawing a connection between EDC people and the increase in crime, Victoria noted that "it was when [EDC people] started coming that safety and crime became a real issue out East because they have money to the degree the island hasn't seen before."

These issues of race and violence came together through home intrusions and burglaries, but also in acts of physical assault. In 2005, the local media across all three of the US Virgin Islands covered the story of the alleged rape of a Black woman that occurred on St. John. While reports of sexual assault are disturbingly regular, what elevated this case to the status of territory-wide news was its racial component. Amid escalating tensions between white and Black residents on St. John following the attack, the online newspaper the *St. Croix Source* published a story in 2005 describing the situation:

> A fire early Friday morning that gutted the interior of Close Reach Imports is under investigation, Deputy Fire Chief Brian Chapman said at the scene. The store, located at Meada's Mall in the heart of Cruz Bay, is owned by Bob Sells.

"The downstairs is a total loss," Chapman said. This is the latest in a series of incidents that appear to be racially motivated. Early Thursday, someone set fire to Sells' Jeep, which was still parked in front of the store Thursday morning. That incident is also under investigation.

The problems at Close Reach Imports appear to have their roots in a feud between Sells and House of Dolls owner Esther Frett. Until she was evicted in June, she had her store at Meada's Mall upstairs from Close Reach Imports.

Sells is white and Frett is black.

On June 3, Sells was arrested on assault charges after he allegedly pushed her. Sells said Thursday that case is still pending.

On June 20, someone wrote racial epithets on a car and fence at the East End home of Esther Frett and her husband, Jerry. No one has been arrested in this case.

Then, on Tuesday, Frett was allegedly raped. While Police Commissioner Elton Lewis stopped short of saying Frett was a rape victim at a Wednesday meeting in Cruz Bay Park, he called her a crime victim. (Lohr 2005a)

While the charge of sexual assault is alarming, the aspect of this case that became the primary topic of discussion was the relationship between white and Black residents on St. John and throughout the US Virgin Islands. In response to this case, a coalition of Virgin Islanders led by an outspoken Crucian radio personality came together under the name "We The People," staging a number of protests on St. John, including sit-ins at local restaurants (Lohr 2005b) and forcing supermarket slowdowns by paying in coins. Asked why he and his fellow Crucians had become involved in this case, the leader of this contingent, Mario Moorhead, responded that St. Croix "views itself as the big sister to the little sister St. John," and that it was the job of the big sister to look after the little sister:

"We came here to take care of business," he said.

He said he was there to exterminate the "rascals and scumbags" who raped Frett.

He said that although St. John may be 51 percent
white, the Virgin Islands is "made up of people of color."
"This is the reality many of you seem to forget," he
said. (Lohr 2005b)

Given the widespread economic and racialized displacement experienced by Black residents on St. John, this intervention was fraught
with fears of a similar fate for St. Croix. While these protests were in
response to a "racially motivated" feud between a white businessman
and a Black businesswoman on St. John as well as an attack on the
woman, the "you" addressed by Moorhead is the entire community
of white residents in the US Virgin Islands. What is more striking is
the fact that when this case was discussed on St. Croix, the "you"
who has forgotten that people of color constitute the majority in
the USVI referred to "EDC people." Like the elision of Indians,
Arabs, Jews, and Puerto Ricans in the wake of the arrival of EDC
people, so too were whites with a long-term presence on the island
erased from the narrative.

This slippage from "white" to "EDC" is momentous. There is
a long presence and history of white, including very wealthy white,[9]
people in the territory. Yet, Moorhead's comments about white people were interpreted on St. Croix as a commentary on EDC people.
Although the man involved in this case was not, in fact, part of the
EDC program, the extravagant wealth and high profile[10] of many
EDC businessmen has resulted in a metonymic relationship between
"EDC people" and "white" in the territory. Moorhead's comment
that "this is the reality many of you seem to forget" echoes the
frequent refrain heard on St. Croix that "EDC people" are intent
on "taking over" and that they would do well to remember both
the Fireburn slave uprising that took place on St. Croix and the
massacre at Fountain Valley. These instances and threats of racial
violence in the context of the EDC that connect plantation slavery,
industrialization, and neoliberal development demonstrate the temporal fluidity with which Crucians engage these moments of capital
accumulation. More than this, the *fears* surrounding a return to the
dystopian past come together in spectral time. Certainly, capitalism
has changed and continues to remake itself—and there are ongoing
struggles over these various iterations. Yet what I am pointing to
are the ways in which these ostensibly discrete moments of time and

capital are brought together by Crucians who have long experienced the brunt of dispossession by capitalism—and who articulate a critique of this ongoing process of wealth accumulation that is predicated on exploiting the Caribbean and its (Black) people.

White Before EDC: Long-Term White Residents

This equation of "EDC people" with "white," as witnessed in the St. John assault, points to the centrality of this community in the USVI while also eliding long-term white residents in the territory. The sizable community of white residents on St. Croix grew significantly after the particularly devastating Hurricane Hugo of 1989 that destroyed much of the island. In its aftermath, large numbers of white contractors from the US mainland arrived and ultimately settled on the island with their families. The emergent direct relationship between "EDC" and "white," however, glosses over both the centuries-long presence of whites in the territory—including descendants of the plantocracy—and this more recent history. Being struck by the way in which the EDC community became linked in the minds of Crucians with "white," as demonstrated by the railing against "EDC people" that took place when the St. John case made its way into conversation and, curious about the displacement of pre-EDC white residents—the former gatekeepers of the social and charitable arenas on St. Croix—I arranged to meet with a family who had moved to the island from the US mainland in the late 1980s.

As I gave my name to the guard charged with protecting the gated community I was about to enter, he eyed both me and my car closely, seeming to assess all the dings, rust spots, and peeling paint on my "ragga."[11] Ultimately deeming me safe to admit to the posh neighborhood, he lifted the arm of the wooden gate, allowing me to pass. I was there, in Caddy Lanes, to have dinner and talk with the parents of a longtime friend, a couple who had moved to St. Croix from the States in the late 1980s, shortly after Hurricane Hugo, and had raised both of their children on the island. The Martins, a well-to-do white family, had agreed to talk with me about their experiences on the island before and after the inception of the EDC program. Sitting on their patio, I asked their impressions of EDC people and what, if any, changes had come about with the arrival of this business community. The vast amounts of capital to which they have access combined with their "flashiness" has resulted in EDC people becoming central figures of social life and charitable giving on St. Croix, often displacing the interests of white residents who formerly held these positions on the island. When, during the course of our conversation, Ann and her husband, Bill, both called EDC people "flashy," I asked them to explain more fully their impressions of this group:

> ANN: There has been a big change in the kind of white people we get here now. We've always had wealthy people move here, but in the '90s, they moved here to get into island life and be part of the community. Now, though, EDC people come here who want to flash their money with fancy cars, instead of driving beat-up Jeeps.

This relationship between the long-term white residents of St. Croix (including "Statesiders," like Karen, who relocated to the USVI decades ago in search of a slower pace of life and general "irieness") and the newly arrived EDC people also demands closer examination. While white residents who have been on St. Croix for some time often side with Crucians in decrying EDC people as racist, it is difficult to assess how much this has to do with their displacement as the patron class by these incredibly wealthy, and often flamboyant, newcomers. In addition to noting the differing approaches to displays of wealth between EDC people and whites with a longer presence on the island, Ann observed that the former are "here just because of the money they're saving and don't have an interest, for the most part, in being part of the community." This assessment of EDC people as unenthusiastic about being integrated into the local community—or belonging—was one that was made frequently on the island. Of all the accusations hurled at the EDC community, including claims of racism, segregation, and hiring discrimination, this charge that EDC people *just don't care* about the Virgin Islands or Virgin Islanders was the one leveled most matter-of-factly by residents, both white and Black.

To shore up this claim, Ann Martin recounted her experiences with a nonprofit started by the wives of several EDC businessmen, a group in which she was no longer a member of because she did not agree with what she called the "outlook" of its members. Ann felt that the members of this group, comprised of wives of EDC businessmen, only "wanted to feel good about giving, and when [she] pointed out deeper issues or other directions for their giving and community service, they didn't want to hear it." Rather than engaging her suggestions of more long-term philanthropy or part-nering with local nonprofit organizations, Ann said, they preferred to focus on more immediate and high-profile acts of philanthropy such as donating books or toiletries to local public schools.

Interested in Ann's comments about tensions between the new forms of philanthropy preferred by the EDC community and preex-isting attempts at community uplift, I decided to attend a popular fundraiser put on by a community foundation on St. Croix, an annual gourmet-dining event known as Island Dining at which restaurants from around the island come together at a local resort and serve smaller versions of their signature dishes. Tickets for this event, costing around $80, are coveted on the island and often sell out in a matter of minutes. Island Dining has been one of the most discussed and anticipated events on St. Croix since its inception in 2001. What is particularly unique about this event is its relatively broad appeal, its ability to diversify attendees at a fundraiser beyond members of the upper middle class and bring island residents together for an evening of fine dining and high fashion at a beachside resort. During Island Dining 2007, I was struck by the finery of the attendees as they circled the resort's infinity pool, chatting and sipping champagne. Equally of note, however, was the diversity of the crowd: near the fondue station was the salesclerk from the grocery store dressed in a silk gown, by the pool was a schoolteacher in organza. In the corner, the wife of a notorious EDC businessman nodded intently along with the jazz band playing on stage. Offering an evening of elegance at a comparatively attainable price has contributed to the widespread appeal of this affair.

In recent years, however, members of the EDC community have taken an interest in this event, volunteering themselves as hosts and their spacious homes as backdrops for new events leading up to Island Dining, such as private dinners ranging in cost from $250 to $750. As a result, Island Dining has been expanded to include a week of food-themed events, culminating in a dinner at a local restaurant priced at $1,000 per person. Staggered by the cost of these events, and curious about their effect on the diverse crowd drawn to Island Dining, I arranged to have dinner with several friends at the restaurant that would soon host the $1,000 dinner. While everyone excitedly discussed what they would wear and which restaurant would have the best offerings, I asked this crowd of middle-class twentysomethings (many of whom were employed by EDC companies) what they thought of the new events surrounding Island Dining and whether any of them were planning to attend these additional events. The first to respond was Jamila, a Black Crucian woman in her twenties who worked as an office manager for an EDC business: "You mean them white people things? (sucks her teeth) Please. Them things is for white people, ok. Why you think it's so expensive? They don't want we there." Like Tyrone, Jamila invoked an excluded "we" that on its face seemed certain, but in reality was anything but. What is more, this invocation of "white people" (a stand-in for "EDC") versus "we" points to the continuing division between EDC people and the local community on St. Croix. As a result of EDC people's interest and participation, the philanthropic circuit on St. Croix has become increasingly exclusive and, as many Crucians—including Jamila—would argue, "segregated."

In order to gather more information about the impact of EDC people on local philanthropy, I arranged to serve as a volunteer for a major art auction put on each year by a local nonprofit group. I had years ago worked at this organization and still counted many of the employees as friends, so in addition to assisting with the planning of the event, I was given a task for the evening of the auction: I was to be a "piece-holder"—one of the volunteers who carried the items for sale onto the stage and displayed them to the crowd. When I arrived at the beachside hotel where the auction was to be held, I was greeted by the sight of hundreds of floating candles in the swimming pool and flowers arranged throughout the resort. As the evening progressed, I began to compare it to Island Dining, an event that is notable for its appeal across racial and (some) class lines. At the auction, which cost $125 per ticket, the attendees were mostly white, including many EDC people and several longtime white residents, including a few of the artists who had designed the pieces being auctioned that evening. I found this mix of EDC people and long-term whites fascinating, as the widely varying levels of wealth between these groups and conflicts over community participation often result in members of these groups socializing separately.

Long-term whites, such as the Martins, often do not socialize with extremely wealthy EDC people and see themselves—and their level of engagement with the community—as far different from this group. On the whole, these former gatekeepers have been displaced by the vast wealth and flashiness of this newly arrived group. This shift of the category of "white" comes at the expense of an older racial hierarchy on top of which long-term whites were found; their subsumption under the umbrella of "EDC," combined with the emergent category of "EDC girls," demonstrates the significance of global elites participating in this program as well as the unpredictability of the outcomes.

While this art auction has been held on the island for the past fifteen years and has long been attended by wealthy white residents, this night it was clear that EDC people, and their wealth, dominated the event. As I stood smiling on the stage wearing high heels and holding a large chair that was being auctioned, a bidding war broke out between an EDC businessman widely known on the island for his large land purchases and a white lawyer who had been practicing on St. Croix for over a decade. As the auctioneer volleyed between these competing bidders, the price rose from $1,000 to $4,000— ultimately ending with the EDC businessman purchasing the piece for $8,000. When I recounted this story the next day to my friend, Beth, a white woman in her twenties who was raised on the island and now worked at a local craft store, she responded: "Yeah, I went to that [auction] last year. I was bidding on chairs [for the store], you know, $5,000, $10,000 . . . People kept telling me, joking I think, that I seemed like a young EDC wife."

My conversation with the Martins demonstrates that there are divisions between EDC people and the longer-term white community on St. Croix. Here, even Ann, a well-to-do long-term white resident of St. Croix, a group that was formerly understood as the patron class on the island, was sidelined by these recently arrived EDC people. This shift is one members of this group object to, as demonstrated by Ann Martin's departure from the philanthropic group. If long-term whites are displeased with the changes in the racial hierarchy and social relations brought about by the presence of EDC people, many Crucians object even more strongly, describing the arrival of these global elites, their selective engagement with the local community and residential and social enclaves, as an attempt to return to plantation-style race relations—that is, "slave days."

The introduction of EDC people, global elites with no ties to St. Croix beyond the program of which they are beneficiaries, marks a shift from the group of former middle- and upper-class whites, many of whom relocated to the island specifically to become incorporated into the local community. These longer-term white residents, however, have become displaced by and are unable to compete with the vast amounts of capital commanded by EDC people. What is more, the resentment toward these recent arrivals for their lack of concern about the local community is related to this shift in the "kind of white people" drawn to the island, as EDC people are seen as failing to fulfill their role as the patron class vis-à-vis the local community. This presumed failure has resulted in local resentment of this group, while their extreme wealth has displaced and alienated white former gatekeepers on the island. The circumvention of former gatekeepers on St. Croix has led to increased stratification in the form of exponentially higher property taxes and real estate costs, rather than new mobilities for poorer Crucians. On St. Croix, the supersession of long-term white residents as power brokers has led to the consolidation of an even wealthier community of whites largely unconcerned with St. Croix beyond an economic program. EDC advocates argue that this rendering is inaccurate. From their perspective, EDC people care very much about St. Croix—about the reliability of the electric grid, about the safety of (certain) neighborhoods, and about the dearth of well-paying jobs in the territory. Like the calls for the privatization of Puerto Rico's utilities following hurricanes Irma and Maria, this model of demonstrating care by way of assuming ownership is in direct conflict with what Crucians envision as community participation.

EDC People as "Racist"

The charge of racism against EDC people is multilayered, with Virgin Islanders pointing to experiences of hiring discrimination, the "segregated" clusters of EDC homes on the island's East End, and the unwillingness of EDC people to engage with either the island or its people beyond the program as evidence. This assessment is connected to historical experiences of race-based economic divisions, and the neoliberal focus on wealth consolidation brings with it attendant—and familiar—racialized divisions as these programs favor (and increase the wealth of) global elites, while worsening economic realities of people of color in small places such as St. Croix. In my interview of an EDC employee named Veronica, a light-skinned woman in her midtwenties, she noted that her employer "doesn't know anything about the other side of the island, because he just stays around [East End] and doesn't really want to get out and interact, [since] . . . he's just here for his job." In limiting his circuit to the East End, Veronica's employer is actually minimizing his engagement with the other *three* sides of the island, the North Shore, South Shore, and West End (Frederiksted)—not to mention the entire cluster of mid-island, working-class, neighborhoods. Many Virgin Islanders I spoke with were angry about this residential divide, a raced and classed split that allowed incredibly wealthy white EDC people to live almost entirely apart from the local population—a pattern of residential separation reminiscent of "company towns."

In talking with Veronica, I mentioned the difficulty I was having engaging EDC people before beginning my internships as I could not afford to rent an East End apartment on my fieldwork stipend. In her response, she pointed to the social insularity of the EDC community:

> VERONICA: Since a lot of the heads of these companies are from the States, and, you know, they're kind of new to the island, it's kind of like a little subculture. I guess they all have things in common and they're new to the island . . .
>
> TN: So, what kinds of activities do they plan [for themselves and their employees]?
>
> V: Well, my boss owns a yacht, so he would have little outings on the . . . yacht. We all went and it was mostly the heads of EDCs and some of their employees. We were just socializing.

Pushing a bit further, I asked Veronica not just about the exclusivity of "EDC" circles but also about the ways in which their presence on the island had changed certain spaces. Having talked with Crucians informally for months, I had heard much about changes to places such as restaurants, bars, and even grocery stores since the arrival of EDC people:

> TN: Have you noticed a split or tension, when just hanging out? Like, "this is where EDC people go," "this is where other people go," and people who aren't part of the EDC circle aren't welcome in certain places?

> V: Maybe to an extent. I try personally not to, like, I mean I come here and I do my work and that's about it. I mean, it's good to make friends with the people you work with, but I don't go out of my way to hang out or get to know other EDC people. Just because a lot of them, I'm not into the whole economics field and a lot of these companies are financial companies, and that's just not my thing so I really don't, I guess, deal with that. But I mean, that I think there probably is a split . . .

> TN: Do you remember [a few years ago] when I was living out East [working at a nonprofit organization] and there was a concentration of EDC people out that way . . .

> V: Yeah, one EDC moves down, then another one. They're new, this one has been there longer, and the first tells them "oh, this is the spot where you should live, this is safer." And a lot of them do live in East End, because it's more expensive to live there, so they kind of . . . it segregates them from the rest of the island, and they just kind of stay on the EDC end. And my boss, I would say, doesn't know anything about the other side of the island, because he just stays around there because it's close to where he works and he doesn't really want to get out and interact and I guess learn about the island and what it has to offer; he's just here for his job and . . . you know, that's what it is.

Here, Veronica navigates her life as an EDC employee and a Crucian by seeing them as distinct roles to be navigated ("I come here and I do my work and that's about it"). In rejecting the wholesale insularity of the EDC sector—not going "out of [her] way to hang out or get to know other EDC people"—she posits a situation in which these worlds are separate and from which she can choose. That is, she can either be sunbathing on her boss's yacht, *or* she can spend her leisure time in ways that involve seeing and engaging with other members of the local community, including visiting easily accessible beaches or attending any of the numerous events celebrating VI history and culture held across the island. While this division between the local community and mainland Americans is long-standing, resentment remains raw. For instance, outrage over "segregation," and the feeling of exclusion it engendered in Virgin Islanders, boiled over during a lunchtime conversation I had with Allison, a Black woman in her forties who worked as a midlevel manager in a government office on St. Croix. As we both talked about work, the politics in our respective offices, and our plans for the upcoming weekend, I mentioned that I was planning to go to Shoy's, a local beach that is located within, and shares its name with, one of the fashionable neighborhoods preferred by EDC people. At the mention of this, Allison became agitated, saying, "You'd better go while you can." When I asked what she meant, Allison explained that she'd recently learned that a group of EDC people were planning to erect a gate, marking off the East End from the rest of the island. In disbelief, I told her that this could not possibly be true, as Virgin Islands law requires that all beaches, and access to them, remain public. Besides, I reasoned, the only road running through the East End was public and maintained by the local government. It would be impossible to cordon off this section of the island.

Not long after my conversation with Allison and still weighing the possibility of a gate marking off an entire section of the island, I ran into Karen, the woman whose debate in the post office about real estate had drawn my attention. Realizing that if anyone would know about such plans on the part of EDC people, it would be her, I asked Karen if she had heard anything about a gate being put up out East. Her eyes immediately lit up, and she shouted, "Yes! I know all about it." Surprised, I asked how such a separation could be created and enforced. While she had the same information as Allison and not much more in the way of details, Karen seemed absolutely certain the EDC community was planning to erect this gate. Although a boundary separating East End from the rest of the island was not erected, the widespread rumor of its impending arrival, much like the swirling rumors concerning the EDC "cult" of Stanford Financial, speak to the anxiety on the part of Virgin Islanders about the EDC program and its participants. This anxiety reflects the haunting of earlier moments of racial capitalism and fears that they are unfolding yet again. These interconnections between slavery, empire, capital, and neoliberalism are at the fore of the deep-seated fears surrounding the EDC program.

While a physical barrier separating the island was not created, many residents I spoke with argued that a separation was accomplished even without it. For instance, Nancy, a Black woman teaching at the St. Croix campus of the University of the Virgin Islands, remarked to me that her young son enjoyed the weekly crab races at a local beachside restaurant—however, the fact that the restaurant was "out East" meant that they were often the only people of color in attendance, a situation that made her feel "as though [she] and [her] son did not belong there." What struck me most about the changes on East End in general, and this restaurant feeling particularly "marked off" as EDC territory, were the vivid childhood memories I have of playing at that very beach before the restaurant was built. This beach, where I spent countless Saturdays making sandcastles and "selling" seashells alongside other Black and brown children to passersby, now felt, to many Crucians, as though it were only for EDC people. This shift in ostensibly public space—that is, the sense that many Crucians now have that certain places are "off-limits" to them—is closely related to another local concern vis-à-vis EDC people—that of land use and real estate accumulation.

EDC People and Land: The Price of Prosperity

Many EDC people have amassed large tracts of land across the island for personal and recreational use, purchases that have incensed some Virgin Islanders while earning others tidy profits. The rising cost of real estate, a development due in large part to EDC interest and capital, has priced out many local residents across the USVI and threatened to displace even those who are existing homeowners with property tax bills that are drastically higher than in years past. Describing the impact of these property tax increases, a 2008 article in the *St. Croix*

Source notes that "in some cases St. John property owners face tax bills six to 10 times higher than their previous bill" (Lohr 2008). These drastic increases in property taxes are not limited to St. John. Throughout the territory, "the value of properties have been revalued and in most cases, dramatically increased" (Lewin 2008). While many beneficiaries of the program live on the "East End," their wealth allows them to purchase large swaths of real estate across the island, a situation that has especially alarmed Virgin Islanders concerned about "locals" being permanently priced out of the housing market on St. Croix. This concern on St. Croix is heightened by the cost of real estate on St. John, a hyperinflated market that many Virgin Islanders are unable to enter.[12]

In both formal and informal interviews, Crucians argued that the greatest social cost of the success of tourism on St. Thomas and St. John has been the phenomenon of whites "taking over." This concern was expressed especially strongly in relation to questions about the island of St. John. During an interview with Albert Bryan, I asked about these issues of escalating real estate costs and increasing property taxes:

> TN: I think perhaps, just in doing interviews, it seems like maybe some of the miscommunication has to do with different aims [of the program], right. So people, you know, Joe on the street, doesn't necessarily [think]. . . . "Great, they're getting tax benefits and our economy is going to get built up, but meanwhile I still can't afford stuff in [the supermarket]."

> AB: You're right, people think that [the program] means, "I'm going to get a job and live a better life." And you're also right that we have no idea, or we don't sit down to think the *price* of economic prosperity. I remember having a conversation with my friend five years ago, telling him, "You see the price of houses? You see how the prices on East End have started spiking?" And he told me, "That's East End. That will never, that ain't have nothing to do with us." I said, "Are you crazy? Construction is construction is construction. Your house is valued more, that means it's going to cost you more to build . . ."

TN: and the [escalating] property taxes . . .

AB: Oh yeah . . . but um, that's the price of prosperity . . . And I can, I can see . . . I remember going to
St. John and all it has was donkeys and jeeps. There was
no, and that's in my lifetime . . .

TN: There was no Caneel Bay?[13]

AB: There was Caneel Bay [but] it was . . . it was smaller
and it was . . .

TN: Not what it is now?

AB: No . . . There was no Westin.[14] You know, there
was none of that. I mean, it was a lot of foot paths and
dirt roads, and you know, now look at St. John now. St.
John has . . .

TN: So do you think that's St. Croix's future? A similar
trajectory?

AB: . . . yeah. And I think that people have a difficult
time seeing that, but because I've seen it in St. Thomas,
I *know* what's going to happen to St. Croix.

While Bryan recognizes the St. Johnian real estate market as an
eventuality for St. Croix, there remain many Crucians for whom St.
John remains a worst-case scenario of development. The issue of
real estate and EDC people became increasingly contentious on St.
Croix fueled by the large land purchases made by EDC people, and
the privatization of space (both in the sense expressed by Nancy that
she and her son "didn't belong" at the crab races and that expressed
in relation to the purchase of the formerly public landmark Grassy
Point). These shifts are hallmarks of neoliberal privatization and have
contributed to tensions between Crucians and whites (now understood to be "EDC people").

Crucians both object to the history of racialized oppression they
see unfolding through the program *and* material inequalities they see

increasing as a result of the program—seen, for instance, through rising property tax rates. As the entity charged with overseeing the program, the EDA has not been unaware of complaints of increased stratification since the inception of the program. The agency has attempted to address these critiques by implementing checks on EDC spending, notably through a subprogram called the Eligible Supplier program, which attempts to ensure that local vendors are given priority vis-à-vis EDC contracts for everything ranging from office supplies to construction materials. As part of this initiative, the USVI government vets local businesses in order to assign the title of "Eligible Virgin Islands" supplier—the category of company that EDCs are required to employ for goods and services.[15] Yet, there is local frustration with this subprogram, as well. Many participants charge that EDC companies either disregard this requirement altogether or work around it by inventing overly specific needs—for example, claiming the need for a particular color of pencil for the completion of basic office tasks. In response to my questions about this subprogram, Jeannette, a white woman who, along with her husband, owns an Eligible Supplier construction company and had lived on St. Croix for several decades, said that she feels as though "the EDCs just get the quote for show" because they are required by contract to obtain local estimates. Jeannette was bothered by this practice, not only because it allowed beneficiaries to sidestep local businesses, but also because "putting the quotes together takes a lot of time, [and] for the most part EDCs end up buying off-island through loopholes." Further, while EDC companies are required to report the outcome of the bidding process to all applicants, Jeannette complained that this frequently did not happen.

In response to complaints about the efficacy of the Eligible Supplier program, such as those lodged by Jeannette, the EDA invited local business owners taking part in the program to a biennial Eligible Supplier conference where the agency attempted to address concerns, as well as to provide participants with a forum in which to share their experiences. In August 2008, I attended one such conference that was held in the conference room of a midrange hotel, a meeting that ended with the forty-plus attendees (all of whom were there representing local small businesses) denouncing the lack of enforcement in this program and the continued practice of EDCs buying the bulk of their supplies off-island.

"New" Ideas

While the EDC is the most well-known program run by the EDA, it is only one of several economic development initiatives under the auspices of this agency. The other programs of the EDA focus on supporting local businesses and entrepreneurs—yet these initiatives do not receive anything like the level of attention garnered by the US capital and its handlers targeted by the EDC. The disproportionate level of attention received by the EDC was addressed during an interview with then-EDA chairman Albert Bryan:

> TN: As the chairman of the EDA board, I'm interested in what you see as the role, the impact of the EDC, particularly on St. Croix in relation to other things like tourism, which has historically been the way most Caribbean islands stimulate their economies.
>
> AB: What the vision is? When you talk about the EDC, you're talking about it as that division of the EDA . . . Not all the tools of the EDA, just that program. I see the EDC as one tool for economic development, if you will. And the way that ties into the economy is attracting new money to the territory. I mean, yeah, people like to concentrate on small business, but if you're spinning the same money around over and over again, it doesn't really make any difference . . . I think it's important for us to create turns in our economy, create opportunities for *new* money to come into the economy . . .

The other "tools" at the disposal of the EDA referred to by the commissioner in the preceding passage are the Government Development Bank (GDB) and the Small Business Development Association (SBDA) that grant loans of varying amounts to business owners who have resided in the Virgin Islands for five years or longer. The agency's other "tool" is the Enterprise Zone, a program that encourages renovation of historic buildings and neighborhoods that have become abandoned and dilapidated as a result of deindustrialization.[16] Again, while the EDC has become the "poster child" for the program—and an unpopular one, at that—these other programs of the EDA are also attempts to revitalize the local economy. It is of note that, of these programs, the EDC is the only initiative focused on attracting outside investors. As with previous tax incentive programs in the region, the many industrialization-by-invitation programs formerly operating in the Caribbean, and tourism in the current moment, the EDC program relies on *foreign* capital for its success. As a result, the structure and requirements of this program are necessarily, at least in part, set elsewhere. Depending on both foreign capital and its agents puts St. Croix at a disadvantage for negotiating these global processes, as was the case with many of these earlier development programs. Unlike that of St. Thomas and St. John, the economy of St. Croix has long been in need of "new money," as noted by Governor Bryan. This need, of course, is what led to the creation of the EDC program in the first place. However, the ostensible "newness" of this money—and EDC people—is also at the foundation of critiques of the EDC.

More specifically, both the "newness" and the "foreignness" of EDC people and their money are of great concern to Crucians. For many residents, while the money circulating through the territory may be new, the processes that facilitate its arrival and the power dynamics it creates on the island hearken back to earlier moments of colonialism and "slave days." This engagement with racialized wealth accumulation is haunted by previous encounters that have been prosperous for some at the expense of Black people. It is possible that Crucians are articulating a critique of broader processes of neoliberalism through the phrase "slave days." However, I take seriously their explicit invocation of slavery as the specter to which they are reacting vis-à-vis the EDC. What is more, these two positions are not necessarily at odds—if slavery is the apotheosis of Crucians' experience of racial capitalism, it stands to reason that this would be the moment to which they collectively refer in their critique of more recent iterations of this project.

Race, Belonging, and Political Dependency

The document known as the Organic Act governs the US Virgin Islands. Instituted in 1936 and revised in 1954, the Organic Act outlines political and fiscal realities for these islands, including the management of tax revenues and exported goods, the establishment of municipal councils, and the guidelines for various local elections (Boyer 1983). Beginning merely a decade after the Revised Organic Act of 1954 (a document that further clarified the position of the USVI vis-à-vis the United States, by formally deeming the islands an "unincorporated" territory and excluding them from representation in the US Congress), there have been political attempts across these islands to increase the autonomy of the territory by supplanting the Organic Act. Since 1964, there have been five such attempts, known as Constitutional Conventions. These gatherings feature concerned citizens, nominated as delegates, and elected officials who have over time advocated for political change, including lobbying for a locally elected governor, separate municipal councils for St. Croix and St. Thomas/St. John, and crucially, a legally binding definition of "native" Virgin Islander in both the fourth and fifth Constitutional Conventions (1980 and 2008, respectively). While I conducted fieldwork on the EDC program in 2008, the territory was in the midst of its Fifth Constitutional Convention—serendipitous timing, as the series of debates and conversations tied to this political intervention shed light on various notions of belonging on St. Croix, with the question of Virgin Islanders with roots in other islands (or "garrotes") becoming an especially heated topic of discussion. While these tensions are long-standing, they became inflamed with the inception of the EDC program in the early 2000s, and these increasingly racialized hostilities were on full display during the territory-wide debates over defining "native" Virgin Islanders through the convention.

Beginning in 2008, the Fifth Constitutional Convention of the USVI began with the election of representatives to the various committees of the convention. There was much excitement on the island surrounding this process, although this optimism was tempered by the fact that the four previous conventions had failed to result in an agreed-upon document that could be submitted to the US federal government. Not long into the proceedings, it became clear that the most divisive issue of these meetings would be defining "native" Virgin Islanders, a vexing process that had divided the island before, most recently in the early 2000s, when the local government attempted to ensure Crucian employment within a casino that was attempting to break ground on St. Croix. During the Fifth Constitutional Convention, an overarching aim of the convention was to create a legally binding category of "native Virgin Islanders," those who could trace their familial presence in the USVI to the year 1927, when residents of the former Danish West Indies were granted American citizenship. This definition relied upon long standing presence as the determinant of allegiance—relying on a combination of colonial authority and linear time as the measure of belonging. This move reinvigorated long-simmering tensions between "natives" and members of the Virgin Islands community who often felt themselves either marginalized or outright excluded from this definition. Critics of this definition contended that it privileged Black Virgin Islanders at the expense of other ethnic groups that have had generations-long presence in the territory. In relation to the Puerto Rican community, Roopnarine (2016) has described the anxiety surrounding the Fifth Constitutional Convention, writing that "the worst fear is that the constitution is drafted in a way to give preference to ancestral and native Virgin Islanders, which excludes most Puerto Ricans, since they arrived on St. Croix in the early twentieth century" (23). While this process was deeply divisive, it is far from unique to the US Virgin Islands. The nearby British Virgin Islands has long grappled with demarcating the boundaries of its community and employs a contentious system that sets "belongers" apart from "nonbelongers."[17] In the BVI, this legislative distinction separates "belongers" who claim this status through birth or parentage from "nonbelongers" who are unable to do so (see Cohen 2010; Maurer 1997; O'Neal 2012). As is the case in the US Virgin Islands, public debate about these identities are fraught.[18] Unlike the USVI, however, the BVI designation of "belonger" carries with it material benefits in the realms of land ownership, employment, and education.[19] During the Fifth Constitutional Convention, delegates attempted to institute a similar set of affairs—moves that were read either as protections or as preferential treatment, depending on the source.

While a number of subcommittees were formed and many meetings held, the issue that captivated the island most during the Fifth Constitutional Convention was that of defining "native" or "ancestral" Virgin Islanders. Although the fear of immigrants from neighboring islands displacing locals has long been a low-level concern and topic of discussion on St. Croix, anxiety surrounding this possibility increased dramatically in the 2000s with the arrival of EDC people, a group with spending power that far outmatched that of most Crucians. In large part as a result of concerns about the continued possibility of local ownership in the face of EDC interest and capital, the debate over "native" Virgin Islanders and their rights—including limiting "foreign" (such as mainland US) land ownership—intensified. As Virgin Islanders confront the EDC program and its "people" as but the most recent iteration of racial capitalism that relies on the dependency of the territory and its inhabitants, one response has been to ramp up processes of "Otherization" in the name of identifying those who "truly" belong in and to the Virgin Islands—that is, those whose allegiance is somehow unassailable. Of course, this is a slippery slope, and the metric by which "belonging" is measured is ever-changing. Nevertheless, this project was under way during the Fifth Constitutional Convention held in the territory.

This debate surrounding "native" Virgin Islanders demonstrates once more that a linear notion of time is inadequate for grasping the economic and raced tensions on the ground: the community of largely migrant laborers from across the Caribbean that began arriving to these US-owned islands in the mid-1950s with the advent of the tourist industry in the USVI once again came under racist attack in 2008 with charges that they didn't *belong* on the island and that St. Croix should benefit "native" Virgin Islanders. This latter claim is connected to the EDC program and thus tied into a larger debate about "outsiders" brought to the island by economic incentives, both Caribbean migrants and EDC people.

Flashes of tensions from the "native" debate informed conflicts I witnessed during my government (EDA) "internship." In the EDA office, these tensions were salient at particular moments: comments such as "me don't ask that gasso gyul nothing,"[20] spoken by a St. Croix–born employee in response to a question about the whereabouts of a misplaced stapler, and factionalizing along lines of birthplace were indicators of the increasing race- and place-based resentments on the island. While there is intense intermigration between the USVI and surrounding islands, due in part to their status as an American territory making them an easily accessed point of entry to the US, there have long been strained relations between USVI-born residents and these settlers. Demonstrated by my fellow office worker's comment that she "don't ask that gasso gyul nothing," this tension has been noted by Dookhan (1974), who argues:

> Some social "unrest can be attributed to the widespread feeling among Virgin Islanders that they have lost control of their economy. . . . The ownership and control of the major industries and big businesses by non-Virgin Islanders with greater competitive power has led the natives to question their role in the future economic development of the islands. (307)

This quote by Dookhan points to the tensions between "Virgin Islanders" and "non-Virgin Islanders"—here, meant to indicate Caribbean migrant workers. However, in the wake of the EDC program, the "non-Virgin Islanders" toward whom may Crucians directed their ire were not Black Caribbean migrants but wealthy white EDC people.

The current status of the USVI as a territory of the US has meant that it is legally impossible to differentiate between long-term residents of the territory and mainland Americans, a difference of "belonging" that is frequently made law on surrounding islands, such as the BVI, vis-à-vis, for instance, land ownership. Escalating concerns over the availability and cost of land on St. Croix and fears of being displaced by either down-islanders or EDC people seeking to "take over" combined to inflame tensions around defining "native Virgin Islanders" during the Fifth Constitutional Convention.

The 2008 Constitutional Convention was largely dominated by racial antagonisms, including frequent charges of racism from all sides, culminating in a debate over the rights of "native" Virgin Islanders—an issue that resulted in renewed hostility between Crucians born on the island and residents from surrounding islands who felt their identity was being called into question and claimed this title was exclusionary. These tensions are linked to the unstable "we" invoked by the eavesdropping Tyrone mentioned earlier: here, instead, the "we" pits St. Croix–born Crucians against residents who have immigrated from surrounding islands.

While the USVI has a continuing history of inter-island travel and residence, the definition of "native" put forth during the 2008 Constitutional Convention disavowed these practices, claiming only those able to trace their lineage in the US Virgin Islands to 1927, the year residents of the former Danish West Indies were granted American citizenship, were true "natives." As the convention progressed, a number of articles began appearing in local news sources, taking issue with the definition of "native" put forth by a former–Virgin Islands senator Adelbert "Bert" Bryan (an entirely different person than Governor Albert Bryan) and his supporters:

Dear Source,

My Webster's New World Dictionary defines the word bully in several ways. . . . This would be a very good description of Bert Bryan and his recent racist tirade in a hearing of the Constitutional Convention.

    Bert reminds me of those old southern American white guys like Strom Thurmond and Bull Connor and George Wallace. Society back then was changing and those self-appointed keepers of the flame didn't like it. They all wanted to hold on to a past that was coming to an end called segregation. Bert doesn't want his conception of the past to end here on our islands. Bert would like for everyone but those of African slave descent to leave our islands. No Puerto Ricans, no Down Islanders, no East Indians, no Arabs, no Caucasians, no nobody. (Monagle 2008)

The notion that Delegate Bryan, and by extension those in support of the category of "native" Virgin Islander, would like nothing better than to have "no nobody" in the territory except for "those of African slave descent" is one that became widespread as the debate engulfed the island.

    This delegate, Bert Bryan, had long been a polarizing figure on St. Croix: adored by some for what they saw as his "tell-it-like-it-is" approach to race relations on the island and reviled by others for what they saw as his own racism, which they argued was most clearly demonstrated by his ongoing prioritizing of Black Virgin Islanders and frequent denigration of essentially everyone else in the territory. Bryan's larger-than-life presence was made more so by his frequent participation in political debates that more often than not devolved into slinging insults as well as his brushes with the law.[21]

    To say I was nervous as I approached the agreed-upon meeting point where Bert Bryan and I were scheduled to conduct an interview would be an understatement. Pulling into the makeshift parking lot of the island's horseracing track, I saw no other vehicles, so I sat in the abandoned bleacher-style seats and waited, going over my notes and the questions I hoped to ask Bryan about his role in the ongoing Constitutional Convention. A few minutes later, I was startled by the sound of an engine revving. Looking up, I saw a large pickup truck with the words "A Knock at Midnight" printed across the top of the windshield. On St. Croix, it is not uncommon for vehicles to have either sayings or nicknames printed across their windshield: for instance, a taxi may read "Road Runner" or "Running the Streets" while a sports car may read "Unstoppable." As Bryan settled into the bleacher seats for our conversation, I remained struck by the inscription and asked him what it meant. Immediately, he screwed up his face and said that people were always misinterpreting him and that this was a prime example. He was bothered, he said, that people regularly took the phrasing on his vehicle to be a commentary on his personal nocturnal activities—assuming it to be a crude, or at the very least illicit, reference. That assumption, he insisted, could not be further from the truth. In reality, he explained, the phrasing was borrowed from Martin Luther King Jr., who used the term in his sermon "Strength to Love" to stress the virtues of preparedness and generosity toward one's friends and neighbors. The sermon draws from the book of Luke in the Bible, which reads, "Which of you who has a friend will go to him at midnight and say to him, 'Friend, lend me three loaves; for a friend of mine has arrived on a journey, and I have nothing to set before him'" (Luke 11: 5–6). Dr. King mines this scripture for insights into, for instance, the persistent need for charity and neighborly love, as he notes that "when the man in the parable knocked on the door of his friend and asked for the three loaves of bread, he received the impatient retort: 'Don't bother me! The door is fastened, and my children and I have gone to bed; I cannot get up and give you any.' In other words, this man was left disappointed at midnight."[22] For Bryan's critics, many of whom viewed him as a figure who trafficked in fearmongering and divisiveness, the selection of this phrase would seem quite ironic. Yet, according to Bryan, all he did in his public life was in the service of his "brothers and sisters" of the Virgin Islands. Seen in that light, King's message of openheartedness made perfect sense to Bryan: To those who *truly* belonged as friends and neighbors, much should be given. Those who did not, however, should expect far less generous treatment. I would next see Bryan at a public meeting in his role as a delegate to the Fifth Constitutional Convention.

While many definitions of "native" Virgin Islander were put forward, the suggestion that was discussed most frequently held that this category was comprised of those able to trace their lineage in the territory to the year 1927.[23] While some on the island clamored for this definition that would allow for legal benefits for "natives," including preference for land purchases and employment, others decried the very attempt to create this category as "racist." The racial grounding of this debate became clear during one convention meeting during which Bert Bryan, the most outspoken proponent of "native" rights, was asked what would become of white residents with long family histories in the territory:

> [Convention] Delegate Frank Jackson brought up the Lawaetzes and the Merwins, families that moved to St. Croix around the end of the 19th century from Denmark and New York, respectively, asking why they shouldn't be considered "ancestral Virgin Islanders."
>
> Delegate Adelbert Bryan . . . walk[ed] to the back of the Fritz Lawaetz Legislative Conference Room and pull[ed] the plaque commemorating Lawaetz from the wall. "Fritz didn't do anything for black people," Bryan said. "We keep changing it because of the media . . . Nobody can convince me Mr. Lawaetz was a native Virgin Islander." (Kossler 2008b)

While this substitution of "black" for "native" found support among some on St. Croix, a large number of residents, including immigrants from surrounding islands, Puerto Ricans, East Indians, and whites, were marginalized in this debate. Writing in support of defining "native" Virgin Islanders, one St. Croix resident submitted an opinion piece to a local newspaper that addressed many of the concerns Crucians have about EDC people. I include much of this letter here, due to its particular salience:

> Here in the VI, there are persons who require programs to pursue and attain the Virgin Islands dream of life, liberty

and the pursuit of happiness here. This dream includes owning land for homes and businesses, so that there will always be natives around to preserve and promote our rich culture and traditions. It all natives disappear from the VI, so will our culture, which even those who are against native rights claim to love so much.

However, the persons who are against programs designed to guarantee the above rights for persons born in the Virgin Islands, argue that everyone should be treated equally based on the 14th Amendment to the U.S. Constitution. This sounds nice in theory and I would agree with it if, in reality, things were equal economically for all persons who live here. However, all things are not equal and many natives cannot afford to buy land or start businesses in their homeland.

Contrastingly, persons from the outside who have access to large sums of money, capital, and who usually get credit easier than natives, are able to come here, purchase large chunks of land, subdivide it and resell it to others who are economically "well-off" at prices that are way beyond the reach of many natives. In other instances, they build extravagant homes that drive up the property values around them. Although both of these actions are perfectly legal in this society, they exclude many natives from ever being able to purchase land, whether for homes or businesses in their own homeland. They do not seem to be concerned about the economic inequality existing between natives and the outsiders mentioned above that facilitates the native land alienation process, which is escalating even as this article is being written. (Emanuel 2007)

It is clear that the "outsiders" to whom the author refers, those wielding vast amounts of "money, capital" and to whom credit is assumed to be easily given, are, in fact, EDC people. The concerns voiced earlier by Karen, who feared "that Stanford man"—and EDC people in general—were going to monopolize the real estate market on St. Croix, the anxiety contained in the editorial focusing on the purchase of Grassy Point, and the unease about rising property taxes are all deployed here in the service of ensuring "native" rights by differentiating "outsiders" from "natives." This division became a slippery slope, however, as the binary between "them" and "us" in the "native" debate ultimately deepened and reinvigorated divisions between both whites and Blacks, as well as St. Croix–born Crucians and immigrants from neighboring islands.

While many community members voiced support for the creation of the category of "native" Virgin Islander, this reaction was far from unanimous. Rather, as the convention—and the "native" debate—progressed, a number of articles began appearing in local news sources, taking issue with both the notion of defining "native" Virgin Islanders and the views of Delegate Bert Bryan in particular. In a letter to the editor entitled "Appalled but Not Surprised!" one local resident wrote that she was "appalled but unfortunately, not surprised, at Adelbert Bryan's racist display. If Mr. Bryan cannot or will not accept the fact that he is to represent all segments of our varied community then [he] is not performing up to the standards of his . . . responsibilities. This is no place to continue to portray his well known attitudes of divisiveness and racism" (Mawson 2008).

The issue of "native" Virgin Islanders captured the attention of many people in the USVI and crossed racial, class, and generational divides. Much of the backlash against the category of "native" came from Virgin Islands–born residents, many of whose parents had long ago immigrated to the territory from surrounding islands, who felt their identity being called into question and argued that they were being unfairly excluded from their home. While the "outsiders" against whom Crucians most vividly imagined themselves in this moment were extravagantly wealthy EDC people, this debate privileged the specificity of place to such a degree that many longtime residents were once again excluded as "Other," extending decades-old antagonisms over economic benefit. My exposure to intra-office politics of belonging at the EDA ("me don't ask that gasso gyul nothing") was but an example of the larger processes of Otherization that enveloped the island. The Fifth Constitutional Convention in 2008 was another.

The overwhelming community response to Delegate Bryan's appearance on a local television call-in show in December 2004, as well as his participation in the 2008 Constitutional Convention, captured the intense level of feeling that surrounded the issue of defining "native" Virgin Islanders.[24] During the 2004 television show, Bryan reinforced the primacy of place in response to a self-identified older Kittitian man who was outraged at what he understood as the divisive nature of Bryan's project:

> BERT BRYAN: I have no fight with you or anybody born in St. Kitts, Antigua, Guam or anywhere. I'm simply saying to you just like how you were saying that you are proud to be born in St. Kitts and you'ze [*sic*] Kittitian, I am saying likewise I am proud to be a native Virgin Islander born in Frederiksted, St. Croix to parents that were born in St. Croix in 1898 and 1911, and I'm saying to you sir, if your children are here, born here in St. Thomas, you know and don't want to admit it, as a naturalized U.S. citizen you can enjoy U.S. citizenship, your child that was born in St. Thomas or St. Croix or St. John can enjoy U.S. citizenship and at the same time they can go to St. Kitts and use you as their father and get a Kittitian passport. I cannot get another passport unless I denounce my U.S. citizenship. There's no fight, there's no war. It's people who want to politically separate and influence people would say it's a war. I am not taking anything from anybody.

Despite Bryan's claim that he is "not taking anything from anybody," it is clear from the response in the Virgin Islands that many residents feel he is, in fact, attempting to take away a defining aspect of their identity. This sentiment is also expressed by the host of this program who, noting his birth in Puerto Rico, stated: "I was born in Puerto Rico and came to the Virgin Islands when I was three days old. I know nothing about Puerto Rico other than that. *All I know is the Virgin Islands.*" This privileging of one's personal experience ("all I know is the Virgin Islands") challenges the temporal grounding of the proposed definition of "native" Virgin Islanders that centers colonial history as the determinant of Virgin Islands identity. Rather than being able to trace one's familial presence to the territory to a particular year (1927 or otherwise), the host's definition of belonging is rooted in something far more intimate—one's personal trajectory and sense of identity. However, Bryan's objection to the ability of this man to identify simultaneously as a Kittitian and an American (albeit naturalized) is rooted in a desire for an essentialized identity, a quantifiable measure of his presence, read as allegiance. Attempting to ameliorate the exclusion engendered by this definition, Bryan said later in this television interview: "In all fairness, everybody have [*sic*] the opportunity to live together, work together and own properties together. There's no definition that would upset that." While this is Bryan's claim in 2004, notably the year of the Jobs Act legislation that resulted in increased scrutiny on the EDC community, by the 2008 Constitutional Convention Bryan and his supporters pointed to a split between Blacks and wealthy whites intent on "purchas[ing] large chunks of land, subdivid[ing] it and resell[ing] it to others who are economically 'well-off' at prices that are way beyond the reach of many natives." During the 2008 convention, the formidable presence of EDC people on St. Croix and anxieties about this scenario made the harmonious situation of "everybody hav[ing] the opportunity to live together, work together and own properties together" increasingly unlikely.

During his final exchange on the 2004 television program, Delegate Bryan and a female caller discussed the tension between St. Croix–born residents and those who have immigrated from surrounding Caribbean islands:

CALLER: I don't see what the big uproar is. There's one thing missing from a lot of the residents here and that's something called nationalism.

BB: National pride . . .

CALLER: Exactly, and because a few native Virgin Islanders want to exhibit national pride, it's a problem. When we have these associations: St. Kitts Association, Antigua & Barbuda, Trinidad & Tobago Association, it's fine. They can put up their flags, they can do whatever. The people from the Dominican Republic can put up a big poster of their governor in town, it's fine. Do not say "Oh, we want to have the Crucian Coalition," it's a crime. Do not say "native Virgin Islander," it's a crime. They exhibit nationalism for their country. They are quick to say, "I am going home." Where is home? You live here, you work here, you contribute your taxes here, everything. Where is home? Home for them is the place where they were born. They don't ever say, when they're in the States, "I'm going home to St. Croix." They don't mean home, they mean St. Kitts or St. Lucia or wherever it is they were born. Why is it a crime for us to have some nationalism?

BB: Because there's no real identity of who we are and that's the problem . . .

While Bryan maintains that the "problem" is that there is no Virgin Islands identity, for many Virgin Islands residents, the "problem" is the definition of "native" that seeks to exclude them and their children from this sense of belonging. Both the caller and Bryan attempt to use national pride as a means through which to posit the true identity of nonnatives elsewhere. By arguing that "home" for longtime Virgin Islands residents is, in fact, "St. Kitts or St. Lucia or wherever," this caller is firmly establishing that the Virgin Islands is not their home, and they are to be excluded from an essentialized category of "native" Virgin Islander. In addition to concerns about an essentialized Virgin Islands identity, the anxieties in this debate are also related to concerns about American citizenship, a possession that is prized, yet one about which many in the Caribbean remain ambivalent. Further, both object to the varying levels of mobility among Virgin Islanders—as this caller presents a hypothetical situation in which Kittitians and St. Lucians travel between the States, their "home" country, and the Virgin Islands. In much the same way, EDC people—and as I will discuss in the following chapters, EDC girls—are begrudged their mobility by many Virgin Islanders.

In the end, the Virgin Islands produced a document out of the Fifth Constitutional Convention that included a definition of "native" Virgin Islander. In the proposed document, Article III outlined this (controversial) definition:

> An **Ancestral Native Virgin Islander** is (a) a person born or domiciled in the Virgin Islands prior to and including June 28, 1932 and not a citizen of a foreign country . . . (b) descendants of an Ancestral Native Virgin Islander residing outside of the U.S., its territories and possessions between January 17, 1917 and June 28, 1932, not subject to the jurisdiction of the U.S. and who are not

citizens or subjects of any foreign country. . . . A **Native Virgin Islander** is (a) a person born in the Virgin Islands after June 28, 1932, and (b) descendants of a person born in the Virgin Islands after June 28, 1932.[25]

After initially demurring because of concerns that the document did not sufficiently recognize the authority of the United States, the then governor of the territory sent the document on to the US Congress, where it was debated and sent back to the USVI to be amended. Ultimately, the delegation was unable to agree upon a set of revisions to the document by the deadline set by Congress. Given this, the document was dismissed and none of the provisions it outlined came into being. Still, the process of the convention was productive, serving as a catalyst for long-standing tensions around belonging on St. Croix—with EDC people serving as the foil for this broader set of anxieties.

The ways the EDC program is rooted in St. Croix's territorial status and earlier race and color hierarchies belie a notion of the current moment as a radically different development intervention— particularly in the Caribbean, a region whose history is steeped in global circuits of people and goods. Clearly, the move toward settling on a legally binding definition of "native" Virgin Islander is rooted in a desire to separate a space of privilege for Crucians—against both Caribbean migrants and mainland Americans. However, the political limits of this exercise were made clear a few months later, in 2009, when the document came to naught after its leaving the US Congress. Beyond this political limit, even the *attempt* to reject the primacy of the United States is rooted in its authority, as the date chosen to prove one's "native" identity is based on the date of the American purchase of the islands. The failure of this document and the larger process that produced it demonstrate the utility of spectral time as the framing through which to apprehend the changes in quotidian life on St. Croix since the advent of the EDC program. Reinvigorating decades-long tensions between Crucians and a multitude of "Others," the Fifth Constitutional Convention worked as a space in which these preexisting divisions were tethered to emergent frustrations about the EDC and its people. If the fear of a return to "slave days" was the primary anxiety surrounding the EDC, the convention served as an attempt to ensure that this remained an impossibility, by juridically producing a space of protection for the "right kind of (Black) people" (that is, those who can trace their ancestry to the appropriate year of colonial rule or transfer). Through the lens of spectral time, it becomes clear that this process was not merely a referendum on the state of affairs in 2008. Instead, it was an attempt to intervene in a centuries-long process of displacement.

The EDC program, an attempt to incorporate St. Croix into the global financial market, has resulted in the creation of a financial sector on this island, while the attendant arrival of a community of wealthy white Americans has had the unforeseen effect of creating an increasingly dystopian set of social relations on St. Croix. Rather than only increasing long-standing tensions between white and Black residents of St. Croix as the framing of "dem deh" suggests at first blush, the consolidation of a community of EDC people has resulted in shifting antagonisms between long-term white residents, St. Croix–born Crucians, and those with roots on neighboring islands. Moreover, as I will detail in the following chapter, concerns about hiring preferences for lighter-skinned employees among EDC companies have attached new forms of privilege to long-standing hierarchies of color.

A racially motivated feud on St. John and the 2008 Constitutional Convention with the ensuing debate over defining "native" Virgin Islanders made clear the degree to which antagonisms in the territory had escalated. Many of these tensions have their roots in the colonial period and the tripartite system of white, Creole, and Black, leading many Virgin Islanders to situate the current moment as a return to "slave days." Yet, contemporary racial relations on St. Croix differ in significant ways from this earlier period: the subsumption of long-term whites into the category of global elites known as "EDC people" (a development to which many members of the former community, like the Martins, object) is made possible by the incorporation of St. Croix—a formerly omitted space—into global financial circulations. What is more, the renewed emphasis on determining and legislating indigeneity is a significant response to the neoliberal ethos of freeing new markets and penetrating new spaces to participate in global capital processes. That the EDC program exists at the nexus of this old racial hierarchy and its new articulations results in its ambivalent reception on St. Croix. While Crucians are wary of the intentions of incredibly wealthy EDC people, they are nevertheless aware of—and enticed by—the opportunities and status their presence makes possible.

Charges of racism levied against EDC people by Virgin Islanders inform my theorization of spectral time. At the same time, these claims must be held in balance with former-EDA chairman Albert Bryan's warning that EDC businessmen cannot be expected to be "super corporate citizens." What these antagonisms demonstrate is the importance of recognizing what Clarke and Thomas (2006) have called "contemporary racialized circulations." That is, increasing racial tensions and new forms of privilege attached to race and color on St. Croix since the advent of the EDC program make it necessary to take these claims seriously and pay attention to who benefits most from the presence of the program on the island. The next chapter will do just that by describing and theorizing the position occupied by the most common Crucian employees of EDC companies, EDC girls—particularly those employed at Stanford Financial. In this chapter, I will describe the stereotypical image of these women, including race, color, gender, class, and behavioral markers. These tightly scripted positions reveal much about both race and gender vis-à-vis the EDC program. Further, analyzing these subject-positions allows me to address the issue of privilege as well as continuing anxieties about belonging on St. Croix.

Chapter 6

Easy Money and Respectable Girls

Gender Ideology and Neoliberal Development

One Thursday morning in 2008, I found myself in Christiansted at six o'clock in the morning. It was December, which is the season both of Christmas and Carnival on St. Croix, and I was participating in one of the island's Carnival celebrations called a J'ouvert, an early-morning street party that features crowds of would-be dancers (including myself) following a large truck carting a band of musicians. On this day, as is the case with most such events, the throngs that followed behind this procession were consuming alcohol and, in many cases, scantily clad. As we danced our way through Christiansted, we wound through the street where the Stanford office I had been interning with was located. As we passed the office, I saw three Stanford employees I had come to know from my time there, standing outside, taking in the scene. When I went over to say hello, surprise—and disapproval—clearly registered on their faces, with one woman saying to me: "Is that you? What are YOU doing in the J'ouvert?" For these women, my decision to participate in early-morning drinking and dancing in the street to calypso music along with hundreds of fellow revelers came as a serious and unpleasant surprise, given their view of me as a fellow EDC girl—or, at my frequent insistence, an anthropologist studying this program. What their surprise revealed was that my participation in this particular form of Crucian culture was a serious miscalculation of the limits of behavior for ambivalently positioned EDC girls, a transgression

151

of feminine ideals of respectability and "appropriate" behavior that they navigate daily.

This chapter explores the position of Crucians—many of whom are women—who find employment in the EDC sector. The contractual obligation that EDC companies hire local workers has resulted in both the deepening of existing hierarchies and the emergence of a new subject-position—the "EDC girl"—a middle- to upper-middle-class Crucian woman who has most often attended a private high school on St. Croix and received a college education on the US mainland. Taken together, these hiring practices are seen by many Crucians as deepening existing divisions of wealth and opportunity in ways that are uncomfortably reminiscent of social hierarchies established in the Caribbean during slavery and colonial rule. These workers are often recruited for either summer internships or, after graduation, full-time jobs by alumni of their private high schools. Crucians from less privileged backgrounds frequently lament their inability to penetrate these networks, as news of internships is often spread by word of mouth and informal recommendations. This exclusion from employment opportunities in the EDC sector has significant financial implications, as the average salary in the US Virgin Islands hovers just above $30,000, while EDC companies pay their employees an average of $66,000. This disparity is particularly stark in a context where 32 percent of the population exists below the poverty line.[1]

While taking seriously the implications of this widened income gap, it remains vital to separate the economically competitive salaries paid in the EDC sector from the vast wealth of EDC employers themselves. On St. Croix, there is widespread speculation of fantastic sums presumably paid to local EDC employees, notions that rarely correspond to the reality of entry-level positions, while nevertheless marking these employees with the social stigma of being affiliated with the program and burdening them with familial and societal responsibilities they often resent as unfair. These responsibilities are primarily financial; for instance, EDC workers frequently receive requests for loans or gifts of money and are often encouraged by local vendors to "spend up the EDC money." This demarcation of their income as EDC money is significant, as it sets this money apart from other forms of capital. In addition, EDC girls are expected by much of the Crucian community to consume and behave in particular ways, including disposing of their generous salaries conspicuously on items such as clothing, cars, and vacations—spending expectations that often frustrate and overextend them, while at the same time pushing against the neoliberal privileging of the individual. Despite these expectations, the lived reality for most of the EDC girls with whom I worked and spoke was that they had preexisting financial responsibilities, including schooling, transportation costs, and family expenses. For EDC girls, then, the money they earn is not simply disposable "EDC money" but necessary income. Despite these financial realities, their salaries have simultaneously placed these women in a unique category of affluence and made them subject to additional financial expectations on the island.

The status category of "EDC girl" has come into being through these women's employment and the salaries they earn in the EDC sector, developments brought about by the introduction of St. Croix into global financial circulations. Additionally, however, the label of "EDC girl" also indicates a new development category, as these women's identities are rooted to a significant degree in their roles as *consumers* of various commodities. For EDC girls, this spending is expected to benefit their networks on the island, positioning these young women in a new role of provider. The expectation that EDC girls will spend their relative wealth around the island is one widely shared by their families, friends—and often mere acquaintances.

In this chapter, I take seriously these expectations that (1) the money these women earn is "EDC money," that is, indelibly linked to the program, echoing Viviana Zelizer's (1997) interventions on the differing moral values of money,[2] and (2) that they should spend this money freely and, vitally, in ways that benefit the local community. Here, I also dwell on my time working alongside women employed in the EDC sector on St. Croix. While our projects were different—I was gathering ethnographic data on the program, and they were largely attempting to carve out new lives and identities for themselves—we worked together closely. The access I gained to these EDC girls created space for us to have conversations about their jobs, their lives, and their hopes for the future.

My work on EDC girls builds on decades of scholarship on women's labor in the Caribbean, work that has often focused on working-class women in the region. For instance, Carla Freeman (2000) has coined the term "pink collar" to describe a new type of labor performed by women. In her theorization of female workers in the informatics industry in Barbados, Freeman attempts to complicate a traditional Marxist class analysis, theorizing these employees as a new "class fraction" and arguing that their "pink collar" identity marks them as different from either white- or blue-collar laborers. Unlike EDC girls, these women are largely drawn from working-class backgrounds and attempt to attain new economic realities through their employment in this sector. Given that tourism is a driving economic force across the Caribbean, there is also a substantial body of scholarship on women at work in that industry (for example, Gmelch 2003; Roland 2011). In her discussion of service-sector work in tourist markets in the Caribbean, Angelique Nixon (2015) brings together the assumptions of women's work and the feminization of the region as a whole. What is more, the emergence of the EDC program out of the history of industrialization in the region in general and in the USVI in particular makes the role of women's labor in factories of particular importance (see Yelvington 1995; Deere 1995; in the maquiladora context, see Prieto 1997; Cravey 1998).

In Carla Freeman's work, she argues that the "clean" atmosphere of "pink collar" office work, along with its "professional" dress code, provides workers with a distinct identity. That these women often do not earn substantially more than blue-collar workers suggests that it is not simply earning potential or salary that Freeman considers when describing the subject-position of these women (or, rather, their relationship to the means of production)—introducing the notion of *gendered* class subjects, cultural capital, and local definitions of distinction. That is, the widespread recognition of the value of being well dressed becomes, with the introduction of the offshore informatics firms Freeman describes, part of the basis of the new "pink collar" professional woman's identity. Importantly, she also notes that the demands of "professionalism" are both repressive and enjoyable, as these women are fashioned into new subjects by corporate demands but also find pleasure in their distinction as "modern" subjects. My work on EDC girls differs in that the women hired for these positions are largely drawn from the existing middle to upper middle class and are quite well paid for their work in this sector, when compared to the average salary in the USVI.

Freeman ultimately concludes that informatics workers occupy an ambivalent space in Barbados, an insight that has much relevance for my analysis of EDC girls who are similarly positioned as a result of the tension between their long-standing community ties and newfound notoriety from working in this sector.[3] The consumption patterns of EDC girls—including trips to the mainland, throughout the Caribbean, and beyond are marked as different from many Virgin Islanders who have limited mobility and access to resources. While these workers' employment at EDC firms is facilitated by their "localness" (that is, being from St. Croix—as businesses receiving EDC benefits are legally required to hire a certain number of local employees), I argue that these workers become seen as something else—something like "local, with a difference" as a result of their relationship to the EDC program as well as capital broadly.

EDC Money

The salaries paid to EDC employees are a site of contention on St. Croix. Local merchants and community members, operating under a widespread assumption that this money is easily gotten for those with access to this sector, often tease, cajole, or outright demand money from these workers, making it plain that, like EDC girls themselves, this money is somehow set apart. In her work on the ways in which money is woven into daily life, Viviana Zelizer (1997) has theorized modern forms of currency—upending a notion of undifferentiated money and pointing to the ways capital is deeply embedded in both social relations and moral assessments. She details, for instance, the ways differently earned monies have varying moral values attached to them: ill-gotten (or "dirty") money—such as the proceeds from a bank robbery—may be subject to limitations on how it can be spent. Zelizer also examines the ways in which money is used to shore up gender imbalances through notions such "a woman's wage" (or pin money), which is presumed to be either disposable or supplementary income. In her work on gender and development, Cynthia Enloe (1989) has also engaged in the notion of pin money and demonstrated how the ideology surrounding women as "ideal" workers has shifted over time, with female factory workers during the moment of industrialization being preferred as laborers who could be paid less, based on the assumption that they were supported by men and merely earning supplementary income. Zelizer renews this insight, pointing to the continued interrelationship between gender relations and payments. This history has particular relevance for the lives and paychecks of EDC girls, as this kind of "moral earmarking" applies to their EDC salaries that are seen by many in the local community as tainted, marked off by the designation of "EDC money" and meant to be spent in ways that benefit the local community broadly. What is more, this expectation demonstrates the extent to which members of the community are comfortable working out anxieties about global capital through the paychecks of EDC girls—resurrecting the assumption that their earnings are a supplement to their household income rather than their primary income.

That well-positioned Crucian women find employment in the EDC sector will come as no surprise to students of Caribbean history: Black women in the Caribbean have always worked and often been either the primary or sole provider for their household (see, for instance, Bush 1990). Enslaved labor, for instance, relied on both race and gender: slavery was inflicted upon Black people, and the combination of white supremacy and gender ideology combined to produce a particular bind for Black women.

In 1995, Helen Safa wrote, "The concept of the male bread winner is becoming a myth as women worldwide become increasingly important contributors to the household economy" (1995: 1). With the unfolding of neoliberal programs across the globe, that myth has receded even further, replaced by a reality of differently positioned women laboring across the region. For the women with whom I worked and spoke, their salaries were not supplementary but rather were absolutely vital, as they all had pressing financial obligations— expenses that were compounded by community demands that their salaries perform the work of community uplift. Finally, while EDC girls do outearn most in the community, as Zelizer notes, "how much money is less important than *which* money" (1997: 21). That is, it is the relation to the questionable EDC sector that leads to community expectations that these workers should rid themselves of it as quickly—and with as much community benefit—as possible.

Respectability

As noted at earlier in this chapter, my participation in the J'ouvert celebration came as an unwelcome surprise to my EDC interlocuters.

This is largely because my behavior had transgressed norms of respectability that inform the behavioral expectations surrounding EDC girls: the discourse of respectability is one in which class, race, color, gender, and behavior combine to produce vastly different life possibilities and expectations. White femininity and respectability have long been central to life in the Caribbean as has been extensively documented (see, for example, Wilson 1964, 1973; Enloe 1989; Alexander and Mohanty 1997; Douglass 1992; McClintock 1995; Austin-Broos 1997; Besson 1993; Reddock 1994). This ranking along a continuum of femininity has shaped the lives of women, particularly women in the Caribbean, for centuries and with devastating effects. For instance, during the period of slavery the rhetoric of hypersexualized and insatiable Black women was used to justify the systematized rape of enslaved African women (see, for instance, Bush 1990 and Hammonds 1997). Black women were also regarded as beasts of burden and forced to work in the public sphere—often in plantation fields.[4] This continuum of femininity also had implications for white women, who were positioned as the most respectable and associated with the "Cult of True Womanhood" (Carby 1987; Welter 1966; duCille 1994), becoming linked to the realm of the household (or private sphere) and largely precluded from working outside of it. This history is central to the contemporary moment, as race and color continue to inform expectations of women's labor, with lighter-skinned women often chosen for the high-paying and sometimes-prized jobs of the EDC sector. In this way, historical experiences of race, color, gender, and labor continue to echo throughout life in the region.

In their daily lives, EDC girls are faced with competing expectations. On the one hand, many in the community expect them to freely dispose of their newfound money, while their employers expect that they will conduct themselves in an "appropriate" (or "ladylike") manner as representatives of their business interests. This notion of respectability that is rooted in ideals of white femininity (and its approximation by women of color) in large part governs the behavioral expectations of EDC girls as they are to be the "respectable" local face of the EDC program, comporting themselves in (business) friendly ways always. If capital and its handlers desire safe harbor, these women are expected to be the physical embodiment of St. Croix's friendly climate. As the representation of the island's openness to capital, EDC girls are expected to not only act "respectably" but also present a business-friendly aesthetic—more often than not, this aesthetic is one that privileges whiteness (or its approximation).

As discussed in the previous chapter, St. Croix—like much of the Caribbean—operates as a pigmentocracy in which higher social status is often linked to lighter skin,[5] a reality that extends to the EDC sector. In relation to EDC girls, the influence of color privilege cannot be overlooked, as a number of these workers are drawn from the existing middle and upper middle class. Historically, both race and color shaped possibilities for women's life and work in the plantation economy, as darker-skinned women often worked outside in the fields, while lighter-skinned women were seen as better suited to indoor domestic labor, and these outcomes of color continue to inform work in the Caribbean, as women continue to be assessed—and assess themselves—by their approximation of respectability. As this is rooted in both phenotype and behavior (that is, one can both "look" respectable and act in a respectable manner—and have both factored into one's social standing), women at work in the EDC sector monitored each other (as shown in my J'ouvert transgression) and themselves for markers of respectability.

As outlined in chapter 5, color functions as social capital in the Caribbean and creates avenues for upward mobility. In her work, Gina Ulysse (2007) describes "uptown" Jamaican "ladies" who are white or lighter-skinned—in Jamaica, known as "brown"—against "downtown" women who are often darker-skinned and work in public spaces, such as vendors' plazas in which they conduct the business of selling goods. These traders, the "informal commercial exporters" of Ulysse's research, navigate expectations of race, color, class, and respectability to travel internationally to purchase goods they will ultimately sell on the island. While phenotype figures prominently in assessments of respectability, there are other factors as well, as noted by Ulysse:

> For dark skinned females of the middle class, color is mediated through observance of the culture of femininity and dress. One of the ultimate symbols of ladyhood is her well-groomed hair. At the time my hair was permed or "colonized"—a term I used much to the shock of the females I encountered. [Shortly after cutting] my hair to a low Afro, a female hairdresser asked me if was going

to "texturize" the new 'fro, that is soften it with more chemicals. Yet I had cut off the hair precisely to get rid of all the chemicals. (2007: 117)

The role of Black women's hair vis-à-vis respectability is something I also encountered during fieldwork. Near the start of my time with Stanford Financial, the company hired a new "concierge" (the company's term for the front desk staff member). The woman hired for the position was Larissa, a darker-skinned local woman in her early twenties. Larissa did not "relax"[6] her hair and generally styled her natural hair into a ponytail at work. A few weeks after she began working in the office, we were chatting when she repeatedly asked me for my advice and opinion on whether she should get the curls in her hair loosened by getting a chemical texturizer. When I asked her why she was concerned about this issue, she said that it was just something she had been thinking about, and that she wanted to have "nicer"—that is, looser—curls. Here, the interplay of expectations related to color and hair come together, as lighter skin is often—though not uniformly—associated with looser curls. Certainly, Larissa's decisions concerning hairstyle and texture are matters of personal choice. However, given her recent employment at this high-profile organization, a company foremost in a sector widely suspected of having unspoken hiring preferences that favor lighter-skinned local young women, I wondered about the connection between Larissa's workplace and her sudden concern with looking "appropriate." Further, the literature on black women's hair and notions of beauty and respectability, including Ulysse (2007), Banks (2000), Candelario (2007), and Jacobs-Huey (2006), points to the significance of hairstyles beyond aesthetics. That EDC employers expect Crucian employees to present themselves in ways that privilege whiteness is noteworthy, considering the revisiting of these racialized hierarchies vis-à-vis beauty that has occurred elsewhere in the region of late—for instance, Deborah Thomas (2004) has documented the emergence of "blackness" as an increasingly valued category in Jamaica. This revisiting of the historical and contemporary denigration of Blackness is not one that has occurred on St. Croix generally—and certainly not in the EDC sector that continues to value plantation-era and colonial markers of privilege, including lighter skin and elite education. This shoring up of color privilege and respectability politics on the part of EDC employers stands out, given that many are largely unfamiliar with the long and trajectory-altering hierarchies of race and color in the Caribbean. Rather than explicitly seeking "brown" (see, for instance, Edmondson 2009) women to work in this sector, these employers achieve the same result by privileging "well-spoken" or "appropriate" job candidates.

The experiences of one Stanford employee demonstrate this point. Near the start of my time at Stanford, I became friendly with a Black woman named Ellen who worked there. She was several years older than most of the other Crucian women in the office and had taken upon herself the role of advisor, always ready with a listening ear or suggestion of how to defuse intra-office conflict. Ellen was a darker-skinned woman in her late forties who had not earned a college degree but had taken a number of courses at the University of the Virgin Islands (UVI). After being employed in the EDC sector for four years, she was excited by the arrival of Stanford Financial and quickly applied to work for the company. When she was hired as an administrative assistant for a manager within the company, she set her sights on a promotion to the position of "concierge," a role Ellen desired as it would allow her to interact more frequently with the public and hopefully put her previous client management experience to use. Ultimately, Ellen was passed over for this role, receiving the feedback that she was not "what [the company] want[s] for the front desk," as she did not have the "right kind of voice," presumably an allusion to the trace of her Crucian accent. After being passed over for this role, Ellen remained at Stanford and was still always ready with a piece of advice, but something had changed for her. Perhaps in recognition of the limits she faced at Stanford, she said that she planned to go back to school, to UVI, to take more classes (courses, she hoped, that would be paid for by her current employer, Stanford) in order to make herself more "marketable." Ellen's experience speaks to the community frustrations with the EDC program: while she had experience and was able to secure employment at Stanford, she did not possess the currency of skin color, mainland education, accent, and background valued in this sector. That Ellen was placed in a less visible position points to the company's willingness to fulfill its requirement of hiring local employees, so long as such hires do not tarnish the company's projected image of carefully scripted propriety. At once, Larissa's concerns about her hair seemed weightier, as Ellen's experience brought home the material effects of one's "look" and "sound."

As EDC girls represent a new subject-position on the island, upwardly mobile employees with significant access to commodities and capital, the material reality of these workers' preexisting positions is relevant. The vast majority of EDC girls have attended one of the two private high schools on St. Croix, either Good Hope School or Country Day School, although these institutions merged in 2013 after the closing of the island's largest private employer (the HOVENSA oil refinery) and the exodus of well-heeled residents whose tuition dollars funded these schools. The tuition for upper school (grades 7–12) at Good Hope Country Day School was $16,450, at the same time that the median household income in the territory was just over twice that figure. This is "considerably lower than the US median household income of $50,112" and places enrollment at this private school squarely out of the reach of the vast majority of Virgin Islanders. What is more, these figures do not highlight the most economically disadvantaged in the territory, as "there is a large segment of the population earning very little money. . . . *About 11% of all households live on less than $10,000 per year*, compared to 7% for the United States as a whole" (emphasis mine).[7] My experience attending parochial high school put me into regular social contact with students at these elite schools through participation in varsity sports and other extracurricular activities, networks I was able to draw on during fieldwork.

These forms of educational privilege and networking that often lead to EDC opportunities are not slavery—yet they figure into Crucians' objections to the EDC program as "slave days." This is how spectral time functions; the specter of slavery as an institution dependent upon formal difference rooted in race indelibly marks the intervening centuries of life on St. Croix such that more nuanced forms of privilege (including colonial education) get bundled into fears about a return to "slave days." Like the erasure of myriad "Others" (including Puerto Ricans, Arabs, and Jews) in response to EDC people, the everyday reality of historically informed spaces of privilege become marshaled as evidence of the impending return of this ultimate moment of racial capitalism.

The use of spectral time is a way to not only make sense of race-based claims (for example, the EDC as the reemergence of "slave days") but also to position this moment in the long history of wealth and power consolidation that has been particularly evident in the Caribbean. It is through this lens that I contextualize Crucians' expectations concerning the spending and behavior of local women at work in the EDC sector. If the EDC exists as yet another instance of racial capitalism in a long line of such projects, the novel figure of the EDC girl who "belongs" both to the EDC program and the local community represents a space where community members are able to intervene in these centuries-long processes. That is, Crucians' insistence that EDC girls spend their paychecks in ways that benefit the wider community marks an attempt to dismantle the larger financial architecture that has long wrought havoc across the region and their lives. That is not to say that this attempt at intervention is without its problems. For instance, that these concerns about the implications of neoliberalism are played out through the bodies—and paychecks—of Crucian women echoes concerns long expressed by feminist scholars, many of whom have noted the multiple ways women and their bodies are used to stand in for "the nation" and its concerns (for instance, see Alexander and Mohanty 1997).

As Crucians provide an alternate theorization of capital vis-à-vis time, they push against an engagement with capitalist processes as discrete moments (for example, plantation economy, colonialism, foreign direct investment) and instead position these within a single process of racial capitalism. This approach is at odds with the notion that Crucians who object to the EDC program and the larger project of neoliberalism simply do not *understand* their benefits. This position, that any objection to the EDC on the part of the local community must be rooted in misapprehension, was widespread among EDC supporters. Again, consider the 2004 newspaper editorial that positioned the "EDC program [as] one of the greatest economic stimulus plans to ever grace the shores of the Virgin Islands. Our ability to understand and engage the opportunity will determine the future of the people of the Virgin Islands" (Difede 2004). My assertion of spectral time allows for a positioning of the EDC program as but an instance of a larger project of racial capitalism and makes clear that Crucians who are critical of this program do not simply misapprehend its benefits but are instead part of a long trajectory of theorists who insist upon the necessity of alternate temporal frameworks. Rather than the *linear* narrative of progress in which development initiatives such as the EDC are rooted, this competing analysis is grounded in spectral time, a recognition of the ways in which elements of the past are (often menacingly) present in contemporary operations of capital. This rendering offers insight into the ways in which such neoliberal initiatives—and the project of neoliberalism more broadly—produce novel outcomes (including the emergent subject-position of the EDC girl that is the focus of this chapter) while drawing on both histories and contemporary relations of power. An engagement with spectral time provides space for a recognition of continuities as well as emergent spaces of agency present in the neoliberal project. Far from being either historically determined or simply being a direct outgrowth of market forces, I argue that the operations of capital in the neoliberal moment allow for the *creation* of new spaces of possibility including, but not limited to, figures such as the EDC girl and emergent geographical connections that have "recharted" the globe (Maurer 1997).

In addition to dress, hair, color, and education, there were other markers related to respectability that set Stanford employees apart: of the twelve workers in my office, only two were unmarried (one of whom was engaged and got married shortly after my internship ended). This fact is of note, as the 2000 Census shows that 41.7 percent of women in the Virgin Islands have never been married.[8] More recent data tells a similar story, as figures from 2015 (the most recent data available) show that 37 percent of women on St. Croix are recorded as "never married."[9] This privileging of marriage among Stanford employees against the norms of the island further set these workers apart from much of the Virgin Islands community. Moreover, the high percentage of married employees at Stanford is striking for the region and hints at employer preferences for "classed" behavior among its workforce. The relationship between marriage, class, and respectability in the Caribbean has been theorized by scholars, including foundational work by Simey (1946), Henriques (1953), R. T. Smith (1996), M. G. Smith (1965), and Edith Clarke (1957). Writing in the Jamaican context, R. T. Smith conceptualized the "dual marriage system" that was pivotal in theorizing marriage and class, as he analyzed the practice of upper-class white men marrying white women—while keeping lower-class Black women as concubines. During the colonial period, the British in Jamaica abhorred such practices as serial monogamy and "visiting unions," yet these were—and remained—extremely common, despite British efforts to increase "low" marriage rates through state-sponsored programs such as the Mass Marriage movement. Thus, the disproportionately high number of married Crucians employed at Stanford is more than simply a coincidence; rather, it is a reflection of the classed and behavioral expectations projected by the company.

The expectations of respectability to which EDC girls remain subjected by much of the local community range widely and extend to marriage and patterns of residence. On St. Croix, as in much of the Caribbean, it is commonly expected that young people, particularly women, will live "at home" (that is, with their parents and/or extended family) until marriage. In part, this has to do with financial considerations and a desire to pool family resources, but this expectation is also rooted in notions of "respectable" behavior, as living in one's family home provides an attendant layer of surveillance, with family members being able to keep track of, and comment upon, one's comings and goings. For many unmarried young women earning EDC salaries, these expectations meant continuing to live with their parents while significantly outearning them—a situation that had the potential to create conflicts over authority and financial responsibilities.

I was confronted with these residential expectations early on in fieldwork. Before arriving on St. Croix, I had decided that although I had family members living on the island, it would be crucial for me to rent an apartment in order to establish my identity as an anthropologist rather than simply a home-goer. As I searched for a rental unit at the start of my fieldwork, immediately ruling out East End as too expensive on my stipend, and other areas as simply too far or secluded for my vehicle to manage, I was frequently met with curious stares and concerned questions such as, "You have family here? Why such a pretty young girl like you looking to rent?" This desire for a space of my own was seen as not just unusual but concerning for my would-be landlords: Was something wrong with me? Would I have unwelcome visitors on their property? In short, what was I *up to* that my family couldn't know about? It did not help matters much when I explained that I was an anthropologist seeking to strike out on my own. In the end, my first home in the field came as a result of a college friend, and I settled into a pool house for which I paid monthly rent. This home was located in the neighborhood of Carambola on St. Croix, a gated community of homes situated within one of the island's more popular golf courses. The Carambola Golf Club, formerly the Rockefeller-owned Fountain Valley golf course, is located on the northwest section of the island. This location was also the site of one of the most notorious crimes in St. Croix's history, the Fountain Valley massacre described in the previous chapter, a crime—particularly in the racial makeup of the victims and assailants—that remains vital to race relations on St. Croix today, as it continues to be remembered, and invoked, in relation to the EDC program.

Working to Get Familiar

During my time conducting fieldwork at St. Croix Fund, I was something of an awkward interloper with an unusual work schedule that brought me to the office only on Thursdays and Fridays. This, combined with some initial uncertainty on the part of Fund workers about the purpose of my project (Why did I want to study their company? Was I there to get the business in trouble with the EDA?) resulted in my fellow workers being reserved around me during my first few weeks as an intern. Even during lunchtime chats in the office kitchen, where Peter Davies often provided lunch for his employees, it was clear that office employees were restrained in their conversations with me. At Stanford, too, employees were standoffish toward me when I began my internship. In addition to the sober environment of the office, I attributed this distance to the fact that I was among the youngest of the workers as well as unmarried, two qualities that placed me squarely in the minority at Stanford. Feeling alienated and unsure of how to develop a warmer relationship with my coworkers, I began to wonder if my long days as an EDC intern would be as productive for my research as I had initially hoped.

One afternoon a month into my unpaid internship at Stanford, I was without either lunch plans or money for a nearby restaurant or café. Given these restraints, I decided to take lunch later in the day and to spend the hour reading the newspaper and eating in the company kitchen for the first time. Unlike the open floor plan at St. Croix Fund that facilitated chatting between the work area and kitchen, at Stanford the lunchroom was separated from the offices by a door. Shortly into my break, two of the women who had have given me the iciest reception walked in, chatting about a wedding they had both attended over the weekend. Surprised to learn that these workers who behaved so formally with me socialized with each other outside of the office, I began making small talk. Seeming slightly put off by my attempts at conversation, they nevertheless involved me in their passing commentary on various articles in that day's newspaper. Thirty minutes later, three more women walked into the room and began punching numbers into the microwave, rummaging around in the refrigerator, and dividing up the newspaper among themselves. As conversations took shape, it became clear that this convergence on the lunchroom was a regular event, and one that I had been missing as a result of my habit of leaving for lunch at noon, along with Joe and many of the other managers.

During that first day in the company lunchroom, I realized that there was something of a second shift for the lunch break, and that the women in the kitchen—a group of local women employed at Stanford in administrative and support positions—worked through their supervisors' absence and took their own lunch break later in the day, at around two o'clock. This revelation stunned me, as I had long been attempting to figure out a way to get to know this group of women in a less formal setting, and there they were, talking about social happenings, the day's events at the office, and hinting at their relationships with their bosses. As I struggled to make conversation, I noticed apprehension on the part of my fellow workers and felt that I was somehow infringing on their space, a hesitance I later learned was born out of confusion about my motives for being there: Was I eavesdropping on their conversations to report back to Joe and the other managers? Would the informality of the exchanges in the lunchroom affect their employment? In my attempt to fall into the rhythms of the office, I had spent my first month unconsciously aligning myself with the managerial staff by leaving the office at noon, thereby missing the daily lunchroom chats between the very EDC girls I had come to study. After realizing the effect my mis-timed break had on my research, and how I was perceived in the office, I began taking a later lunch hour and eating in the company lunchroom with these female employees. While these workers were paid well and widely assumed to have disposable income to spend frequenting restaurants in the area for lunch, they did not do so. Instead, they either brought cooked meals from home or purchased lunch at a nearby café, returning to the lunchroom to eat and chat with their fellow workers.

Whereas I would often run into Joe and other members of the managerial staff while eating lunch in Christiansted, that was not the case with the local employees. Although they ate lunch later than their supervisors, an arrangement that meant these workers ran virtually no risk of encountering their bosses during lunch, the women still preferred to spend their lunch hour with one another in the shared space of the office lunchroom, eating and talking. These daily lunch sessions contributed to a sense of community among this group of women who were viewed on the island as incredibly fortunate, newly prosperous—and somewhat suspicious—as a result of their employment within the EDC sector, and at Stanford Financial especially. By taking my lunch hour later in the afternoon and eating in the office lunchroom, I was able to see behind the stoic "professionalism" on display in the office. In its place, I witnessed a network of personal relationships among and between my fellow workers. I learned, for instance, that a wedding I had heard about during my first day in the lunchroom had been of a former "concierge," and that the two women who had been discussing the event had both been bridesmaids. This purposeful formation of a community among EDC girls employed at Stanford Financial—away from both their supervisors and the demands of the wider community—is a demonstration of how these workers curated the opportunity of working in this sector to develop both personal and professional relationships that enabled them to express their multiple positions. Here, they could complain about their bosses' unreasonable demands or share frustrations about financial expectations they faced from family members. In this space that these EDC girls created for themselves, they were free from either recrimination or expectations around their finances and spending.

As a result of the time I began to spend in the company lunchroom with women working at Stanford, the dynamic between us began to change. Rather than the cool professionalism that characterized our exchanges throughout much of the workday, our conversations during lunch became friendly and somewhat intimate. As Crucians who had been selected to work at the highest-profile company on the island, an organization whose CEO continued to be a primary topic of conversation in the island's rumor mill and its newspapers, our lunchtime conversations began to feel like a time of commiseration. Not everyone on St. Croix, however, welcomed the nuanced position of EDC girls, as Crucians outside this space still placed untenable financial expectations on these workers.

Easy Money

The general assumption regarding work in the EDC sector is that it pays well and requires little labor—making these salaries, in effect, "easy money." For instance, recall that in the 2008 legal proceedings against Company X (mentioned in the previous chapters) that was charged with tax evasion, the federal government claimed, "The business of [this company] was not the sale of business services, but the sale of tax evasion. . . . The government can find no evidence of any substantial business services performed by anyone. Specifically, we can find *no* evidence of *any* work performed."[10] This assessment that local employees are hired in support positions and then not expected to perform much labor was echoed by the CEO of one EDC company with whom I spoke, who stressed that his office had a difficult time hiring local employees as "the candidates all came in with a wink and a nod," expecting to be paid handsomely for very little labor. Ellen too conceded that—as many Virgin Islanders suspect—there "was not a lot of work to do" for local employees. When I asked Ellen about her impression of EDC companies and the amount of work they entrust to their employees on St. Croix, she said: "Some of the companies are legitimate, and some of them are not. They just want the tax benefits. They will have a Stateside secretary transfer some work to a secretary on St. Croix—but it's just busywork that could be done in the States. Now I see how the rich get rich and stay rich. You and me won't even think of some of these things." This money, then, is seen as, if not ill-gotten, then certainly questionably obtained, and combined with the hiring preferences that favor lighter-skinned, relatively privileged young women, results in the sentiment on St. Croix that this money is easily—and unfairly— earned and that EDC girls who receive this capital should spend it freely and conspicuously such that it benefits the Crucians without access to EDC capital. Beyond reorganizing the ways opportunities are gendered, the presence of the EDC program has created an environment in which social, cultural, and economic capital—not to mention the human capital so prized by the neoliberal project—are being renegotiated.

In the EDC program, the long-standing hierarchies of race and color in the Caribbean merge with the neoliberal project of becoming an entrepreneur of the self to produce the figure of EDC girl. This liminal position requires EDC girls to be nimble, ever aware of their interlocutors. This state of hyperawareness is necessary for EDC girls, given their relationship to global capital and Crucians' attempts to intervene in racialized wealth accumulation through their paychecks and consumption patterns. The investment of EDC girls in the social networks of St. Croix remain vital to this intervention—particularly in light of the instability of global capital in general and the EDC program in particular.

It is no coincidence that the workers understood to be the custodians of maximum human capital on St. Croix are female, an imbalance tied to the feminization of labor that emerged from the relocation of industrialization to areas like the Caribbean and one that continues in the current moment of development. Given that these workers are generally in their twenties and early thirties, it is of note that they are identified as EDC "girls," as scholars have marked neoliberalism's preoccupation with not just femininity, but particularly with "girls" as the agents most capable of neoliberalism's processes of self-transformation (for instance, see Murphy 2013; Hayhurst 2013; Scharff 2012). Beyond their classification as "girls," Crucian women employed in the EDC sector are further positioned for inclusion in this neoliberal project by their middle- and upper-middle-class backgrounds, the aspiration for the neoliberal, consuming subject (Ringrose and Walkerdine 2008). As I engage with local women employed in the EDC sector and the raced/color/class/gender histories and expectations that shape their experiences, I take seriously the implications of *expectation* as well as the possibilities—both liberatory and oppressive—they create. In a different context, James Ferguson (1999) has written about expectation, examining modernity and the dashed hopes on the part of those in the Global South who had come to believe they might find a place in the ostensibly global march toward "progress." Not only is that narrative flawed, Ferguson argues, but it remains exclusionary—with the neoliberal "future" often excluding the abject category of blackness just as did the colonial past. Given these failures, Crucians root their hopes for an improved economic future—to the degree that there is such a space as "the future"—in EDC girls privileging their community above their individual mobility and consumption patterns.

In addition to examining the expectations that inform and shape the experiences of these workers, I also take up the way they engage with and frustrate these expectations. For instance, these women owe their employment, at least in part, to their presumed *difference* from "other" Crucians—that is, their preexisting position of relative priv- ilege, including access to private education and the (lack of) a local accent. However, it is through their *sameness* as fellow Crucians that members of the local community make their claims on these women. This, then, is the ostensible space of privilege occupied by female EDC employees: afforded singular opportunities and possibilities as a result of their affiliation with the program yet also part of, and—in the view of many of their fellow Crucians—financially responsible to and for, the broader community on St. Croix.

The exceptional opportunities available to EDC workers go beyond contextually high salaries and the occasional catered recep- tion. Some EDC companies highlight team building exercises that can happen either off or on island. While I was in the midst of the difficult process of cold-calling EDC companies and asking them to meet with me, a longtime friend of mine employed by an EDC took pity upon me and invited me for a fun weekend away. The trip would, she thought, take my mind off the daunting task in which I was engaged—trying to get a clear sense of the ways EDC people and EDC girls are positioned on St. Croix. My friend explained that the occasion was an all-expenses-paid company trip to Las Vegas that her employer was offering to her and her coworkers. As part of the incentive, each employee was allowed to invite one guest. Several of the employees invited their spouses or significant others, while others brought friends with whom they could pass a long weekend in Las Vegas. Falling into the latter category, I packed my suitcase, squeezed into my seat on a lost-cost airline, and flew to Las Vegas, unsure of how I would fit in and unclear on the value of this trip for my research.

The EDC company my friend worked at was small, having fewer than a dozen employees, and they—along with the company's owner and his domestic partner—flew by private aircraft to Las Vegas. This arrival, I was sure, was a far more glamourous experience than mine, which involved boarding a shared shuttle van from the airport to our hotel for the weekend. I had never been to Las Vegas before, and the stunning heat and overwhelming noise of the Strip struck me immediately. While my friend and her colleagues were eager to start seeing the sights of the city, I retreated to the room she and I would share for the weekend and begged off any sightseeing until the following day. As I rested, I began to think more about the purpose of this trip: What would we do all weekend? Why were we here? And perhaps most importantly, what did any of this have to do with the EDC program and how it impacted St. Croix, an island we were now more than three thousand miles away from?

My concerns about the itinerary of the weekend were unfounded, as we undertook what seemed to be a record number of tourist activities during the three days we spent in Las Vegas. From nightly group dinners and after-dinner group drinks, to attending a circus performance, to taking an indoor gondola ride, to visiting the casinos in our hotel and those surrounding us, the group and I were to be fully occupied and the expenses paid by the company. On the morning of the second day of the trip, several EDC girls and I met for breakfast in the lobby of our hotel and discussed our options for the day above the sounds of clicking cameras and dinging slot machines. What I began to realize was that what was significant about this scene was the fact of the trip itself, the reality that the EDC program created opportunities such as this weekend escape. For employees in the EDC sector, getaways such as this provide an unusual–for–St. Croix degree of mobility and proximity to wealth. For supporters of the initiative, trips like this demonstrate the success of the program: by and large, the employees on this weekend were Virgin Islanders—that is, they had lived on St. Croix since at least high school, and the vast majority were born and raised there. Pointing to this employment—and improved economic situation—of these Crucians, proponents of the EDC claim success for the program. Critics, however, point to selective hiring preferences as leading only to the repositioning of *some* Crucians through this program. Why is it that these Crucians have access to these opportunities, while many others do not?

While I was initially confused about the location of the company trip, I began to realize that Las Vegas, a place that is perhaps the most famous site of coming into large sums of money "magically" and without labor, is the embodiment of the way the EDC program is perceived on St. Croix. For Crucians not connected to or employed within this sector, these opportunities for both leisure and network/community building are foreclosed, further deepening existing divisions of wealth and mobility. In their work on millennial capitalism, Comaroff and Comaroff argue that all of the signs surrounding capitalism at the millennium "have a single common denominator: the allure of accruing wealth from nothing. These alchemic techniques defy reason in promising unnaturally large profits—to yield wealth without production, value without effort" (2000: 310). Trips such as this weekend in Las Vegas and the often-accurate assessment that EDC girls receive generous salaries for minimal labor shore up this rendering. As the end of the trip approached, my friend and I sat in the hotel room we had shared for the weekend, and I asked her what her friends back on St. Croix thought of her weekend off island at her boss's expense. In response she said: "Oh, they were excited, I guess. But I didn't tell everyone. You know, you can't tell everyone everything because they might either take it the wrong way or expect me to hook them up with a job."

EDC Money

In the extensive history of research on gender and labor in the Caribbean, scholars have long noted the feminization of labor during industrialization.[11] Yet while women were preferred employees in factories, their labor was devalued, as women were not considered serious members of the workforce. Rather, they were presumed to be supported by their fathers, working only to earn "pin money" for themselves (Enloe 1989). With the shift toward information and financial management, young women have remained desirable employees, although the logic for this preference has changed: in the current moment, women are understood as "stable" employees, workers who will report for duty without fail as a result of familial and financial obligations. What is more, the neoliberal project is particularly invested in "girls" as agents of self- and community transformation, as evidenced for instance in the Nike Foundation's focus on "the girl" as point of entry for ending global poverty (Murphy 2013). I argue that while they are performing a different kind of labor from that of women who work in factories or in the tourism industry, EDC girls can be understood as a part of this trajectory.

My focus here is on EDC "girls," yet their almost-always white mainland bosses are also vital to my analysis, as they are responsible for local hiring. Much like the EDC girls they hire, who are alternately bombarded with requests for employment assistance and maligned for deigning to work in this questionable sector, these managers are ambivalently positioned on the island: while Crucians recognize their economic power, these mainland Americans are viewed as being unconcerned with St. Croix beyond an economic initiative. That is, they are understood as being inadequately socially invested in—not caring about—the island beyond the financial benefits afforded by the EDC program. In light of this, many Crucians expect EDC girls to patronize local vendors, spreading their relative and newfound wealth more widely than would otherwise occur.

These community expectations vis-à-vis the consumption patterns of EDC girls came into relief one Saturday on St. Croix when I was window-shopping with a friend who had recently begun working at an EDC company. As we stood outside, the salesman at one locally owned clothing store (also a longtime friend who had heard the news of her recent hire) encouraged us to come in, goading her that she ought to "spend up that EDC money." In response, the newly minted EDC girl laughed awkwardly, shrugging off his attempts to lure her inside. This exchange is telling both because he targeted her specifically as a potentially valuable customer and because of the way he framed her capital as "EDC money" that should be spent as easily as it was presumably earned. For this vendor, her money was tainted by its connection to the EDC program and the way to recapture its value was to have it circulate throughout the broader community and benefit community members in ways that would not otherwise occur. The generous salaries EDC girls are understood to be paid combined with the sometimes-correct assumption that they are not expected to perform much work in EDC offices result in the expectation on St. Croix that these women will dispose of this EDC money, quickly and lavishly.

Sandra, an EDC girl with whom I worked at St. Croix Fund, majored in economics at a well-respected mainland college yet now found herself making coffee and gathering lunch orders in her office.

TAMI NAVARRO: Have you felt like there's a split in the kind of work done [between local and Stateside employees]?

SANDRA: Definitely. At least from the EDC companies I've seen, I've seen more [local] women in the roles of office manager, receptionist, you know, personal assistant and what not. And then, we have one female here that's a research associate, and she has an MBA and I guess, you know, that's why. But a lot of us are hired to kind of just fill, fill in spots so that we, you know, we can comply to the EDC rules and thus get the benefits. Well, I guess the higher ups get the benefits. [The EDC companies] have to hire locals, but there isn't enough work to do—or they don't trust [us] enough to do the real work.

TN: Does that seem, when a local person is hired, does it seem just to be to get the benefits, or is it to lift up the VI?

S: [My boss] wants us to grow and develop, and any way he can help, he does. But, I think for the most part, it's just to fill spaces, for other companies, they just do what they have to do so they can get their benefits. And, and I've seen that.

In this instance, neoliberal expectations of privatization (of property, of identity, of spending decisions) clash with community demands for solidarity and more equitable dispersal of EDC capital, as these workers are expected to right the perceived wrongs of the EDC program. As the EDC program and EDC people themselves are understood to be engaged with the Crucian community in limited and problematic ways, EDC girls are expected to broaden the circuits of this capital to include local vendors. Here again, Crucians are articulating a critique of neoliberal logic by both naming its unevenness (by, for instance, positioning the program as an attempt to return to "slave days") and demanding restitution. At the same time, the expectation that these women both meet the demands of their employers and resolve the contradictions of larger economic systems on behalf of their communities creates layers of complexity for living this critique.

These competing expectations—the right of an employee to be the sole arbiter of how her paycheck is spent versus a community demand for financial inclusion—index the degree to which neoliberal logic has failed to convince the vast majority of Crucians. Through the financial pressure they exert on EDC girls, Crucians emphasize the significance of social solidarities against the individualism privileged by neoliberalism. The former is a worldview shored up by the manifold failures, implosions, and cruelties of capital in the region and in their very lives over time. Once again, the program is haunted by all that has come before.

The spending expectations surrounding EDC girls include that they regularly dine out at the island's posh restaurants, participating in the burgeoning "restaurant culture" (a term used by several interviewees to describe the scene created by EDC people and middle- to upper-class Crucians—including EDC girls—dining out several times each week). That is, being able to frequent the "right" restaurants is an expectation of EDC girls. However, this assumption that EDC girls will spend their evenings drinking wine and socializing applies particularly to unmarried women. As noted by Cynthia Enloe (1989), the logic for this preference has been that young *unmarried* women are more "nimble" and "docile" on the job. Yet while it is the case that many EDC girls are unmarried—with the notable exception of the women working at Stanford—the financial expectations these women face from their parents and communities make their salaries more than disposable income. The expectation for married women working in the EDC sector is that their salaries—and many of their evenings—will go to their nuclear families. Married Crucian women working at Stanford were not expected to be seen at restaurants in the evenings. Rather, these women were held to a different standard of respectability and socialized with one another at small group functions and at company-sponsored events that they attended with their husbands.

I attended one such event, a Stanford-sponsored arts fair, one evening in the summer of 2008 where I looked on as each of my Stanford coworkers settled themselves, their husbands, and small children under the large domed tent reserved for Stanford employees. This event was held at a restored plantation on St. Croix and tickets that included a chair under a tent sold for $30, while "under the stars" tickets that required attendees to bring their own blankets and sit on the ground cost $15. The performance was well attended,

featuring the usual crowd such events draw on St. Croix: EDC people, some of their employees, and upper- to middle-class residents
of varying backgrounds (including Black, white, and Puerto Rican).
This event had a particularly strong showing of Stanford employees, as Allen Stanford had recently endowed this concert series and
employees were strongly encouraged to attend with their families.
As a result, I sat "under the stars" that evening and made small talk
with the Stanford employees I had been getting to know through
my internship, although there were a number of people employed
in the company I had yet to meet, given the number of Stanford
offices, a number that seemed to grow daily. At any rate, as I sat
on the lawn, I was surrounded by the remains of a sugar plantation
and the artifacts of slavery. This particular estate, the Estate Whim
Museum, was a restored sugar plantation that offered regular tours
of the grounds, including a restored Great House, slave quarters,
and the remains of the factory where sugarcane had been processed
during Danish rule. I had vivid memories of this plantation from my
childhood, during which I, like hundreds of other schoolchildren on
the island, was taken on numerous field trips to the site to see what
life on the island was like during slavery. During these childhood
trips two things stood out to me: The first was the sugarcane mill,
used for crushing the cane and extracting sugar that I struggled to
envision as anything but a rusty assemblage of wood, metal, and
stone. The second was the planter's chair, a reclining chair that was,
as the name implies, the domain of the planter, which featured long
arm/footrests, facilitating the process of having his boots removed
by enslaved people.[12]

As I sat on the plantation's lawn that evening waiting for the
concert to start, surrounded by Stanford employees and the ves-
tiges of slavery, I was struck by the juxtaposition. My informants
were insistent in their framing of the EDC program, and Stanford
in particular, as desirous of a return to the social order of slavery:
Black bodies at work and wealthy white people enjoying leisure. In
the midst of this scene, it was clear that the effects of the EDC
were more nuanced than that, as I, a mixed-race woman sat in the
audience awaiting the start of the jazz concert alongside a number
of other people of color. What *did* ring true, however, was the complex interplay of past and present such that it made an eerie kind of
sense to have this Stanford-sponsored event at the plantation: the

picturesque grounds and idyllic Great House masked the violence (both structural and individual) that enabled this plantation to exist. Similarly, in the midst of this evening of privilege, the structural imbalances of racism, colorism, and imperial rule were obfuscated. In the face of this erasure, the framing of spectral time insists on naming the temporal complexity of the systems of oppression that have come before.

Neoliberal Development

Crucians' expectations vis-à-vis the spending of EDC girls belie the notion that deepened inequality is an unintended effect of neoliberalism[13] and instead name its intent and insist upon intervening in this cycle of racialized wealth accumulation. The notion of neoliberalism's inevitability masks the historical and continuing structural inequalities that facilitate this program and countless others like it. Inherent in this rendering is the idea of "luck" and being the fortunate recipient of a prize for which all are equally eligible (see Comaroff and Comaroff 2000 and Piot 2010). On this point, I spoke with Jasmine, a mixed-race (Black and Puerto Rican) Stanford employee in her midtwenties. I asked her if the EDC program was beneficial to the USVI as a whole:

JASMINE: [The program] definitely brings something we didn't have before because for me personally, I was working at another job where I wasn't very happy, I wasn't making as much money as I do now, and so, once I got hired here, it was just a better opportunity, more money. [But] I think people, you know, resent me. Like, for example, I went out last week and I was hanging out with some waitresses and waiters and I used to . . . be a hostess at that restaurant, and it was so weird, because I felt like there was a division, like we were very different and that they looked at me different because "oh, I work for [an EDC]" and "oh she must be making a lot of money and think that she's better than us." And I [thought], "I used to work [at this restaurant!]" It's just, I guess I got lucky! And I feel I did, I did get lucky! And . . . that does make

me feel [badly] because this job doesn't define who I am.
I mean, I'm grateful for it, because I'm able to do things
that I wasn't able to do before.

Neoliberalism's logic of self-transformation and maximizing human
capital are in tension with Jasmine's assertion that her fortunate
employment in the EDC sector does not define who she is. As the
expectation surrounding Crucian women's employment at EDC
companies is that their salaries should be spent in visible ways, EDC
girls capitulate in some ways, taking trips to the US mainland and
beyond, sometimes buying expensive cars and clothes, and dining
out regularly. Yet, Jasmine's encounter with her former restaurant
coworkers during one such evening out, and her rejection of being
made synonymous with her job, serves as a push-back to the widespread community insistence that employment at an EDC company
does, in fact, affect one's identity on the island. In this way of thinking, the new self—that is, the neoliberal subject—she is becoming
is a consuming, market-driven improvement on her previous self.
This emphasis on consumption is not unique to this program and
is a central element of the privileging of market forces in all areas
of life—in this instance, identity. Rather than being rooted in one's
relationship to production, identity is now linked to consumption—
and the neoliberal self must consume (see Davies and Bansel 2007).

Crucians who, like many people of color, have been integrally
involved in and negatively affected by global circulations of capital,
have expectations regarding the ameliorative potential of the spending
of EDC girls. At the same time, EDC employers also have expectations
regarding the behavior of these women who are to be the local face
of the program. These conflicting demands demonstrate the gendered
nature of expectation, as the disappointments felt by Crucians vis-
à-vis financial-services-as-development are expected to be addressed
through the position of EDC girls. That is, as they recognize the
ways they are *structurally* disempowered in global financial circuits,
Crucians seek to exert increased authority and societal pressure on
these local women. These expectations are only more strongly felt
by EDC girls given that they come from, on the one hand, their
bosses and on the other their parents, cousins, friends, and neighbors.
This bind in which EDC employees (that is, "girls") find themselves
is telling—particularly as these groups with competing agendas feel

equally at ease mapping their structural concerns and interests onto the behavior and spending patterns of these local women.

In this awkward positioning, EDC girls are subject to new expectations based on their employment within this sector, yet they remain subject to long-standing local gendered and generational expectations in the wider community. For instance, Ava and Beth, two unmarried and childless EDC girls in their late twenties with whom I spoke, both continued to live with their parents despite the salaries they earned through their employment in the EDC sector. For Ava, whose solidly middle-class, but not extravagantly wealthy, background included having attended Country Day School for high school and obtaining a college degree from the US mainland, this living arrangement provoked tensions around household expenses between her and her parents: Who should foot the bill for remodeling the kitchen? What of a possible addition to the house? These were struggles over financial responsibility and expectations brought on by the salary Ava earned at her EDC job. These conflicts differ from those of many young college graduates living with their parents, as Ava earned the largest salary in the home and thus often felt obligated to support the household rather than to make small contributions, an inversion of traditional generational roles she often lamented. For Beth, who came from a wealthy family, the financial expectations she faced at home were different—but equally frustrating. Given the generous salary earned by their daughter, Beth's parents assigned certain household bills to her, despite their comfortable economic position. This expectation of financial parity between her parents and herself was a relationship to which Beth objected, as she felt less would be expected of her if she worked at what she called a "regular"—that is, non-EDC—job.

Despite this shift in their positioning because of their relationship to global capital and the neoliberal project, EDC girls are more than simply the victims of this global moment, dupes who are paid well by EDC firms to ensure the continued existence of the program, as I understand them as drawing on both their background (their sameness) and their current status as EDC employees (their difference)—a combination that results in this new subject-position. Through their decisions about spending, community building, and choices about when and how to reveal their affiliation with the EDC program, these women not only inhabit but play a role in crafting their new subject-position. The power dynamics of the EDC program are skewed toward wealthy EDC people, the agents of global capital, yet EDC girls (the direct recipients of EDC dollars) also consume and shape the program to their needs and wants. While the limited training many EDC girls receive make it difficult to transfer their skills to new positions, the money and office experience they gain allow them to "use" the program to their benefit. During my interview with Lakisha, I asked her whether the program was beneficial to the territory or if—as many on St. Croix suggest—it merely takes advantage of the island and its resources:

> TN: Do you think the [EDC] program is a good idea?
>
> LAKISHA: I do. A lot of people on St. Croix think the companies are coming to take advantage of the island. I think "they use us, we use them." I can get training and eventually move up in the company or even a transfer within the company to an office in the States. That wouldn't happen in my old job [in the local government]. There, you had to wait for somebody to retire or die to get a promotion. This is progress.

Lakisha's optimism about the possibility of moving up within the company was rooted in a hope that her job in the EDC sector represented something different—a new trajectory for her life. As it would happen, the debacle that was the closing of Stanford belied this possibility. Still, her suggestion that EDCs both "use" and become used by the Virgin Islands and its people remains useful. Rather than the pro-EDC position that posits the program as the saving grace of the territory, Lakisha's position (one shored up by the actions of other Crucians) is that the program marks a moment of possibility, *despite* the intentions of its creators. That is, it is through the relationships created by EDC girls and the community-based spending expectations that they navigate that a new relationship to global capital becomes possible.

Pursuing this notion, I went on to ask Lakisha if the program meant "progress" for everyone in the territory:

> LAKISHA: No—but those who can benefit from it, those who can move back from the States, they can do good.

> Like, with land. The land was there all the time and you
> [that is, Crucians] didn't buy it. Land is for sale and there
> are too many people on St. Croix who think the land is
> theirs. The land ain't yours. I talked with my father about
> Stanford buying up all this land and he said "tell him
> come." I think a lot of people on St. Croix still have a
> "horse-and-cart" mentality about development.

By arguing that Crucians continue to have a "horse-and-cart mentality" (that is, old-fashioned) vis-à-vis development, Lakisha is pointing to the fact that many people on St. Croix are critical of development, particularly initiatives such as the EDC, that they see as detrimental to the island. This skepticism is often countered by EDC businessmen who describe it as "anti-business," with the excitement with which development programs are generally received on St. Thomas. Lakisha's argument that Crucians are able to "use" the EDC program and EDC people introduces a space of agency for local actors and undermines a reading of the program as entirely predatory.

Spaces of Consumption

For their part, EDC people generally shop in the island's tony downtown area, Christiansted (or simply, "town"). This section of the island and points east ("East End") are synonymous with wealth and feature an independent bookstore, a growing number of cafés, and an emerging crop of high-end women's clothing boutiques—subsidiary industries that have developed to cater to those in possession of EDC money. In her research on female workers in Barbados, Carla Freeman (2000) argues that women working in the island's "informatics" sector are able to "fashion" new identities, influencing transformations in notions of style and fashion in Barbados. For EDC girls, clothing purchases are equally significant as they balance the expectations of their community against those of their employers. While many EDC offices are casual in a way that is unfamiliar to most Crucians—with EDC employees adopting a surfer-chic approach to office wear, including shorts, T-shirts, and flip flops—some EDC offices, notably Stanford Financial, adhere to the opposite extreme, requiring a level of formality in dress uncommon on St. Croix. These differences in office norms, as demonstrated through dress, tie into what are seen as larger "cultural" divisions between Crucians and EDC people. While the relatively relaxed dress codes in many EDC offices mean that local women employed in this sector may be appropriately dressed for work in jeans and modest tops, it matters very much *where* these articles of clothing are purchased. As local residents, these women traverse the island (unlike EDC people who generally remain in the exclusive neighborhoods in which they live and work), yet their regular presence in Christiansted—for either dining or shopping—rather than in other shopping districts that feature mass-market chain stores, is significant to their position. Despite their individual financial situations, EDC girls are expected to shop in the area, patronizing smaller boutiques over mass-market retail stores.

Curious about the impact of consumption patterns of EDC girls beyond clothing, I interviewed John Partner, the manager of a large car dealership on the island. John, a white man in his fifties from the US mainland who had moved to St. Croix in the mid-1990s, was the manager of one of the island's more successful car dealerships. When we met at a local fast-food restaurant, I asked about the impact of the EDC program on his business—specifically, if the kind of car he sold most had changed. In response, he told me that "the level of opulence has increased, and the income level seems to be up on the island." When I asked what he meant by "opulence," he said that his customers on St. Croix had gone from wanting to purchase a vehicle, for instance, the Ford F-150, and now shopped for "the next level," the Ford F-250, a pricier model with leather seats and pricier amenities. When I asked John how much of this change he attributed to the EDC community, including local employees, he said that about 10 to 15 percent of his business came from EDC people, and that he thought they had contributed significantly to this increased "opulence" on the island. None of the EDC girls with whom I spoke or was familiar with drove the model of vehicle described by Partner—yet his observation about the "opulence" of this group immediately rang true. For instance, Xio, the twenty-six-year-old Crucian woman alongside whom I worked at St. Croix Fund was so proud of her newly purchased SUV that she often volunteered to run office errands as an excuse to drive around the island. At the time of my fieldwork, her coworker Beth, too, had recently purchased a new SUV, while a third woman working in the office bought a sedan with leather interior—costly investments they made willingly.

Whether out of pride or sympathy, these women always insisted on picking me up when we were to spend time together, lest they be seen in the battered sedan that I drove around the island. It is impossible to discern with any certainty how much of this spending came as a result of these women's desire for more "opulent" transportation and how much arose as a result of expectations of what a "respectable" EDC employee should drive. Nevertheless, it is of note that these workers purchased new, more luxurious, transportation once they began their EDC employment. Certainly, this could be an instance of their new salary filling a long-standing need, but members of the local community viewed these as necessary, almost predetermined, purchases. Again, this insistence on intervening in the centuries-long process of racialized wealth accumulation is rooted in a competing engagement with capital and time. Viewed through the lens of "spectral time," these spending expectations placed on EDC girls mark a singular opportunity to rupture this cycle, while placing these workers in the often-untenable positions of attempting to meet competing expectations: these women are simultaneously (and newly) expected to serve as breadwinners—both within their family units and across the local community.

The Space of EDC Girls

The category of EDC girl represents a new subject-position, informed by gender and one's relationship to the new kinds of social and economic capital that have been generated by the EDC program. This emergent identity is central, as it demonstrates the ongoing relationships between gender, capital, and processes of subject formation in the current moment of neoliberalism in general and the EDC program in particular. Neoliberalism has been described as an "enterprise society" (Foucault 2004) and the neoliberal subject as an "entrepreneur of [her] self" (Gill and Scharff 2011). Pushing beyond this, EDC girls are expected to transform both themselves *and* their community—maximizing both their sameness (as Crucians) and difference (as the relatively privileged entry points for capital) to alter the outcome of this instance of capital circuiting through the Caribbean. While the white male managers of EDCs represent a new kind of development initiative for St. Croix, one that is in line with other trends within neoliberal capitalist processes, the kind of "development" performed by women is also different as they stimulate the local economy in myriad ways. While much recent scholarship on female workers engages with women performing affective labor—particularly in the Caribbean where the service-sector jobs of the tourism industry are often the most attractive options provided to island residents—my focus on EDC girls is an exploration of *middle-class* Caribbean women and their dynamic relationship to neoliberalism that yields significantly different conclusions. Rather than simply being pawns in global supply chains, EDC girls perform a fraught and vital mediating role between processes of neoliberal globalization, development initiatives, and their communities. What is more, it is central that these women face expectations concerning their spending, behavior, and allegiance from both the local community and their employers in the EDC sector, as I argue that these women nimbly navigate these expectations and actively participate in the crafting of new social and economic realities.

Perhaps because employment at Stanford Financial was understood to be particularly lucrative or perhaps because of the suspicion surrounding the company since its arrival on St. Croix, it was here that I most clearly and immediately witnessed EDC girls navigating their emergent position. During our conversations at work, many female employees at Stanford expressed concern about the fact that employment at this company carried it with both behavioral expectations and assumptions about one's financial position and decision-making ability within the company. For example, a frequent complaint had to do with the fact that they often received unsolicited résumés and requests for money from friends, family, and in many cases strangers on the street. In an attempt to negotiate their new social role determined by employment at this particular firm, many women at Stanford adopted strategies such as removing company-specific identification before leaving the office and responding with vague descriptions when asked about their line of work (for instance, "I work at a financial company" or, if pressed, "an EDC company," rather than at Stanford Financial, the company that was seen as the most exploitative of the EDCs). For women working at Stanford, this often meant removing the much-commented-upon golden eagle lapel pin that marked them as employees, a negotiation of their role that points to the ways in which they are active participants in crafting their new position.

From the outset of my fieldwork, I was interested in the ways EDC girls, both at Stanford and beyond, were understood on the island and the strategies they used to navigate these assumptions. While at St. Croix Fund, I interviewed Xio about her experiences in the EDC sector and how friends and family treated her now that she worked there:

> TN: Do you have other friends that work for EDCs? Do people treat you differently when they find out where you work?

> X: I have four friends that work at EDCs. Yeah, I've gotten negative comments: "They aren't permanent. This job isn't reliable." If [St. Croix Fund] closes, I'll look for another EDC job. The pay is great, I'm happy to be part of the program, to have this job. You know next week I'm starting college online . . . Now my kids go to a good [parochial] school.

The opportunities discussed by Xio are indeed benefits of EDC employment. The counterweight to these, however, includes the community perception that EDC girls are undeservedly wealthy and arrogant (as shown in Jasmine's concern that her former restaurant coworkers thought she now felt herself "better than them").

During my time at Stanford Financial, I became increasingly curious about the ways in which Crucian women working at Stanford in particular were set apart by the mandatory brooch that marked these women as participants in the EDC sector in general and at Stanford in particular. To gather more information on what reactions this identity engendered, I asked Lakisha if she felt that people treated her differently since she began working in the EDC sector eight months earlier, as well as whether this brooch affected the way she was identified and treated on the island:

> L: Before I started working [at Stanford], someone told me it was cult and you have to wear the brooch to work

there. I told them "the bank has a uniform, and the brooch
is part of the Stanford uniform."

TN: But does the pin affect the way people treat you?

L: In town, it means good treatment, good service because
they think you have money. Other places, though, you hear
rumors, people ask a lot of questions. Everybody wants
you to help them with a job. Car dealers show you the
most expensive cars in the lot when you wear that brooch.
Everybody thinks you have money. To avoid all that, I
take the pin off when I leave the office. But really, if you
work in any EDC people think you rich.

This negotiation of EDC identity was also noted by Lakisha's
friend, Sandra, a woman who worked in the next cubicle and joked
that she takes off her brooch before going into the supermarket
to avoid being given résumés and fielding job requests. Lakisha's
annoyance at being singled out as a result of her job by, for instance,
being shown the "most expensive cars in the lot" rubs up against
John Partner's assessment of an increased demand for "opulence" on
the island. As a result of their employment in the EDC sector, EDC
girls are understood to be the beneficiaries of an undeserved windfall
built upon their existing backgrounds of relative privilege. Because of
this reading, EDC girls are expected to dispose of their salaries, EDC
money, in "opulent" ways. However, the increased financial burdens
of car notes, expensive lunches, and personal loans are not necessarily
what these women want from their employment. In order to counter
these expectations, local women working at Stanford removed the
most clearly identifying marker of their employment, the golden
logo of their company. When asked if there were other ways she
downplayed her link to the EDC program, Lakisha responded that
she was often vague about her place of employment, telling people
she "works at an EDC. They don't need to know it's Stanford."

New Identities through Consumption

The relationship between state, market, and nation has often been
summarized by the assumption that the market has superseded the

state, rendering it empty, useless (as in the many panics around "failed states"). However, the argument of this text is that one has not replaced the other but that these relationships are dynamic (Appadurai 1996; Hansen 2006; Hardt and Negri 2000; Kelly and Shah 2006; Ong 1999, 2006; Sassen 2003; Shah 2006; Singer 2003; Slocum 2006). For instance, St. Croix and its neighboring islands pit themselves against one another, slashing labor costs and legislating precarity for their residents in order to attract capital to their shores. In this way, the market triumphs over the state's ability (and presumed willingness) to concern itself with the economic well-being of its people. Alternately, however, the EDC program exists and largely rests upon St. Croix's geopolitical positioning as a possession of the United States, a reality that forces a reconsideration of the notion that state power has been done away with entirely. As politically liminal spaces like St. Croix demonstrate, neoliberalism has eroded the power of many states to ensure economic protections, but it has simultaneously furthered the project of consolidating American supremacy in the form of political and economic power.

Despite my insistence on the interplay between states and markets, it is clear that engaging with the market through consumption has become the primary vehicle through which one inhabits and performs one's subject-position. As the neoliberal self is expected to be an agent of self-transformation—the CEO of one's own life—the primary method of this transformation is through consumption (see Davies and Bansel 2007; Ringrose and Walkerdine 2008).

The subject-position of the "EDC girl" comes into being through the relationship between labor and identity, as these employees become understood as more than mere representations of the program but instead as the *embodiment* of St. Croix's interpolation into the global financial market, as well as the centrality of consumption. Through their consumption, neoliberal subjects are able to craft and occupy their place in the spaces created by neoliberalism's sweep across the globe. Key here is that the ability of *some* to consume is meant to stand in for the potential buying power of all. This is a space of tension on St. Croix whose residents largely have not internalized neoliberal logic. The expectations—manifested as economic pressures—that Crucians place on the spending habits of EDC girls belie the notion that EDC money is equally available to all. It is precisely because EDC hiring so clearly builds on preexisting hierarchies of race, color, class, and gender in ways that exclude great swaths of the

Crucian community that these residents expect relatively privileged/appropriately positioned EDC girls to ensure some economic benefit to the wider community. As capitalism has run roughshod through the region before, the expectations that EDC employees will spend their salaries in ways that benefit Crucians broadly marks an attempt to intervene in the cycle of wealth consolidation. Certainly, anyone can be a millionaire—if only she or he applies enough pressure on EDC girls to spend more freely.

Given the centrality of consumption to my analysis of the EDC program, it would be tempting to understand the initiative as one that allows white people from the mainland US to relocate to the USVI and "consume" the island and its resources (for instance, Mimi Sheller [2003] has suggested this relationship in her work on the Caribbean). However, this reading discounts the agency of the Crucians with whom I talked and worked. Instead, as suggested by Lakisha, the opportunities afforded female employees of EDC companies allow for the mutual consumption of the island *and* the EDC program: I understand these women as drawing on both their background and their current status as EDC employees—a combination that results in a new subject-position. EDC girls are neither ideal neoliberal subjects, convinced of the primacy of the market above all, as they are sympathetic to their fellow Crucians' critiques of the program and remain invested in their community against neoliberalism's emphasis on the entrepreneurial individual; nor are they, according to many Crucians, ideal community members, as (1) their ability to be worked into systems of global capital mark their already-present privilege, and (2) they often frustrate spending expectations by consuming as they choose. EDC girls occupy neither of these positions perfectly. Rather, they straddle these worlds precariously, navigating the demands that come from all sides.

There is, of course, a darker reading. If the new subject-position occupied by female EDC employees represents something like a midpoint between local and foreign, it stands to reason that they are expected—to some degree—to perform a mediating function in society: the local grist for the mill of global capital. I argue that while these employees *do* serve as something like a buffer between EDC people and Crucians (an arrangement more than a little reminiscent of the island's societal structure under colonialism), there is more going on. Rather than merely being appropriated and performing a legitimizing function for the EDC program, I argue that through their everyday practices, these women are crafting—and are themselves occupying—new spaces on St. Croix. Crucians are *consuming* this development initiative—actively negotiating its presence, reception, and possibilities on St. Croix.

However, while EDC girls are "consuming" the EDC program, their relationship to this initiative consistently places them in a precarious position on St. Croix. EDC girls, perhaps, are in the best position to "use" this development program (in Lakisha's language), as they are the Crucians with access to EDC connections and capital. Their access, being beneficiaries of EDC opportunities not otherwise available locally while at the same time viewed as responsible to the broader community, results in these "lucky" women actively crafting their role in their community and workplaces. This balancing act was summarized by one former Stanford employee, who said to me, "Everybody wants to talk bad about the EDC, but everybody wants a job." As demonstrated by the indictment of Stanford and the closure of many EDCs following the 2008 financial crash, this "luck" would result in a number of EDC employees finding themselves unceremoniously unemployed in short order.

Conclusion

The fieldwork for this project was conducted during the unfolding of the 2008 economic crisis that would have devastating implications for the USVI. In the American media, the collapse of the US economy was frequently linked to a number of images: beggared Wall Street bankers; shuttered windows where formerly thriving businesses once stood; foreclosure signs stretching along blocks of manicured lawns bearing American flags. What the downturn did not immediately bring to mind for most participant-observers were visions of the sandy shores of the US Virgin Islands (USVI)—yet the US financial crisis had particular resonance in this US territory as the EDC connected St. Croix to Wall Street, as the primarily American capital that funded the program would largely dry up within a year.

The exodus of EDC beneficiaries began in 2008 as financial management companies found themselves without much in the way of capital to manage. St. Croix Fund was one of the casualties of this financial contraction, leading the company to close its doors on St. Croix. Allen Stanford was eventually charged, tried, and sentenced to over one hundred years in US prison for a laundry list of crimes, including fraud and obstruction. He was also stripped of his knighthood that had been conferred by Antigua—he was "Sir Allen" no more. While the initiative continues to exist, its impact—socially, culturally, and economically—is a shadow of what it was during its heyday in the mid-2000s. A 2015 study commissioned by the government of the US Virgin Islands found that "about 32 companies terminated or suspended their [EDC] certificates, causing a loss of 347 jobs and $619 million in employee taxes over the term of benefits which ranged from 10–15 years."[1] By 2019, there were just seventeen EDC companies of the type theorized in this text—those marked as "Category 2A,"[2] offering financial management services in the USVI. Of these, less than half of that number operated on St. Croix, with the remaining beneficiaries based on St. Thomas. There remain a handful of these companies on St. Croix today, but the vast majority of EDC employees I interviewed have had to forge new lives for themselves.

Since the 2008 crisis, the economic well-being of St. Croix has only declined, compounded by the closing of the largest private employer on the island, the HOVENSA oil refinery, leading to a massive increase in unemployment: in 2012, unemployment on St. Croix rose to 14.1 percent, up from 9.8 percent the previous year.[3] The combination of closures led to a staggering number of St. Croix's residents fleeing the island. It would be difficult to overstate the impact of this brain drain, which has been keenly felt across industries, schools, neighborhoods, and communities. For many of these emigrants, their destination is the US mainland, travel made possible by their status as American citizens. The realities of massive outmigration are not new to the region in general or the US territories in particular, as Puerto Rico saw tremendous numbers of emigrants fleeing economic stagnation on the island and seeking new lives on the US mainland following World War II and the introduction of industrialization-by-invitation programs. This pattern has seen a resurgence in recent years, with Puerto Rico's debt crisis resulting in an estimated eighty-four thousand island residents leaving the island for the mainland in 2014[4] and thousands more after the devastation of hurricanes Irma and Maria. Anecdotally, this has resulted in the island losing "a doctor a day," a frequently recounted statistic that points to the gutting of Puerto Rico's healthcare system specifically,[5] but the losses cut across all sectors. As the many Crucians who found themselves unemployed by departure of EDC companies can attest, none of this is particularly new. These effects were seen, most recently, after the closure of the industrial plants that were once the economic focus of the region, and here they were again.

If the Caribbean is indeed a "small place," as suggested by Jamaica Kincaid (1988), its role in global economic developments—often serving as a space of exception or experimentation for capital—continues to loom large. The similarity of effects between the industrial moment and neoliberal development (with particular attention to programs characterized by "virtuality," notably finance) are striking, certainly. Yet, there are specific characteristics of the current moment that are significant: the primacy of the market as the arbiter of moral correctness combined with the intense focus on the role of individual actors (over and against an analysis that considers community effects and concerns) has resulted in a particular set of consequences for the region. In the case of St. Croix, it has meant that former EDC girls and their broader community are left to sort out the implications of this most recent brush with global capital and its handlers. What of the hierarchies created and deepened by EDC wealth and opportunity, spaces of privilege afforded to some, but not all, on the island? The decline of the program has meant the upending of the associated forms of privilege. Yet such programs, instances of racial capitalism, build upon processes of racialization, including color as social capital—and these systems remain in place after each (ostensibly new) iteration of this project.

Given this, the preexisting hierarchies of race, color, and class that facilitated entry to this sector for some Crucians generally braced their fall as the program waned. In the wake of St. Croix's post-2008 economic downturn, a number of former EDC girls, whose network and backgrounds continue to provide them increased opportunities for mobility, have been among those who have left the island for the US mainland. As before, their relative privilege continues to serve them well. Lakisha, who had formerly been employed as an administrative assistant at Stanford, moved to Atlanta and translated the administrative experience she gained in the EDC sector to secure a position in the human resources department of a major retailer. For her, the model of "they use us, we use them" vis-à-vis the EDC program and its beneficiaries resulted in a desired move to the US mainland. Leslie, who spoke of her concern about the "cultural gap" between EDC people and the wider St. Croix community, also capitalized on her EDC experience and network and now lives and works on the US mainland. Other former EDC girls, however, have forged paths for themselves while remaining on St. Croix. After the 2008 financial crisis, Veronica left the island to pursue an advanced degree and has since returned to operate her own small business. Sandra (Lakisha's workplace friend who often made a point of removing her company brooch when leaving the office and felt underutilized during her time at Stanford Financial) earned an advanced degree and now works for the Virgin Islands government, while Ava and Allison now both work in the non-profit sector on St. Croix. The new lives these women have crafted for themselves demonstrate the extent to which they consumed some advantages from the presence of global financial capital and reworked it to their advantage. Yet, in capitalizing on these histo-ries and opportunities they remain paradoxically implicated in the reproduction of dependent development and racialized/gendered systems of neoliberalism. While these former EDC employees have managed to curate new livelihoods, this has not been the case for everyone who lost a job in this sector, and there have been broader impacts of the decline of the program, including a perilous drop in philanthropic giving and the closure of EDC-adjacent businesses such as boutiques, cafés, and EDC "handlers."

At best, program supporters had hoped that the EDC would inject much-needed new capital into St. Croix and jump-start its long-struggling economy. At the very least, the legal requirement that each beneficiary employ Virgin Islanders seemed to ensure increased employment prospects for Crucians. Even this, however, was not to be the case, as EDC companies often imported existing workers who would legally become Virgin Islanders after spending just 183 days in the territory. Like earlier experiences St. Croix (and the Caribbean in general) has had with mass circulations of people and wealth, the EDC program largely benefited those with existing privilege and did damage to the people and places it was ostensibly put in place to help. Today, residents have not forgotten the tensions, fractures, and resentments that surrounded the EDC. Certainly, they have receded from the territory's newspaper headlines and opinion columns but they remain beneath the surface of everyday conversations, ready to resurface at an opportune moment.

My focus on St. Croix as a "new" node in global financial circulations has been rooted in the island's status as an English-speaking US territory only a short plane ride away from the mainland United States. These unique geographic and political factors made the USVI especially attractive to American investors and were central to the existence of the EDC program. However, for all the partic-ular advantages, it remained situated within its broader global and regional context: the abject lessons learned by many Caribbean islands following their experiences with industrialization programs, including the minimal benefit to their "host" countries compared to that received by foreign corporations; increased unemployment; migration in search of employment; and a continued—often increased—reliance on foreign capital. As demonstrated by the Stanford debacle and the steep decline of the program post-2008, initiatives like the EDC produce many of the same negative effects as attempts at economic development that have come before. Far from a turn away from service, the move toward global circulations has resulted in but another *type* of service: employing lighter-skinned, middle-class young women on St. Croix, EDC companies have built upon long-standing local relations of privilege, frustrating many on the island who had hoped the program would provide inroads toward economic development for Crucians more broadly.

The historical continuities of race, color, and class that the EDC program shares with earlier circulations in the Caribbean, such as slavery and colonialism, made real the concerns of Crucians who feared an increase in existing stratification on the island. However, advocates who heralded the initiative as beneficial and unprecedented also told part of its story, as it brought desperately needed capital into the territory and provided opportunities for some local residents. This text serves as an attempt to situate the initiative in its nuanced reality: neither a return to "slavery" nor an unproblematic step of "progress," the EDC has been some of both and all of neither. As it is both new *and* rooted in relations that are centuries old, the EDC created unprecedented circulations and opportunities that were never entirely free from what came before them.

A central preoccupation of *Virgin Capital* has been the question, "How might we theorize the interplay in the Caribbean between past and present, then and now, in relation to both manifestations and experiences of capital accumulation?" I have articulated spectral time as a way to name the ever-looming threat of repetition and violence vis-à-vis capital. Rather than sidestepping the question of "what comes next," it inverts the query, insisting upon an examination of what has come before. It is by grappling with previous iterations of racial capitalism that we can begin to apprehend their "new" forms.

In 2017, the USVI experienced what was termed its "Centennial Year," the one-hundred-year mark of the sale of the islands from Denmark to the United States. This occasion was marked by celebrations in the USVI and Denmark and featured a number of cultural and political gatherings, where speeches from elected officials from the US, Denmark, and USVI were given.[6] In these speeches, which often waxed poetic about Denmark's longing for its long-lost colony in the Caribbean or the present-day importance of these islands to the United States, it largely went unsaid that the people of the USVI had never been consulted about this sale, nor were they fully included as citizens of the US to date, given their continued inability to vote in presidential elections.

Later that year, the US response to the damage wrought by hurricanes Irma and Maria in its territories shed renewed light on the precarious positioning of America's possessions and its people in the Caribbean. As I have written elsewhere, "The recognition of the contributions made by Virgin Islanders quickly vanished in the aftermath of the two devastating hurricanes, Irma and Maria, that decimated the islands. By September 2017, American news outlets began to fret about how Hurricane Irma might make landfall on 'American soil'—that is, Florida—while entirely eliding the damage done to the US owned Virgin Islands that were also directly in the path of the Category 5 storm" (Navarro 2018). This same precarity, and repetition, was demonstrated both by the arrival of the EDC program and its dismal fall, as American companies capitalized on the status of the USVI as an American territory to conduct business and lead lives characterized by classed insularity, over the widespread objections of local residents.

Throughout this analysis of the continuing implications of colonial history, American empire, and processes of racialization in contemporary neoliberal development, I have theorized the inter-relationship between past, present, and future. Far from arguing that the past is bound to reoccur, the notion of spectral time is an argument for engaging with the often-terrifying experiences of capital accumulation in the Caribbean. At the same time, it remains crucial to be attentive to the *particular* hierarchies and histories that facilitate contemporary attempts at development—that is, the ground upon which new initiatives are built. In the end, for many formerly colonized spaces, particularly those in Latin America and the Caribbean, such attempts at economic improvement are all too often a haunting refrain.

Epilogue

Given that mobility was one of the characteristic traits defining the position of "EDC girls," it is apropos that the spaces in which I now most often encounter my former interlocutors are airport terminals. Sometimes this occurs on the tiny seaplanes that connect St. Croix and St. Thomas, and sometimes it happens as I am attempting to connect to a flight servicing St. Croix from the mainland. After the 2017 hurricanes, air service to St. Croix was cut dramatically, such that it became increasingly difficult to travel to St. Croix from the Northeast, where I now live. As a result, I often found myself spending long periods of time in the terminal of the Miami airport in particular. This was the case in 2019 as I waited for my flight to St. Croix. I was traveling to the USVI to conduct community forums for a project I had recently begun.[7] As I milled around, I heard someone call my name. Turning, I saw that it was a woman with whom I had worked during my time at Stanford. I had not seen her in the better part of a decade, so we spent a few moments chatting and catching up. She was on her way back to St. Croix after a trip to visit family who had left the island after the hurricanes, and I explained that, yes, I was still an anthropologist and that my travel was work related. She recounted that in the years since she had opened a small business of her own and said that she enjoyed the flexibility it afforded her, particularly the ability to spend much-desired time with her children, something she felt she would not have had in her previous position at Stanford. While we talked, we simultaneously attempted to corral the small children we each now had, a difficult feat in the confined space of the terminal. As our conversation wound down, there was a call over the loudspeaker for our flight. We each turned to gather our things and head to our shared gate. Despite all that had happened in the intervening years, we were going to the same place. We were both going home.

Notes

Chapter 1

1. See Hudson (2017) on the long history of connection between Wall Street and the Caribbean.

2. The annual average gross pay in the USVI in 2007 was $36,510 (http://www.usviber.org/wp-content/uploads/2016/11/ECON17july.pdf).

3. The USVI consists of three major islands, St. Croix, St. Thomas, and St. John.

4. A number of scholars have noted this shift; see especially David Harvey (1989).

5. For instance, A. W. Maldonado has written (1997) on the Puerto Rican economy during Operation Bootstrap.

6. From the Virgin Islands Department of Labor; Virgin Islands Annual Labor Economic Analysis: Occupational Data; https://www.vidolviews.org/admin/gsipub/htmlarea/uploads/2016%20Labor%20Economic%20Analysis.pdf.

7. This comment roughly translates to "Slavery is over!," indicating an unwillingness on the part of the speaker to return to the social order of slavery in which Black bodies were surveilled, exploited, and tortured in the name of increasing white wealth.

8. See, for instance, Appel (2019), Murch (2010), Rosenthal (2018), and Smallwood (2007).

9. US Securities and Exchange Commission Statement, https://www.sec.gov/news/press/2009/2009-26.htm.

10. In December 2008, businessman Bernie Madoff was arrested and charged with what is currently the biggest investor fraud ever perpetrated by a single individual, resulting in his imprisonment for 150 years. Allen Stanford's Ponzi scheme is the second largest in US history.

11. While the EDC program continues to operate in the USVI, its numbers have been drastically reduced. In June 2019, there were seventeen

companies receiving EDC benefits for financial management in the USVI (known as "Category 2A" companies). Of these, only nine were located on St. Croix (https://www.usvieda.org/resources/beneficiaries/pdf).

12. Scholarship that argues for alternative temporal frameworks vis-à-vis capital includes the generative work of Braudel (1972), whose *longue durée* approach creates space for my argument against discrete historical events and units of time. Walter Benjamin's (1942) foundational writings and Johannes Fabian's (1983) insights on nonlinear time are profoundly instructive vis-à-vis conceptualizations of the relationship between past, present, and future.

13. See also Scott (2016), who has engaged the Grenada Revolution to call into question the notion of futurity and its relationship to revolutionary emancipation. Katherine McKittrick (2013) also troubles a linear notion of time in her work on "plantation futures," which she argues is a "conceptualization of time-space that tracks the plantation toward the prison and the impoverished and destroyed city sectors and, consequently, brings into sharp focus the ways the plantation is an ongoing locus of antiblack violence and death" (2013: 2). Crichlow (2009) employs the term "creole time" to attend to the ways in which "colonial and postcolonial formations appear less as succeeding linear histories than as complex, dependent, relational, material, and discursive formations" (2009: 43).

14. This long and repeating history is enough to haunt all who continue to live in what Christina Sharpe (2016) has called the afterlives of slavery, and those who inhabit the still-unfolding wake of slavery's effects on Black life.

15. In her work on the francophone Caribbean, Yarimar Bonilla (2015) has pointed to the complexity of such spaces and the ways in which their position complicates any easy division between sovereignty and non-sovereignty.

16. Working in Barbados, Carla Freeman (2000) has put forth the term "pink collar identities," suggesting a refeminization of the labor process with the turn toward service industries, resulting in an upward repositioning of (some) women within local status hierarchies, an insight that resonates in the positioning of EDC girls.

17. Bolles (1983), Deere et al. (1990), Harrison (1997), McAfee (1991), Safa (1995), Sen and Grown (1987).

18. Rules and Regulations Economic Development Commission, Title 29 V.I.R.R, December 22, 2004, Sections 708–601 and 604.

19. The list of requirements to obtain EDC benefits requires that "individuals and companies must commit $100,000 of capital, employ 10 local residents, buy goods and services from local suppliers and promise to make charitable donations. They must also establish residency, and are

advised to buy or lease a house and car, obtain a local driver's license and join local clubs" (Kossler 2009a).

20. In 2008, the average cost of a home on St. John was $560,006. See "U.S. Virgin Islands Annual Tourism Indicators" (USVI Bureau of Economic Research n.d.).

21. The average cost of a home on St. Croix was $181,335 in 2001. In 2008, it had risen to $385,665. See "U.S. Virgin Islands Annual Tourism Indicators" (USVI Bureau of Economic Research n.d.)

22. PricewaterhouseCoopers 2004: 8.

23. It is significant that this work is rooted in the Caribbean. Caribbeanist scholars have long pointed to the lessons to be learned from this region vis-à-vis the workings of capital, as it has long been noted as a model of modernity. While scholars have critiqued the unproblematic taking up of Caribbean societies as both historical and contemporary centers of global mixing (notably Khan 2001), the dominant understanding of the region has long recognized its early cosmopolitanism—an urbanity that was part and parcel of the international meetings of ideas and people as a result of the transatlantic slave trade, as well as the related plantation-based production of sugar that served as the basis of prosperity for most Caribbean islands during this period (see especially Mintz 1985). There is also foundational scholarship that positions the Caribbean as central to global circulations of capital (Mintz 1985; Sheller 2014). This link connecting the Caribbean to broader global developments and history is one that scholars, particularly Caribbeanists, have pointed to for decades. In his landmark text *Sweetness and Power*, Sidney Mintz, for example, uses the circulation of sugar to point to the ways in which the Caribbean and the plantation economy were central to global developments like the Industrial Revolution. This need to illuminate the links between the Caribbean and global financial and political developments is one that informs my work.

24. See, for instance, Baucom (2005), Mintz (1985), Trouillot (2003), Yelvington (2001).

25. Bill Maurer (1997) has written on this point in relation to the British Virgin Islands, outlining the ways this formerly British holding attempts to capitalize on its colonial history in order to lure capital to its shores today. See also O'Neal (2012).

26. In her work on circulations and consumption in the Caribbean, Mimi Sheller describes this between-ness with the term "binding mobilities of consumption," an attempt to point to the continued implications(s) of older circulations in the contemporary Caribbean (Sheller 2003), while I find the term "spectral" more useful to describe the often-menacing experience of capital in the region.

Chapter 2

1. See Gore (2009).

2. Hurston uses this phrasing in relation to anthropology in the introduction to her text *Mules and Men* (1935).

3. One woman, Ellen, was in her late forties and had not been educated in the States.

Chapter 3

1. Arnold Highfield has written that "between 100,000 and 125,000 African captives [were sent] to the Danish colonies in the West Indies" (2018: 533) during the period of slavery, while Isaac Dookhan (1974), citing Philip Curtin (1969) and Waldemar Westergaard (1917), has argued that only 28,000 slaves were imported to these islands. At any rate, the highest number of slaves in the Danish West Indies was 35,727 in the year 1803. Of this number, 27,161 slaves arrived on St. Croix (Boyer 1983: 22). Eltis and Richardson (2010) estimate the number of slaves imported to the Danish West Indies at 109,000.

2. For instance, Westergaard (1917) notes in the census reports in 1720 and 1725 "that there came to be not fewer than eight full-grown slaves for each adult white person" (1917: 158).

3. "From the outset, Danish colonization in the West Indies was characterized by the paucity of a Danish colonial population. . . . In the absence of a sufficiently large indigenous Amerindian population, Denmark sought to resolve the colonial manpower problem in the approved manner of the 1630s and 1640s. But Danish indentured servants, the 'servingers' sent out to St. Thomas as plantation labor and militia footmen, suffered high mortality rates. . . . As for the British and French, the Danish flirtation with indentured labor lasted well into the 18th century, but long before then the indenture system as a mechanism for affixing an imperial presence in the West Indies was a certifiable failure" (Hall 1992: 6).

4. For example, see Lewis (1972). Also, Svalesen (2000): "The Danish king in the 1700s ruled over a worldwide Lilliputian empire. Denmark-Norway never became a colonial power of international importance. [Its] possessions in Asia and Africa were only small trading posts, open on the basis of rental and trading agreements with the local authorities. Only the three West Indian islands were real colonies, and they were of the most modest size" (8).

5. In a self-described attempt to educate Danish about the horrors of the Middle Passage, the Danish gaming company Serious Games Interactive

launched a jigsaw puzzle–like video game in 2013 entitled *Playing History 2: Slave Trade*, in which players were to contort and dismember Africans' bodies to fill slave ships more efficiently.

6. https://www.virgin-islands-history.org/en/history/slavery/barbaric-punishment-for-enslaved-laborers-with-an-urge-to-rebel/.

7. https://stcroixsource.com/2000/11/03/remnant-christiansted-whipping-post-unearthed/.

8. The formerly enslaved women who led this charge were "Queen" Mary Thomas, "Queen" Agnes (née Axelina Solomon), and "Queen" Matilda (Matilda Macbean).

9. Verene Shepherd at the Centre for Reparation Research at the University of the West Indies (Mona) has conducted research on the history of female-led slave rebellions in the Caribbean. See also Hillman and D'Agostino (2003), Beckles (1989), Mair (1995), Sheller (1998).

10. *Nordisk Tidsskrift for Informationsvidenskab og Kulturformidling* 8(2), https://tidsskrift.dk/ntik/article/view/118478/166419.

11. Remarkably, however, slaves continued to outnumber whites in the Virgin Islands despite this edict: "even after freedmen obtained their civil liberties and were enumerated with whites in the free category, slaves never lost their numerical superiority within the population as a whole until the termination of slavery" (Hall 1972: 3).

12. The title of this essay is drawn from a reggae song by Buju Banton entitled "Love Me Browning," which has as its chorus the lines: "Me love me car Me love me bike; Me love me money and ting. But most of all, Me love me browning."

13. See also the *Jamaica Gleaner* article on color privilege vis-à-vis waiting times throughout the Jamaican medical system: http://jamaica-gleaner.com/article/news/20190616/faster-healthcare-brownings-doctors-raise-concerns-colour-prejudice.

14. https://www.vanderbilt.edu/lapop/insights/IO873en.pdf.

15. https://www.vanderbilt.edu/lapop/insights/ITB031en.pdf.

16. "Is Mexico a Post-Racial Country? Inequality and Skin Tone across the Americas," https://www.vanderbilt.edu/lapop/insights/ITB031en.pdf, 1.

17. The central uprising on the island of St. John occurred in 1733 and was smaller than those that would occur on St. Croix, as 146 slaves on St. John were found to be involved in that rebellion (Westergaard 1917: 176). See Anderson (1975) for a history of this rebellion.

18. Earthquakes, tsunamis, drought, and hurricanes all befall these islands in the late 1800s, contributing to economic stagnation.

19. The Danish did attempt to stabilize the sugar economy on these islands through peasant cultivation, however it was largely unsuccessful: "In order to achieve the dual goals of community stability and agricultural pro-

duction, the parceling-out system was adopted; It involved the subdivision of plantations or parts of plantations and their sale to those laborers who wished to establish themselves as peasant proprietors. The policy seems to have been applied to all three islands . . . though it acquired greater significance in St. Croix." Sellers participated in this program largely as a result of falling land values that declined after emancipation. Prices fell "to such an extent that the total plantation wealth of St. Croix, which was estimated at $2.9 million in 1851 had been halved by 1870" (Dookhan 1974: 233).

20. The sale took place during World War I, and it was seen as advantageous for the United States to have an outpost in the Caribbean. While the islands were purchased by the US in 1917, it was not until 1927 that islanders were granted the status of American citizens. Initially, the US Navy administered the islands, and it was not until 1931 that they were transferred to the jurisdiction of the Department of the Interior (see Harrigan and Varlack 1977).

21. Harrigan and Varlack (1977).

22. This relationship between race and class was hardly unique to these islands. Lewis (1972) writes that "what 19th century observers reported was a highly stratified society based on caste and color. . . . The usual West Indian scheme of the small white European class at the top, the mulatto from colored in the middle, and the Negro freedmen and slaves at the bottom repeated itself, with the usual numerical imbalance" (26). While common, this system of racial relations was not appreciated by all. Lewis goes on to lambast wealthy Blacks (or "coloreds") who did not advocate on behalf of poorer Blacks, arguing that "social snobbery . . . supplanted racial brotherhood, and the Virgin Islands' free coloreds, like their counterparts elsewhere in the Caribbean, became known as a group given more to lavish social display than radical mental activity" (Lewis 1972: 29).

23. Schools were not an entirely new presence in these islands, as the Danish government, "in keeping with its relative benevolence," established four public schools for the education of Blacks in 1787. Under American rule, however, the number of schools increased and their curriculum became standardized (see Harrigan and Varlack 1977: 390).

24. *Public Papers of the Presidents of the United States, Herbert Hoover, Containing the Public Messages, Speeches, and Statements of the President, January 1 to December 31, 1931* (Washington, DC: United States Government Printing Office, 1976), 154.

25. Caneel Bay resort was largely demolished in 2017 by Hurricane Irma and has remained inoperable.

26. In his work on the US Virgin Islands, Lomarsh Roopnarine (2011) dates these intra-territorial tensions to the introduction of the Organic Act in 1954, a document that provided Virgin Islanders with an increased measure

of self-governance: "An inter-island rivalry has emerged . . . and has persisted into the contemporary period in the USVI. Specifically, Crucians have claimed that liquor prices are lower on St. Thomas even though liquor has been manufactured on St. Croix . . . most departments have larger budgets on St. Thomas . . . St. Croix's school system has not received equal treatment with regard to finance and infra-structural development . . . St. Thomas has been marketed and promoted more for tourism than St. Croix, and as a result, fewer cruise ships come to St. Croix . . . the University of the Virgin Islands is larger on St. Thomas and the St. Croix campus is treated like a Community College . . . airfares are cheaper from St. Thomas . . . St. Croix generates quite a bit of revenue but more money goes to St. Thomas and St. John" (Roopnarine 2011: 47)

27. In addition to this dust, the processing of bauxite produces a red mud that contaminates water. A class action suit begun in 2005 charges that this aluminum processing plant on St. Croix polluted groundwater, damaged marine life, and compromised potable water in residential cisterns across the island.

28. In her text *Aluminum Dreams* (2014), Mimi Sheller examines this narrative of the Caribbean as a space of "backwardness" and the backdrop against which North American modernity and development took place following World War II.

29. See Macarena Gomez-Barris (2017) for a history of racialized and colonial relations of extraction as well as possibilities for moving beyond this framework.

30. Deere notes that "between 1951 and 1960 the Gross National Product of Puerto Rico grew by an annual real rate of 5.3% as a result of new investment in the manufacturing sector" (Deere et al. 1990: 129).

31. "By the end of the decade most of the countries that were to later form the Caribbean Community and Common Market (CARICOM) had put in place the requisite legal and infrastructural framework by which 'industrialization by invitation' was to function. The similarity of these programs with Operation Bootstrap was that the expansion of manufacturing took place with the assistance of government subsidies, tax benefits, and government provision of infrastructure; that is, industrialization required active government intervention in the economy" (Deere et al. 1990: 130).

32. Dookhan writes, "As early as 1949 legislation was passed providing for designated tax exemption and industrial subsidies for eight years to new industries which qualified with a minimum investment of $10,000. The Act, however, lay idle. . . . Until 1959 the only attempt to intro an industry was made in 1951 when an experimental button factory was established in St. Thomas. Then in 1959 watch assembly operations were started in the Virgin Islands, utilizing parts imported from various foreign countries. By the

mid-1960s production had jumped to 4.5 million units despite the shortage of skilled labor, and by 1967, sixteen watch companies were located in the Virgin Islands" (Dookhan 1974: 287).

33. Gordon Lewis writes, "Since the 1950's the [Virgin Islands'] economy has increasingly turned first to organized tourism and second to incentive-based industrialization after the Puerto Rican style. Both of these enterprises, however, are notoriously hazardous as foundations for permanent prosperity to replace the old agricultural and trading economy. . . . Even the success of such a program, paradoxically, may prove harmful, for, based as it is on expatriate capital, it tends to repeat all of the traditional features of the West Indian sugar structure: a structure of local demand shaped by expatriate needs; the destruction of industry, as can be seen in the disappearance of the St. Thomas handicraft industry; and the growth of absentee landlordism under a new guise, in which the outsider shareholder replaces the colonial planter. All of those features are already far advanced in the Puerto Rican situation; it is ironic that the Virgin Islands seek to emulate 'Operation Bootstrap' at the moment when the Puerto Rican planners themselves have begun to be aware of the massive alienation of the local economic patrimony that it has entailed" (Lewis 1972: 16–17).

34. Deere notes that "as a model of industrial organization, this outward looking development strategy favors US interest by facilitating the location of US multinational corporation processing facilities in low-wage areas, allowing them to maintain the competitive edge. Under such an arrangement there are no foreign aid obligations, as in the Alliance for Progress, or public transfer of funds, as in Operation Bootstrap. . . . Besides government incentives, the other major factor attracting new industries to the region are the low labor costs. For example, garment workers in the Dominican Free Trade Zone earn 47 cents an hour compared to the $3.35 for their US counterparts" (Deere et al. 1990: 144).

35. Operation Bootstrap was marketed primarily by Industrial Representatives (IR's), a "carefully selected corps of salesmen who were mostly young Puerto Ricans with educational and practical experience in business and attracted to public service." These salesmen "served as the heart of the mainland operation" (Maldonado 1997: 85).

36. In his analysis of Operation Bootstrap, A. W. Maldonado argues that "as a model for economic development, Puerto Rico was indeed a special case due to its unique political and economic relationship to the US. . . . It was evident that without its unique association to the US, Puerto Rico's economy would not be much better than those of neighboring Caribbean nations, such as the Dominican Republic, or of the small Central American countries" (1997: 225).

37. See, for example, see Stephanie Black (2001) on banana farming in Jamaica. Regarding the structure of Operation Bootstrap, Carmen Deere

(1990) writes: "Puerto Rico's government chose an industrialization strategy explicitly designed to integrate Puerto Rico more closely to the US market. Known as 'Operation Bootstrap,' the strategy consisted of attracting US investors through tax incentive schemes to establish manufacturing plants on the island geared to the US market. The foundations of the model rested on the structural advantages Puerto Rico could offer to US manufacturing industries. These included low wages (Puerto Rico's wages were 27% of average US manufacturing wages in the 1950s); selective minimum-wage exemption; generous tax exemptions, including exemptions on US and local corporate income taxes, income taxes on dividends distributed to individuals, municipal taxes, license fees, and property taxes; duty-free access to the US market; geographic proximity to the US and a government infrastructure which enforced and managed the development model" (Deere et al. 1990: 129).

38. "Behind the glowing figures [of Operation Bootstrap], lay a different reality. Puerto Rico's rapid industrialization was accompanied not by rising employment, but by relentlessly rising unemployment. Official unemployment stood at around 12% in the mid-1960's; by 1975 it had risen to 20%, and this was considered an underestimation of true joblessness. Over this same period, and especially after 1970, Puerto Rico became heavily dependent on subsidies from the US federal budget. These subsidies, which stood at US$119 million per year in 1950, soared to US$3.1 billion per year in 1979. Contrary to the self-reliance its name implied, the Bootstrap model made Puerto Rico dependent on foreign capital. This capital became increasingly mobile as the transnational corporations extended their operations around the globe. The result was an erosion of investment in Puerto Rico, and mounting dependence on subsidies" (Ferguson 1990b: 28).

39. Even in Jamaica and Trinidad, the two island nations that received the majority of such projects, the unemployment numbers remained troubling: "By June 1963 in Trinidad and Tobago 99 factories employing a mere 4,666 workers had been put in place under that country's Pioneer Industries Program. Adding to that number the 40 factories under construction and anticipating an additional 2,255 jobs that would be created, Edwin Carrington wrote in 1967 that "the estimate of 6,921 jobs from these 139 establishments and an investment of $257.8 million (TT) is to say the least disappointing." It was all the more so in view of the fact that between 1950 and 1963 Trinidad and Tobago's labor force increased by nearly 100,000 and employment in the country's sugar industry declined by about 3,800. A similar pattern of inadequate employment creation occurred in Jamaica" (Ferguson 1990b: 67).

40. "The growth in manufacturing employment did not keep up with the rate of agricultural labor-force displacement. Moreover, the manufacturing sector which developed in the 1960s was increasingly characterized by capital-intensive technologies, reducing the demand for labor. As a result,

other measures had to be adopted to maintain the model of capital accumulation: along with the introduction of population control and sterilization programs, migration to the US became virtually institutionalized" (Deere et al. 1990: 129).

41. Deere writes that "Caribbean migration to the US . . . accelerat[ed] in the late 1960s. [During this period] the Caribbean islands contributed 20% of the legal migrants to the US compared with only 5% in the decade of the 1950s and 9% in the early 1960s. In the 1960s, Cubans represented the majority of Caribbean migrants, followed by Dominicans and Haitians; in the latter half of the 1960s migration by Jamaicans increased significantly. In the early 1970s migration from Cuba was surpassed by that from the English-speaking Caribbean—Jamaica, Trinidad-Tobago, Barbados, and Guyana—a trend repeated in the 1980s" (Deere et al. 1990: 133).

42. Shoring up this argument, Maldonado writes that "Puerto Rico averted a catastrophic increase in unemployment in the early part of [the 1950s] as a result of the migration of working-age Puerto Ricans" (1997: 143).

43. Hillman and D'Agostino argue that "as important as emigration has been to the West Indies in serving as an escape valve for population growth, it should not be viewed as a solution to mounting population pressures. . . . Some countries that once received significant numbers of immigrants from the Caribbean are now tightening immigration requirements. In addition to Great Britain's Commonwealth Immigration Act of 1962, Canada tightened its immigration policy in 1972, as did the US in 1986, 1990, and 1996. Even within the Caribbean, serious efforts have been made to reduce interisland movement. For example, Haitian and Jamaican migrations to Cuba have been stopped. The Netherlands Antilles has halted the influx from the British and French islands. Jamaica and Barbados have forbidden the entry of unskilled laborers. Trinidad and Tobago, much of whose Black population initially came from the Windward and Leeward Islands, now has legal barriers against further unrestricted entry" (Hillman and D'Agostino 2003: 40).

44. Examples of this trend include the 1965 revolt in the Dominican Republic, the 1974 election of Michael Manley in Jamaica on a platform of democratic socialism, and the 1970 protest by the Black power movement in Trinidad and Tobago (see Deere et al. 1990).

45. Including the 1974 election of Michael Manley in Jamaica on a platform of democratic socialism, which included a plan to nationalize that country's bauxite industry.

46. See Bolles (1993) for a gendered analysis of IMF restructuring.

47. This preference for female workers occurs within the EDC program as well as among the "pink collar" workers theorized by Freeman (2000).

Chapter 4

1. *United States of America and the People of the Virgin Islands v. James A. Auffenberg, Jr.*, Appendix to Government's Response (2008).

2. Informally, this space is referred to as "the Park." Taken together, these warehouses spread over 150,000 feet and are officially known as the William D. Roebuck Industrial Park.

3. At present, the Park is largely empty. At 11 percent occupancy by EDC companies, this area is in need of repair, including attention to leaking roofs and peeling paint (Economic Development Authority 2007: 15).

4. The representative of the USVI in Washington, Delegate to Congress Donna Christensen, was outspoken in her objection to the EDC requirements included in the Jobs Act, stating in the same article that "the only good thing we can say about this is that they are out, and the companies now know what they need to know." Rather than the 183-day residency requirement, "Christensen and others had advocated that an average of 122 days in the territory over three years be sufficient" (Buchanan 2006).

5. A 2002 opinion piece in the *Virgin Islands Daily News* reflects this position:

> The territory's high employment rate is the result of the V.I. Legislature and the business community taking no action to change. Unless changes are made, the unemployment rate will continue to grow and will help plunge the territory into deeper economic turmoil.
>
> For 22 years the territory's employment has stagnated. Why? Business is disconnected and the Legislature continues to send anti-business messages, and both of these entities have done little to change things for more than two decades.
>
> The Legislature must drop its persistent, anti-business attitude. It completely defeats the opportunities offered by the Economic Development Commission, and blocks any thoughts of expansion by existing businesses. And, businesses must stop financially supporting the anti-business senators in the hopes that these legislators "will at least leave me alone." (Editor 2002)

6. In 2018 Albert Bryan would go on to be elected governor of the US Virgin Islands.

7. Companies operating in export-processing zones have used worker lockouts to curtail attempts at unionizing as well as a means of notifying workers of the company's closure. Dunn (1999) writes that for EPZs "there is still a far way to go in accepting the principle of workers' rights, as some

companies have moved their operations elsewhere rather than accept a unionized workforce" (602). Films such as *Life and Debt* and *Zoned for Slavery* depict such instances of worker lockouts, while Brooks (2007) describes the lockout of more than five thousand from a Bangladeshi EPZ in her work.

8. In her work, Mimi Sheller (2003) also links current global processes circulating through the Caribbean to histories of piracy and evasion, writing: "In contrast to the restrictions on labour mobility, the Caribbean has become a leader in the free-booting flight of capital across international borders. Money itself is a crucial liquid asset which has been subject to wrangling over the ease of its illegal movement into and out of weakly regulated banking sectors in the Caribbean. . . . As in the days of piracy and 'freebooting,' the Caribbean has come to be associated with interruptions of the 'normal' flows of capital, as well as with forms of smuggling and drug-running which subvert (yet support) the formal regulated economy" (Sheller 2003: 33).

9. "Stanford Sentenced to 110-Year Term in $7 Billion Ponzi Case," *New York Times*, June 14, 2012.

10. "Allen Stanford: A Mini Madoff?," *Newsweek*, February 20, 2009.

11. "Found! Accused Scammer Stanford Turns in Passport in Washington," ABC News, February 19, 2009.

12. "Jury Convicts Stanford in $7 Billion Ponzi Scheme," MSNBC, March 6, 2012.

Chapter 5

1. This converts to 945,000 gallons of sugar and 840,000 gallons of rum.

2. From Bill 2019, Act 1076, February 20, 1964.

3. Christiansted, one of two town centers on St. Croix, is generally referred to as "town." The other center, located on the western end of the island, is Frederiksted.

4. This expression roughly translates to "those people over there" and marks a clear separation between the speaker and the people he or she is describing.

5. The EDA offers an internship program that encourages undergraduate students to work in the office for approximately six weeks, performing front office duties including answering telephones and faxing documents.

6. On St. Croix, there are a number of derogatory names for residents who have migrated from surrounding islands, including "down island," "garrote," and "gasso."

7. *Virgin Islands On-Line Coconut Telegraph* 2005.

8. Part-time residents who generally spend the winter season on the island.

9. For instance, Caneel Bay, the St. John resort, and Carambola Beach Resort on St. Croix were both created by the Rockefeller family.

10. In addition to large land purchases, members of the EDC community have generally maintained greater levels of visibility on St. Croix than the island's long-term white residents through such measures as establishing nonprofits, charity events, and in one instance a private school. One particularly well-known EDC businessman has unsuccessfully run three times for the political office of Delegate to Congress for the USVI. In 2018, he ran for the office of Governor of the USVI.

11. This word is used on St. Croix to describe a jalopy.

12. Shifts in the housing market that negatively affect Black homeowners are not limited to St. Croix. In her work on the real estate market in the US, Keeanga-Yamahtta Taylor (2019) has turned to the phrase "predatory inclusion" to name the ways in which racial capitalism continues to react nimbly to new parameters like legislation and produce the continued marginalization of Black people.

13. A hotel started by Laurance Rockefeller on the island of St. John.

14. The Westin hotel on St. John operates on the island as part of the luxury Westin chain of hotels.

15. The Procurement subsection of the Rules and Regulations governing the program states:

> It is the purpose of this Division to provide clear guidelines for the implementation of a workable program by which local suppliers of goods and providers of services may benefit from the increased commercial and industrial activity produced by the Program. To this end these rules provide (and they shall be so construed) for responsible United States Virgin Islands business enterprises to have the maximum practicable opportunity to participate in procurement activities of beneficiaries, as suppliers of goods or providers of services. Beneficiaries shall do their utmost to facilitate the participation of United States Virgin Islands businesses pursuant to these rules.

> Section 708–702. Procurement Requirements.

> 1. Each Beneficiary shall employ or contract, and require all contractors retained by him to employ or subcontract, for services and to purchase goods, materials and supplies with and from those persons, firms, and corporations who are

residents of the United States Virgin Islands, or incorporated under the laws of the United States Virgin Islands, and who are duly licensed to do business in the United States Virgin Islands and have been so duly licensed for one year or more prior to the initial date of any such employment, contract, subcontract, or purchase.

2. Each Beneficiary shall invite competitive bidding, and require all contractors retained by it to invite competitive bidding for all such services, goods and materials pursuant to the publication requirements [listed in] the U.S. Virgin Islands Code, and to notify each bidder in writing of the name of the successful bidder and amount of his bid.

3. Each Beneficiary shall advise the Economic Development Commission, in writing with a copy to the Commissioner of Licensing and Consumer Affairs when goods and materials are not available under the above-defined Virgin Islands sources and demonstrate in writing of efforts to obtain such services, goods and materials, and to require contractor or subcontractors retained by the applicant to likewise comply with this requirement. (Rules and Regulations Economic Development Commission, Title 29 V.I.R.R., December 22, 2004, Section 708-601 & 604)

16. For more on the project of deindustrialization and its effects on cities and urban minorities, see, for example, Kelley (1997).

17. Clashes between "belongers" and "nonbelongers" in the BVI echo increasing invocations of autochthony and indigeneity more broadly (Geschiere and Nyamnjoh 2000; Geschiere 2009; Starn and Cadena 2007).

18. http://www.virginislandsdailynews.com/bill-to-expand-belonger-status-on-hold/article_5b0a1fee-bd4b-58f3-8d54-c03a06c164ba.html.

19. In his work, Bill Maurer (1997) has traced legislation in the BVI and demonstrated the conflation of BVI citizenship with "belonger" status. Yet, these distinctions have significant impact on life in the BVI: Cathy Cohen (2010) writes, "By law, only BVI citizens have unrestricted rights to buy BVI land, and BVI citizens are given preference in all hiring and in the awarding of trade licenses, college scholarships, and low-interest development bank loans. *In conventional practice and discourse*, BVI citizenship is equated with *belonger* as opposed to *nonbelonger* status" (106; emphasis mine).

20. This roughly translates to "I don't ask that girl from another island anything."

21. In 1996, Adelbert Bryan shot and killed his son in what was later determined by the VI Police Department to be an act of self-defense.

22. https://kinginstitute.stanford.edu/king-papers/documents/draft-chapter-vi-knock-midnight.

23. This date was selected as it provided then residents ten years to select between American and Danish citizenship following the 1917 sale of the islands to the US. During the convention, there were a number of competing definitions of "native" Virgin Islander. As noted in one 2008 newspaper article: "In the draft [convention] language, an ancestral native Virgin Islander is a person born or living in the territory before 1927, the date U.S. citizenship was first conferred on people living in the territory, as well as any direct descendants of someone who meets that criteria. A native Virgin Islander is defined as anyone born in the territory after 1927, plus anyone who is 'a descendant of at least one parent who was born in the Virgin Islands after 1927.' A simple 'Virgin Islander' is someone who has resided in the Virgin Islands for at least five years" (Kossler 2008b).

24. As Jacqueline Nassy-Brown (2005) argues in her work on diaspora through the lens of Britain, "local belonging is reckoned through rhetorics of continual, generations-long presence in a place" (110).

25. https://www.uvi.edu/files/documents/College_of_Liberal_Arts_and_Social_Sciences/social_sciences/OSDCD/Fifth_Constitution_Proposed_US_Virgin_Islands_to_Governor_deJongh2009.pdf.

Chapter 6

1. The per capita personal income in the US Virgin Islands in 2003 was $31,000—"significantly lower than in any U.S. state" (Pricewaterhouse-Coopers 2004: 6).

2. See also Maurer (2015) on the complexity of forms of currency.

3. Freeman's more recent work (2014) on neoliberalism in Barbados is more closely related to the situation created by the EDC program, as she explores the impacts primarily on middle-class entrepreneurs—yet even here there are key differences, as the neoliberal flexibility noted by Freeman has not affected EDC girls in ways she describes. Rather than moving toward starting businesses of their own, the "entrepreneurialism" of neoliberalism has, for them, translated into the long-standing hierarchies of race and color in the Caribbean merging with the neoliberal project of becoming an entrepreneur of the self—that is, managing one's human capital such that one has the best possible outcome in the market—to produce the figure of the "EDC girl."

4. This is not to suggest, however, that enslaved women who were performing indoor, domestic, labor had an immediately improved situation, as they were frequently subjected to sexual assaults, given their placement inside the planter's house. These women were often lighter-skinned and

not infrequently the offspring of a planter and an enslaved woman. What is more, historian Barbara Bush (1990) has noted that these assaults were frequently positioned as part of their work, as "female domestics were often expected to perform sexual duties in addition to their official duties" (44).

5. In her work on female vendors in Jamaica, Gina Ulysse (2007) points to the centrality of *color* or shade—in addition to race—that informs how one is positioned in relation to notions of respectability.

6. That is, apply a chemical treatment to her hair in order to alter the texture such that hair becomes straighter for a period of time.

7. http://www.usviber.org/wp-content/uploads/2017/04/Self-Sufficiency-Standard.pdf.

8. https://www.census.gov/prod/cen2000/phc-4-vi.pdf.

9. file:///Users/tnavarro/Downloads/2015%20Virgin%20Islands%20Community%20Survey%20(1).pdf.

10. *United States of America and the People of the Virgin Islands v. James A. Auffenberg, Jr.*, Appendix to Government's Response (2008).

11. Abraham-Van der Mark (1983), Anderson (1986), Barrow (1995), Barrow (1998), Bolles (1983), Ellis (2003), Kempadoo (2004), Leo-Rhynie (1997), Mohammed (2002), Mohammed and Shepherd (1988), Momsen (1993), Yelvington (1995).

12. There have been interventions into the power dynamics inherent in this piece of furniture: in 2011, the Virgin Islands artist LaVaughn Belle created an art installation entitled *The Planter's Chair* based at Whim plantation. For this work, Belle had visitors sit in the planter's chair in order to "allow each participant to reimagine themselves into this colonial narrative" (LaVaughn Belle, *The Planter's Chair*, http://www.lavaughnbelle.com/island/abwadoi9sxjdgasd9qtnqyn4b10r18).

13. Davies and Bansel (2007) and Harvey (2007) argue that increased global economic disparities and the simultaneous obfuscation of this end product with terms like "freedom," "individuality," and "market logic" are central to the neoliberal project. Picking apart the notion of neoliberalism's inevitability, the persistent "habit of treating the very idea that [increased inequality] is a mere and in some instances even unfortunate byproduct of neoliberalization," David Harvey insists that this consolidation of class power is at the core of the neoliberal project (2007: 119).

Conclusion

1. "The United States Virgin Islands: Comprehensive Economic Development Strategy"—CEDS, https://www.usvieda.org/sites/default/files/pdf_document/CEDS_Plan_2015.pdf.

2. https://www.usvieda.org/resources/beneficiaries.

3. On the joint district of St. Thomas/St. John, the 2012 figure held at 9.6 percent.

4. Pew Research Center, "Puerto Ricans Leave in Record Numbers for Mainland US," http://www.pewresearch.org/fact-tank/2015/10/14/puerto-ricans-leave-in-record-numbers-for-mainland-u-s/.

5. "Puerto Ricans Brace for Crisis in Health Care," *New York Times*, August 2, 2015, http://www.nytimes.com/2015/08/03/us/health-providers-brace-for-more-cuts-to-medicare-in-puerto-rico.html.

6. One such speech, given by the US Secretary of the Interior, included the following sentiments about the importance of the USVI to the United States: "Today is a testament to the Virgin Islanders whose commitment, vision, expertise, and sacrifice built these islands, enriched our shared history and contributed to our national security. Since joining the American family, Virgin Islanders have distinguished themselves in education, medicine, engineering, politics, law, entertainment, and sports. And many of their sons and daughters have honorably served and are serving with distinction in the U.S. Armed Forces to provide for our Nation's defense" ("Secretary Zinke Lauds Virgin Islanders' Progress and Delivers President Trump's 'Warm Wishes' at Ceremonies Marking 100th Anniversary of Islands Transfer to America," US Department of the Interior website, March 31, 2017, https://www.doi.gov/pressreleases/secretary-zinke-lauds-virgin-islanders-progress-delivers-president-trumps-warm-wishes).

7. In 2017, a group of colleagues and I founded the Virgin Islands Studies Collective, which is "committed to centering the Virgin Islands as the intellectual, cultural and political center of our inquiry. We engage with other sites, including Denmark, the United States, and the wider Caribbean and African Diaspora secondarily but vitally" (Virgin Islands Studies Collective Founding Statement).

References

Abraham-Van der Mark, Eva E. 1983. "The Impact of Industrialization on Women: A Caribbean Case." In *Women, Men, and the International Division of Labor*, edited by June Nash and María Patricia Fernández-Kelly, 374–388. Albany: State University of New York Press.

Aikau, Hōkūlani, and Vernadette Vicuña Gonzalez, eds. 2019. *Detours: A Decolonial Guide to Hawai'i*. Durham: Duke University Press.

Aldrich, Robert, and John Connell. 1998. *The Last Colonies*. Cambridge: Cambridge University Press.

Alexander, M. Jacqui. 2005. *Pedagogies of Crossing: Meditations on Feminism, Sexual Politics, Memory, and the Sacred*. Durham: Duke University Press.

Alexander, M. Jacqui, and Chandra Talpade Mohanty, eds. 1997. *Feminist Genealogies, Colonial Legacies, Democratic Futures*. New York: Routledge.

Anderson, John. 1975. *Night of the Silent Drums: A Narrative of Slave Rebellion on the Virgin Islands*. New York: Scribner's.

Anderson, Patricia. 1986. "Conclusion: Women in the Caribbean." *Social and Economic Studies* 35(2): 291–324.

Appadurai, Arjun. 1990. "Disjuncture and Difference in the Global Cultural Economy." *Public Culture* 2(2): 1–24.

———. 1996. *Modernity at Large: Cultural Dimensions of Globalization*. Minneapolis: University of Minnesota Press.

Appel, Hannah. 2019. *The Licit Life of Capitalism: US Oil in Equatorial Guinea*. Durham: Duke University Press.

Austin-Broos, Diane. 1997. *Jamaica Genesis: Religion and the Politics of Moral Orders*. Chicago: University of Chicago Press.

Babbington, Anthony. 2000. "Reencountering Development: Livelihood Transitions and Place Transformations in the Andes." *Annals of the Association of American Geographers* 90(3): 495–520.

Banks, Ingrid. 2000. *Hair Matters: Beauty, Power, and Black Women's Consciousness*. New York: New York University Press.

Ballentine, Jabriel. 2009. "Pipe Dreams and Ponzi Schemes: Is This the Promise of the EDA?" VirginIslandsWatch.com. http://virginisland-swatch.com/blog_post/show/148.

Barrow, Christine. 1998. *Caribbean Portraits: Essays on Gender Ideologies and Identities*. Kingston: Ian Randle.

Barrow, Eudine. 1995. "Postmodernist Feminist Theorizing and Development Policy Practice in the Anglophone Caribbean: The Barbados Case." In *Feminism/Postmodernism/Development*, edited by Marian H. Marchand and Jane Parpart, 142–158. New York: Routledge.

Baucom, Ian. 2005. *Specters of the Atlantic: Finance Capital, Slavery, and the Philosophy of History*. Durham: Duke University Press.

Baur, John. 2009. "V.I. Plant Law Applied to Stanford Lockdown." *St. Croix Source*, March 6.

Bear, Laura. 2015. *Navigating Austerity: Currents of Debt Along a South Asian River*. Stanford: Stanford University Press.

Bear, Laura, Karen Ho, Anna Tsing, and Sylvia Yanagisako. 2015. "Gens: A Feminist Manifesto for the Study of Capitalism." *Cultural Anthropology*. https://culanth.org/fieldsights/gens-a-feminist-manifesto-for-the-study-of-capitalism.

Beckles, Hilary. 1989. *Natural Rebels: A Social History of Enslaved Black Women in Barbados*. New Brunswick, NJ: Rutgers University Press.

Benería, Lourdes, and Martha Roldán. 1987. *The Crossroads of Class and Gender: Industrial Homework, Subcontracting, and Household Dynamics in Mexico City*. Chicago: University of Chicago Press.

Benjamin, Walter. 1940. "Theses on the Philosophy of History."

Benítez-Rojo, Antonio. 1997. *The Repeating Island: The Caribbean and the Postmodern Perspective*. Durham: Duke University Press.

Bermúdez-Ruiz, Johanna, dir. 2010. *Sugar Pathways*. Cane Bay Films.

Besson, Jean. 1993. "Reputation and Respectability Reconsidered: A New Perspective on Afro-Caribbean Peasant Women." In *Women and Change in the Caribbean*, edited by Janet Momsen, 15–37. Bloomington: Indiana University Press.

Black, Stephanie, dir. 2001. *Life and Debt*. Tuff Gong Pictures.

Bolles, Lynn. 1983. "Kitchens Hit by Priorities: Employed Working-Class Jamaican Women Confront the IMF." In *Women, Men, and the International Division of Labor*, edited by June Nash and María Patricia Fernández-Kelly, 138–160. Albany: State University of New York Press.

Bond, David. 2017. "Oil in the Caribbean: Refineries, Mangroves, and the Negative Ecologies of Crude Oil." *Comparative Studies in Society and History* 59(3): 600–628.

Bonilla, Yarimar. 2015. *Non-Sovereign Futures: French Caribbean Politics in the Wake of Disenchantment*. Chicago: University of Chicago Press.

Bonilla, Yarimar, and Marisol LeBron. 2019. *Aftershocks of Disaster: Puerto Rico Before and After the Storm*. Chicago: Haymarket Books.

Boyer, William. 1983. *America's Virgin Islands: A History of Human Rights and Wrongs*. Durham: Carolina Academic Press

Braudel, Fernand. 1972. *The Mediterranean and the Mediterranean World in the Age of Philip II*, vol. 1. Translated by Sean Reynolds. New York: Harper and Row.

Brent, E. D. 2004. "While the Rich Gets Richer." *Virgin Islands Daily News*, June 8.

Briggs, Laura. 2002. *Reproducing Empire: Race, Sex, Science, and U.S. Imperialism in Puerto Rico*. Berkeley: University of California Press.

Brooks, Ethel Carolyn. 2007. *Unraveling the Garment Industry: Transnational Organizing and Women's Work*. Minneapolis: University of Minnesota Press.

Buchanan, Don. 2006. "V.I. Official Disappointed with New EDC Residency Regulations." *St. Croix Source*, January 30.

Bush, Barbara. 1990. *Slave Women in Caribbean Society, 1650–1838*. Bloomington: Indiana University Press.

Campbell, A. A. 1943. "St. Thomas Negroes—A Study of Personality and Culture." *Psychological Monographs* 55(5): 1–90.

Candelario, Ginetta. 2007. *Black Behind the Ears: Dominican Racial Identity from Museums to Beauty Shops*. Durham: Duke University Press.

Carby, Hazel. 1987. *Reconstructing Womanhood: The Emergence of the Afro-American Woman Novelist*. Oxford: Oxford University Press.

Caruso, A. F. 2003. *Ishmael Was Paradise Lost*. Book Publishing Division of Ad Sales III, Inc.

Clarke, Edith. 1957. *My Mother Who Fathered Me: A Study of the Family in Three Selected Communities in Jamaica*. London: G. Allen & Unwin.

Clarke, Kamari, and Deborah Thomas, eds. 2006. *Globalization and Race: Transformations in the Cultural Production of Blackness*. Durham: Duke University Press.

Cohen, Cathy. 2010. *Take Me to My Paradise: Tourism and Nationalism in the British Virgin Islands*. New Brunswick, NJ: Rutgers University Press.

Cohen, Judah. 2011. "Arabs and Jews in the Virgin Islands: A Search for Caribbean Paradigms." *Latin American and Caribbean Ethnic Studies* 6(2): 213–223.

Corbridge, Stuart. 1993. *Debt and Development*. Oxford: Blackwell.

Comaroff, Jean, and John Comaroff. 2000. "Millennial Capitalism: First Thoughts on a Second Coming." *Public Culture* 12(2): 291–343.

Cravey, Altha. 1998. *Women and Work in Mexico's Maquiladoras*. Lanham, MD: Rowman & Littlefield.

Crichlow, Michaeline. 2009. *Globalization and the Post-Creole Imagination: Notes on Fleeing the Plantation.* Durham: Duke University Press.

Curtin, Philip. 1969. *The Atlantic Slave Trade: A Census.* Madison: University of Wisconsin Press.

Davies, Bronwyn, and Peter Bansel. 2007. "Neoliberalism and Education." *International Journal of Qualitative Studies in Education* 20(3): 247–259.

Davis, Dana-Ain, and Christa Craven, eds. 2016. *Feminist Ethnography: Thinking through Methodologies, Challenges, and Possibilities.* Lanham, MD: Rowman & Littlefield.

Davis, Olasee. 2009. "Grassy Point Development Is Cause for Concern." *Virgin Islands Daily News*, September 8.

Deere, Carmen Diana. 1995. "What Difference Does Gender Make? Rethinking Peasant Studies." *Feminist Economics* 1(1): 53–72.

Deere, Carmen Diana, et al. 1990. *In the Shadows of the Sun: U.S. Policy and Development Alternatives in the Caribbean.* Boulder, CO: Westview Press.

Dello Buono, Richard, and José Bell Lara. 2007. *Imperialism, Neoliberalism, and Social Struggles in Latin America.* Studies in Critical Social Sciences. Boston: Brill.

Derrida, Jacques. 1993. *Specters of Marx.* New York: Routledge.

Difede, Richard. 2004. "EDC Program a Godsend." *Virgin Islands Daily News*, June 10.

Donmoyer, Ryan. 2007. "Hedge Funds Flee Tax Haven in Virgin Islands, Hounded by IRS." Bloomberg.com, January 25. https://www.hedgeco.net/news/01/2007/hedge-funds-flee-tax-haven-in-virgin-islands-hounded-by-irs.html.

Dookhan, Isaac. 1974. *A History of the Virgin Islands of the United States.* St. Thomas, USVI: Caribbean Universities Press in association with Bowker.

Douglass, Lisa. 1992. *Politics of Sentiment: Love, Hierarchy, and the Jamaican Family Elite.* Boulder, CO: Westview Press.

duCille, Ann. 1994. "The Occult of True Black Womanhood: Critical Demeanor and Black Feminist Studies." *Signs* 19(3): 591–629.

Dunn, Leith. 1999. "Export Processing Zones: A Caribbean Development Dilemma." *Development in Practice* 9(5): 601–605.

Economic Development Authority. 2004. Virgin Islands Economic Development Authority Annual Report FY 2002–2004.

———. 2007. Virgin Islands Economic Development Authority Annual Report FY 2007.

———. N.d. Message from the Governor. http://www.usvieda.org/.

Editor. 2002. "Bleak Employment Picture." *Virgin Islands Daily News*, December 17.

Editorial. 2008. "Stanford Financial Group Expanding in Caribbean." *St. Croix Avis*, January 9.

Edmondson, Belinda. 2009. *Caribbean Middlebrow: Leisure Culture and the Middle Class*. Ithaca, NY: Cornell University Press.

Ellis, Pat. 2003. *Women, Gender, and Development in the Caribbean: Reflections and Projections*. London: Zed Books.

Elson, Diane, and Ruth Pearson. 1986. "Third World Manufacturing." In *Waged Work: A Reader*, edited by Feminist Review, 67–92. London: Virago.

Eltis, David, and David Richardson. 2010. *Atlas of the Transatlantic Slave Trade*. New Haven, CT: Yale University Press.

Elyachar, Julia. 2005. *Markets of Dispossession: NGO's, Economic Development, and the State in Cairo*. Durham: Duke University Press.

Emanuel, Gerard. 2007. "Equality for All in the Territory." *St. Croix Avis*, August 12.

Enloe, Cynthia. 1989. *Bananas, Beaches and Bases: Making Feminist Sense of International Politics*. Berkeley: University of California Press.

Escobar, Arturo. 1994. *Encountering Development: The Making and Unmaking of the Third World*. Princeton, NJ: Princeton University Press.

Evans, Luther Harris. 1945. *The Virgin Islands, from Naval Base to New Deal*. Westport, CT: Greenwood Press.

Fabian, Johannes. 1983. *Time and the Other*. New York: Columbia University Press.

Ferguson, James. 1990a. *The Anti-Politics Machine: "Development," Depoliticization, and Bureaucratic Power in Lesotho*. Cambridge: Cambridge University Press.

———. 1990b. *Far from Paradise: An Introduction to Caribbean Development*. New York: Distribution in North America by Monthly Review Press.

———. 1999. *Expectations of Modernity: Myths and Meanings of Urban Life on the Zambian Copperbelt*. Berkeley: University of California Press.

———. 2006. *Global Shadows: Africa in the Neoliberal World Order*. Durham: Duke University Press.

Fernández-Kelly, María Patricia. 1983. *For We Are Sold, I and My People: Women and Industry in Mexico's Frontier*. Albany: State University of New York Press.

Fisher, Melissa, and Greg Downey, eds. 2006. *Frontiers of Capital: Ethnographic Reflections on the New Economy*. Durham: Duke University Press.

Fortwrangler, Crystal. 2007. "Friends with Money: Private Support for a National Park in the US Virgin Islands." *Conservation and Society* 5(4): 504–533.

Foucault, Michel. 2004. *Abnormal: Lectures at the Collège de France, 1974–1975*. London: Picador.

Freeman, Carla. 2000. *High Tech and High Heels in the Global Economy: Women, Work, and Pink-Collar Identities in the Caribbean*. Durham: Duke University Press.

———. 2014. *Entrepreneurial Selves: Neoliberal Respectability and the Making of a Caribbean Middle Class*. Durham: Duke University Press.

Fryer, Peter. 1984. *Staying Power: The History of Black People in Britain*. London: Pluto Press.

Fuentes, Annette, and Barbara Ehrenreich. 1983. *Women in the Global Factory*. Boston: South End Press.

Galvin, Anne. 2012. "Caribbean Piracies/Social Mobilities: Some Commonalities between Colonial Privateers and Entrepreneurial Profiteers in the 21st Century." *Anthropological* Quarterly 85(3): 755–784.

George, Abosede. 2013. "Getting the Hang of It." *Scholar and Feminist Online: Gender, Justice, and Neoliberal Transformations*. 11.1–11.2 (Fall 2012/Spring 2013).

Geschiere, Peter. 2009. *The Perils of Belonging: Autochthony, Citizenship, and Exclusion in Africa and Europe*. Chicago: University of Chicago Press.

Geschiere, Peter, and Francis Nyamnjoh. 2000. "Capitalism and Autochthony: The Seesaw of Mobility and Belonging." *Public Culture* 12(2): 423–452.

Gill, Rosalind, and Christina Scharff. 2011. *New Femininities: Postfeminism, Neoliberalism, and Subjectivity*. London: Palgrave Macmillan.

Glick-Schiller, Nina, and Georges Fouron. 2001. *Georges Woke Up Laughing*. Durham: Duke University Press.

Gmelch, George. 2003. *Behind the Smile: The Working Lives of Caribbean Tourism*. Bloomington: Indiana University Press.

Goldstone, Brian, and Juan Obarrio, eds. 2016. *African Futures: Essays on Crisis, Emergence, and Possibility*. Chicago: University of Chicago Press.

Gomez-Barris, Macarena. 2017. *The Extractive Zone: Social Ecologies and Decolonial Perspectives*. Durham: Duke University Press.

Gonzalez, Vernadette. 2013. *Securing Paradise: Tourism and Militarism in Hawai'i and the Philippines*. Durham: Duke University Press.

Gordon, Avery. 2008. *Ghostly Matters: Haunting and the Sociological Imagination*. Minneapolis: University of Minnesota Press.

Gore, Akia. 2009. *Garrote: The Illusion of Social Equality and Political Justice in the United States Virgin Islands*. New York: Wadadli Press.

Greene, Jerome, and William Cissel. 1988. *Historic Furnishings Report: Fort Christiansvaern, Christiansted National Historic Site*. Washington, DC: Harpers Free Center, National Park Service.

Greene, Julie. 2009. *The Canal Builders: Making America's Empire at the Panama Canal*. New York: Penguin Press.

Grewal, Inderpal. 2005. *Transnational America: Feminisms, Diasporas, Neoliberalisms*. Durham: Duke University Press.

Guyton, Lori. 2008. "Stanford Financial Group Breaks Ground on Caribbean Expansion." Reuters.com, February 21. https://www.slideshare.net/JoeWeisenthal/stanford-bush.

Hall, Neville A. T. 1992. *Slave Society in the Danish West Indies: St. Thomas, St. John, and St. Croix.* Baltimore: Johns Hopkins University Press.

Hall, Stuart. 1997. "Old and New Identities, Old and New Ethnicities." In *Culture, Globalization, and the World-System: Contemporary Conditions for the Representation of Identity*, edited by Anthony King, 41–68. Minneapolis: University of Minnesota Press.

Hammonds, Evelynn. 1997. "Toward a Genealogy of Black Female Sexuality: The Problematic of Silence." In *Feminist Genealogies, Colonial Legacies, Democratic Futures*, edited by M. Jacqui Alexander and Chandra Talpade Mohanty, 170–182. New York: Routledge.

Hansen, Thomas Blom, and Finn Stepputat, eds. 2005. *Sovereign Bodies: Citizens, Migrants, and States in the Postcolonial World.* Princeton, NJ: Princeton University Press.

Hardt, Michael, and Antonio Negri. 2000. *Empire.* Cambridge: Harvard University Press.

Harrigan, Norwell, and Pearl Varlack. 1977. "The US Virgin Islands and the Black Experience." *Journal of Black Studies* 7(4): 387–410.

Harrison, Faye. 1997. *Decolonizing Anthropology: Moving Further toward an Anthropology for Liberation.* Arlington, VA: American Anthropological Association.

Harvey, David. 1989. *The Condition of Postmodernity.* Oxford: Blackwell.

———. 2005. *A Brief History of Neoliberalism.* Oxford: Oxford University Press.

———. 2007. "Neoliberalism as Creative Destruction." *Annals of the American Academy of Political and Social Science* 610(1): 21–44.

Hayhurst, Lyndsay M. C. 2013. "Girls as the 'New' Agents of Social Change? Exploring the 'Girl Effect' through Sport, Gender and Development Programs in Uganda." *Sociological Research Online* 18(2): 1–12.

Henriques, Fernando. 1953. *Family and Color in Jamaica.* London: Eyre & Spottiswoode.

Highfield, Arnold. 2014. *Crucian Recollections: From the Compelling Past of a Storied Island.* Christiansted: Antilles Press.

———. 2018. *The Cultural History of the American Virgin Islands and the Danish West Indies: A Companion Guide.* Christiansted: Antilles Press.

Hill, Roger. 1983. *Clear de Road: A Virgin Islands History Textbook.* St. Thomas, USVI: US Virgin Islands Department of Conservation and Cultural Affairs, Bureau of Libraries, Museums and Archaeological Services.

Hillman, Richard, and Thomas D'Agostino, eds. 2003. *Understanding the Contemporary Caribbean*. Boulder, CO: Lynne Rienner.

Ho, Karen. 2009. *Liquidated: An Ethnography of Wall Street*. Durham: Duke University Press.

Holt, Thomas. 2000. *The Problem of Race in the Twenty-First Century*. Cambridge, MA: Harvard University Press.

Hook, Derek. 2007. *Foucault, Psychology and the Analytics of Power*. Basingstoke: Palgrave Macmillan.

Hudson, Peter. 2017. *Bankers and Empire: How Wall Street Colonized the Caribbean*. Chicago: University of Chicago Press.

Hurston, Zora Neale. 1935. *Mules and Men*. Philadelphia: J. B. Lippincott.

Jacobs-Huey, Lanita. 2006. *From the Kitchen to the Parlor: Language and Becoming in African American Women's Hair Care*. New York: Oxford University Press.

Jackson, John. 2008. *Racial Paranoia: The Unintended Consequences of Political Correctness—The New Reality of Race in America*. New York: Basic Books.

Jensen, Peter Hoxcer. 1998. *From Serfdom to Fireburn and Strike: The History of Black Labor in the Danish West Indies, 1848–1916*. Christiansted: Antilles Press.

Kastner, Jamie, dir. 2017. *The Skyjacker's Tale*. Strand Releasing.

Kaye, Kerwin. 2012. "Rehabilitating the 'Drugs Lifestyle': Criminal Justice, Social Control, and the Cultivation of Agency." *Ethnography* 14(2): 207–232.

Kelley, Robin D. G. 1997. *Yo' Mama's Disfunktional! Fighting the Culture Wars in Urban America*. Boston: Beacon Press.

Kelly, Tobias, and Alpa Shah. 2006. "Introduction: A Double-Edged Sword: Protection and State Violence." *Critique of Anthropology* 26(3): 251–257.

Kempadoo, Kamala. 1999. *Sun, Sex, and Gold: Tourism and Sex Work in the Caribbean*. Lanham, MD: Rowman & Littlefield.

———. 2004. *Sexing the Caribbean: Gender, Race, and Sexual Labor*. London: Routledge.

Khan, Aisha. 2001. "Journey to the Center of the Earth: The Caribbean as Master Symbol." *Cultural Anthropology* 16(3): 271–302.

———. 2004. *Callaloo Nation: Metaphors of Race and Religious Identity among South Asians in Trinidad*. Durham: Duke University Press.

Kiely, Ray. 1999. "The Last Refuge of the Noble Savage? A Critical Assessment of Post-Development Theory." *European Journal of Development Research* 11(1): 30–55.

Kincaid, Jamaica. 1988. *A Small Place*. New York: Farrar, Straus and Giroux.

Klein, Naomi. 2007. *Shock Doctrine: The Rise of Disaster Capitalism*. New York: Picador Paper.

———. 2018. *The Battle for Paradise: Puerto Rico Takes on the Disaster Capitalists*. Chicago: Haymarket Books.

Kossler, Bill. 2007. "United States Would Help Itself by Helping the Caribbean, Billionaire Says." *VI Source*, September 21.

———. 2008a. "Bigwigs Join Billionaire Stanford in St. Croix Groundbreaking." *St. Croix Source*, February 22.

———. 2008b. "Structure of Legislature, 'Native' Questions Dominate Constitutional Session." *St. Croix Source*, October 14.

———. 2009a. "Feds: Auffenberg and Accomplices Nailed by IRS Sting." *St. Croix Source*, January 29.

———. 2009b. "Labor Reaches Out to Jobless Stanford Employees." *St. Croix Source*, March 4.

Krauss, Clifford, Julie Creswell, and Charlie Savage. 2009. "Questions Rise as Billionaire's Island Realm Comes Apart." *New York Times*, February 21, A1.

Larsen, Jens. 1950. *Virgin Islands Story: A History of the Lutheran State Church, Other Churches, Slavery, Education, and Culture in the Danish West Indies, Now the Virgin Islands*. Philadelphia: Muhlenberg Press.

Lefever, Harry. 1992. *Turtle Bogue: Afro-Caribbean Life and Culture in the Costa Rican Village*. Selinsgrove, PA: Susquehanna University Press.

Leo-Rhynie, Elsa. 1997. "Class, Race, and Gender Issues in Child Rearing in the Caribbean." In *Caribbean Families: Diversity Among Ethnic Groups*, edited by Jaipaul Roopnarine and Janet Brown, 25–55. London: Ablex.

Lett, Christine. 2004. "Gov't to Weather Expected EDC Storm." *St. Croix Avis*, October 13.

Lewin, Aldeth. 2008. "Gov. Submits Revised Property Tax Proposal." *St. Croix Avis*, February 6.

Lewis, Gordon K. 1972. *The Virgin Islands: A Caribbean Lilliput*. Evanston: Northwestern University Press.

Lightfoot, Natasha. 2015. *Troubling Freedom: Antigua and the Aftermath of British Emancipation*. Durham: Duke University Press.

Lim, Bliss Cua. 2001. "Spectral Times: The Ghost Film as Historical Allegory." *positions: east asia cultures critique* 9(2): 287–329.

Lipuma, Edward, and Benjamin Lee. 2004. *Financial Derivatives and the Globalization of Risk*. Durham: Duke University Press.

Little, Peter, and Michael Painter. 1995. "Discourse, Politics, and the Development Process: Reflections on Escobar's 'Anthropology and the Development Encounter.'" *American Ethnologist* 22(3): 602–609.

Lohr, Lynda. 2005a. "Meada's Mall Fire Likely Sparked by Racial Tensions." *St. Croix Source*, September 2.

———. 2005b. "Frett, Injured While at Sit-in, Files Police Reports." *St. Croix Source*, October 19.

———. 2005c. "Protesters Stop Shoppers at Starfish Market." *St. Croix Source*, November 23.

———. 2005d. "Many Calls for Unity at St. John Rally." *St. Croix Source*, October 1.

———. 2008. "Municipal Government Hot Topic at Constitutional Convention Meeting." *St. Croix Source*, March 12.

Lourdes Dick, Diane. 2015. "U.S. Tax Imperialism." *American University Law Review* 65. https://digitalcommons.law.seattleu.edu/faculty/729.

Lowe, Lisa. 2015. *The Intimacies of Four Continents*. Durham: Duke University Press.

Mair, Lucille Mathurin. 1995. *The Rebel Woman in the British West Indies during Slavery*. Kingston, Jamaica: Institute of Jamaica.

Maldonado, A. W. 1997. *Teodoro Moscoso and Puerto Rico's Operation Bootstrap*. Gainesville: University Press of Florida.

Mandle, Jay. 1996. *Persistent Underdevelopment: Change and Economic Modernization in the West Indies*. Amsterdam: Gordon and Breach.

Marcus, George. 1998. *Corporate Futures: The Diffusion of the Culturally Sensitive Corporate Form*. Chicago: University of Chicago Press.

Maurer, Bill. 1997. *Recharting the Caribbean: Land, Law, and Citizenship in the British Virgin Islands*. Ann Arbor: University of Michigan Press.

———. 2005. "Due Diligence and 'Reasonable Man,' Offshore." *Cultural Anthropology* 20(4): 474–505.

———. 2015. *How Would You Like to Pay? How Technology Is Changing the Future of Money*. Durham: Duke University Press

Mawson, Alana. 2008. "Appalled but Not Surprised!" *St. Croix Source*, May 13.

Mbembe, Achille. 2001. *On the Postcolony*. Berkeley: University of California Press.

McAfee, Kathy. 1991. *Storm Signals: Structural Adjustment and Development Alternatives in the Caribbean*. Boston: South End Press.

McClaurin, Irma. 2001. *Black Feminist Anthropology: Theory, Politics, Praxis, and Poetics*. New Brunswick, NJ: Rutgers University Press.

McClintock, Anne. 1995. *Imperial Leather: Race, Gender and Sexuality in the Colonial Contest*. London: Routledge.

McKittrick, Katherine. 2013. "Plantation Futures." *Small Axe* 7(3): 1–15.

Mintz, Sidney. 1985. *Sweetness and Power: The Place of Sugar in Modern History*. New York: Penguin Books.

Mohammed, Patricia. 2000. "'But Most of All Mi Love Me Browning': The Emergence in Eighteenth- and Nineteenth-Century Jamaica of the Mulatto Woman as the Desired." *Feminist Review* 65(1): 22–48.

Mohammed, Patricia, ed. 2002. *Gendered Realities: Essays in Caribbean Feminist Thought*. Barbados: University of the West Indies Press.

Mohammed, Patricia, and Catherine Shepherd, eds. 1988. *Gender in Caribbean Development: Papers Presented at the Inaugural Seminar of the University of the West Indies, Women and Development Studies Project*. Kingston, Jamaica: Center for Gender and Development Studies, University of the West Indies.

Momsen, Janet. 1993. *Women and Change in the Caribbean: A Pan-Caribbean Perspective*. Bloomington: Indiana University Press.

Monagle, Michael. 2008. "Bert Needs to Be Relegated to Our Past." *St. Croix Source*, May 13.

Morales, Ed. 2019. *Fantasy Island: Colonialism, Exploitation, and the Betrayal of Puerto Rico*. New York: Bold Type Books.

Munasinghe, Viranjini. 2001. *Callaloo or Tossed Salad? East Indians and the Cultural Politics of Identity in Trinidad*. Ithaca, NY: Cornell University Press.

Murch, Donna Jean. 2010. *Living for the City: Migration, Education, and the Rise of the Black Panther Party in Oakland, California*. Chapel Hill: University of North Carolina Press.

Murphy, Michelle. 2013. "The Girl: Mergers of Feminism and Finance in Neoliberal Times." *Scholar and Feminist Online* 11(2). https://sfonline.barnard.edu/gender-justice-and-neoliberal-transformations/the-girl-mergers-of-feminism-and-finance-in-neoliberal-times/.

Nash, June, and María Patricia Fernández-Kelly, eds. 1983. *Women, Men, and the International Division of Labor*. Albany: State University of New York Press.

Nassy-Brown, Jacqueline. 2005. *Dropping Anchor, Setting Sail: Geographies of Race in Black Liverpool*. Princeton, NJ: Princeton University Press.

Navarro, Tami. 2017. "But Some of Us Are Broke: Race, Gender, and the Neoliberalization of the Academy." *American Anthropologist* 119(3): 506–517.

———. 2018. "After the Storms: Reflections on the US Virgin Islands." *Transforming Anthropology* 26(2): 173–180.

Nixon, Angelique. 2015. *Resisting Paradise: Tourism, Diaspora, and Sexuality in Caribbean Culture*. Jackson: University Press of Mississippi.

Oliver, Cynthia. 2009. *Queen of the Virgins: Pageantry and Black Womanhood in the Caribbean*. Jackson: University Press of Mississippi.

Olwig, Karen Fog. 1985. *Cultural Adaptation and Resistance on St. John: Three Politics of Culture in Jamaica*. Durham: Duke University Press.

O'Neal, Michael. 2012. *Slavery, Smallholding, and Tourism: Social Transformations in the British Virgin Islands*. New Orleans: Quid Pro Books.

Ong, Aihwa. 1999. *Flexible Citizenship: The Cultural Logics of Transnationality*. Durham: Duke University Press.

———. 2006. *Neoliberalism as Exception: Mutations in Citizenship and Sovereignty*. Durham: Duke University Press.

Palan, Ronen. 2003. *The Offshore World: Sovereign Markets, Virtual Places, and Nomad Millionaires*. Ithaca: Cornell University Press.

Peet, Richard, and Elaine Hartwick. 1999. *Theories of Development*. New York: Guilford.

Peterson, Marina. 2006. "Patrolling the Plaza: Privatized Public Space and the Neoliberal State in Downtown Los Angeles." *Urban Anthropology and Studies of Cultural Systems and World Economic Development* 35(4): 355–386.

Pieterse, Jan Nederveen. 1998. "My Paradigm or Yours? Alternative Development, Post-Development, Reflexive Development." *Development and Change* 29(2): 343–373.

Piot, Charles. 1999. *Remotely Global: Village Modernity in West Africa*. Chicago: University of Chicago Press.

———. 2010. *Nostalgia for the Future: West Africa after the Cold War*. Chicago: University of Chicago Press.

———. 2019. *The Fixer: Visa Lottery Chronicles*. Durham: Duke University Press.

Plambech, Sine. 2014. "Between 'Victims' and 'Criminals': Rescue, Deportation, and Everyday Violence among Nigerian Migrants." Special issue, *Sexual Economies and New Techniques of Governance*, edited by Elizabeth Bernstein, of *Social Politics: International Studies in Gender, State and Society* 21(3): 382–402.

PricewaterhouseCoopers. 2004. Economic Impact of H.R. 4520 on U.S. Virgin Islands.

Prieto, Norma Iglesias. 1997. *Beautiful Flowers of the Maquiladora: Life Histories of Women Workers in Tijuana*. Austin: University of Texas Press.

Probasco, Matt. 2007. "Four Charged with Multiple Counts in EDC Tax Fraud Case." *St. Croix Source*, October 18.

Putnam, Lara. 2002. *The Company They Kept: Migrants and the Politics of Gender in Costa Rica, 1870–1960*. Chapel Hill: University of North Carolina Press.

Randall, Barry. 2008. "Caribbean Tax Havens under Attack in US Senate." *Caribbean Net News*. http://www.caribbeannetnews.com/archivelist. php?news_id=9360&pageaction=showdetail&news_id=9360&arcyear= 2008&arcmonth=7&arcday=24=&ty=.

Reddock, Rhoda. 1994. *Women, Labour and Politics in Trinidad and Tobago: A History*. London: Zed Books.

Reilly, Matthew. 2019. *Archaeology below the Cliff: Race, Class, and Redlegs in Barbadian Sugar Society*. Tuscaloosa: University of Alabama Press.

Ringrose, Jessica, and Valerie Walkerdine. 2008. "Regulating the Abject: The TV Make-Over as Site of Neoliberal Reinvention toward Bourgeois Femininity." *Feminist Media Studies* 8(3): 227–246.

Robinson, Cedric. 1983. *Black Marxism: The Making of the Black Radical Tradition*. London: Zed Books.

Roitman, Janet. 2005. *Fiscal Disobedience: An Anthropology of Economic Regulation in Central Africa*. Princeton, NJ: Princeton University Press.

Roland, Kaifa. 2011. *Cuban Color in Tourism and La Lucha: An Ethnography of Racial Meanings*. Oxford: Oxford University Press.

Roopnarine, Lomarsh. 2009. "The First and Only Crossing: Indian Indentured Servitude on Danish St. Croix, 1863–1868." *South Asian Diaspora* 1(2): 113–140.

———. 2011. "St. Croix's Secession Movement in the United States Virgin Islands: Sentimental or Serious." *Journal of Eastern Caribbean Studies* 36(1): 43–66.

———. 2016. *Indian Indenture in the Danish West Indies, 1863–1873*. New York: Palgrave Macmillan.

Rosenthal, Caitlin. 2018. *Accounting for Slavery: Masters and Management*. Cambridge, MA: Harvard University Press.

Sachs, Wolfgang, ed. 1992. *The Development Dictionary: A Guide to Knowledge as Power*. London: Zed Books.

Safa, Helen. 1981. "Runaway Shops and Female Employment: The Search for Cheap Labor." *Signs* 7(2): 418–433.

———. 1995. *The Myth of the Male Breadwinner: Women and Industrialization in the Caribbean*. Boulder, CO: Westview Press.

Sassen, Saskia. 1998. *Globalization and Its Discontents*. New York: New Press.

———. 2003. "Economic Globalization and the Redrawing of Citizenship." In *Globalization, the State, and Violence*, edited by Jonathan Friedman, 67–86. Walnut Creek, CA: AltaMira Press.

Scharff, Christina. 2012. *Repudiating Feminism: Young Women in a Neoliberal World*. Farnham: Ashgate.

Scott, David. 2016. *Omens of Adversity: Tragedy, Time, Memory, Justice*. Durham: Duke University Press.

Sen, Gita, and Caren Grown. 1987. *Development Crises and Alternative Visions: Third World Women's Perspectives*. New York: Monthly Review Press.

Shah, Alpa. 2006. "The 'Terrorist' Maoist Movement and the State in Jharkhand, India." *Critique of Anthropology* 26(3): 297–314.

Sharpe, Christina. 2016. *In the Wake: On Blackness and Being*. Durham: Duke University Press.

Sheller, Mimi. 1998. "Quasheba, Mother, Queen: Black Women's Public Leadership and Political Protest in Post-Emancipation Jamaica, 1834–65." *Slavery and Abolition* 19(3): 90–117.

———. 2003. *Consuming the Caribbean: From Arawaks to Zombies.* New York: Routledge.

———. 2014. *Aluminum Dreams: The Making of Light Modernity.* Cambridge: MIT Press.

Silber, Carlota Irina. 2007. "Local Capacity Building in 'Dysfunctional' Times: Internationals, Revolutionaries, and Activism in Postwar El Salvador." *Women's Studies Quarterly* 35(3/4): 167–183.

Simey, T. S. 1946. *Welfare and Planning in the West Indies.* Oxford: Clarendon Press.

Singer, P. W. 2003. *Corporate Warriors: The Rise of the Privatized Military Industry.* Ithaca, NY: Cornell University Press.

Sircar, K. K. 1971. "Emigration of Indian Indentured Labour to the Danish West Indian Island of St. Croix 1863–68." *Scandinavian Economic History Review* 1971(2): 133–148.

Slocum, Karla. 2006. *Free Trade and Freedom: Neoliberalism, Place, and Nation in the Caribbean.* Ann Arbor: University of Michigan Press.

Slocum, Karla, and Deborah Thomas. 2003. "Rethinking Global and Area Studies: Insights from Caribbeanist Anthropology." *American Anthropologist* 105(3): 553–565.

Smallwood, Stephanie. 2008. *Saltwater Slavery: A Middle Passage from Africa to American Diaspora.* Cambridge, MA: Harvard University Press.

Smith, M. G. 1965. *The Plural Society in the British West Indies.* Berkeley: University of California Press.

Smith, R. T. 1996. *The Matrifocal Family: Power, Pluralism, and Politics.* New York: Routledge.

Spillers, Hortense. 1987. "Mama's Baby, Papa's Maybe: An American Grammar Book." *Diacritics* 17(2): 64–81.

Starn, Orin, and Marisol de la Cadena, eds. 2007. *Indigenous Experience Today.* New York: Berg.

Stoler, Ann Laura. 2016. *Duress: Imperial Durabilities in Our Times.* Durham: Duke University Press.

Strom, Stephanie. 2007. "Tax Proposal from Rangel Could Benefit His Donors." NY Times.com, November 8.

Svalesen, Leif. 2000. *The Slave Ship Fredensborg.* Bloomington: Indiana University Press.

Tadiar, Neferti. 2013. "Life-Times of Disposability in Global Neoliberalism." *Social Text* 31(2): 19–48.

Taylor, Keeanga-Yamahtta. 2019. *Race for Profit: How Banks and the Real Estate Industry Undermined Black Homeownership.* Chapel Hill: University of North Carolina Press.

Thomas, Deborah A. 2004. *Modern Blackness: Nationalism, Globalization, and the Politics of Culture in Jamaica*. Durham: Duke University Press.

———. 2016. "Time and the Otherwise: Plantations, Garrisons and Being Human in the Caribbean." *Anthropological Theory* 16(2–3): 177–200.

Thurland, Karen. 2014. *The Sugar Industry on St. Croix*. Bloomington, IN: AuthorHouse.

Torres, Arlene, and Norman Whitten, eds. 1998. *Blackness in Latin America and the Caribbean: Social Dynamics and Cultural Transformations*. Bloomington: Indiana University Press.

Trouillot, Michel-Rolph. 2001. "The Anthropology of the State in the Age of Globalization: Close Encounters of the Deceptive Kind." *Current Anthropology* 42(1): 171–186.

———. 2003. *Global Transformations: Anthropology and the Modern World*. New York: Palgrave.

Tyson, George. 1996. *Bondmen and Freedmen in the Danish West Indies: Scholarly Perspectives*. St. Thomas: Virgin Islands Humanities Council, Caribbean Universities Press in association with Bowker.

Tyson, George, and Arnold Highfield, eds. 1994. *The Danish West Indian Slave Trade: Virgin Islands Perspectives*. St. Thomas: Virgin Islands Humanities Council.

Ulysse, Gina. 2007. *Downtown Ladies: Informal Commercial Importers, a Haitian Anthropologist, and Self-Making in Jamaica*. Chicago: University of Chicago Press.

USVI Bureau of Economic Research. N.d. http://www.usviber.org/publications.htm.

Virgin Islands Investment Analysis. 2002. Islands News. May.

Virgin-Islands-On-Line's Coconut Telegraph. 2005. "State of the Territory Address Tonight." http://www.virgin-islands-on-line.com/coconut-telegraph/archives/2005_02.shtml.

Vlcek, William. 2017. *Offshore Finance and Global Governance: Disciplining the Tax Nomad*. London: Palgrave.

Waters, Anita. 2003. "Presenting the Past: The Construction of National History in a Jamaican Tourist Site." In *Modern Political Culture in the Caribbean*, edited by Holger Henke and Fred Reno, 141–180. Trinidad and Tobago: University of the West Indies Press.

Welter, Barbara. 1966. "The Cult of True Womanhood: 1820–1860." *American* 18(2): 151–174.

Westergaard, Waldemar. 1917. *The Danish West Indies under Company Rule (1671–1754)*. New York: Macmillan.

Wilkinson, Alec. 2009. "Not Quite Cricket." *New Yorker*, March 9.

Wilson, Peter. 1964. "General and Ethnology: Kinship and Community in Carriacou, M. G. Smith." *American Anthropologist* 66(1): 172–174.

————. 1973. *Crab Antics: The Social Anthropology of English-Speaking Negro Societies of the Caribbean.* New Haven, CT: Yale University Press.

Wiltshire, Shari. 2006. "VI Watch Industry Wins Important Victory." *St. Croix Avis*, July 7.

————. 2008. "'I am home': Stanford Breaks Ground on STX Headquarters." *St. Croix Avis*, February 22.

Yanagisako, Sylvia. 2002. *Producing Culture and Capital: Family Firms in Italy.* Princeton, NJ: Princeton University Press.

Yelvington, Kevin. 1995. *Producing Power: Ethnicity, Gender, and Class in a Caribbean Workplace.* Philadelphia: Temple University Press.

————. 2001. "The Anthropology of Afro-Latin America and the Caribbean: Diasporic Dimensions." *Annual Review of Anthropology* 30: 227–260.

Zaloom, Caitlin. 2006. *Out of the Pits: Traders and Technology from Chicago to London.* Chicago: University of Chicago Press.

Zelizer, Viviana. 1997. *The Social Meaning of Money: Pin Money, Paychecks, Poor Relief, and Other Currencies.* Princeton, NJ: Princeton University Press.

Index

Olwig, Karen Fog, 48, 58
Ong, Aihwa, 67
Operation Bootstrap. compared
  to CARICOM, 205n31; Deere
  on, 206n34, 206n37; emulation
  of, 206n33; impact of, 62–64,
  207n38; Maldonado on, 76–77,
  206n36; marketing of, 206n35;
  purpose of, 4
Organic Act, 135–36, 204n26
"Otherization," 138
outmigration, 5, 63, 192,
  208nn41–42, 208n43
"outsiders," 113–16, 138, 144

Palan, Ronen, 96
Partner, John, 182, 186
Pendergest, Laura, 87–89
philanthropic circuit, 123–26
phone etiquette, 110–11
pigmentocracy, 53–54, 158
"pink collar" workers, 153–54
"pin money," 155, 172
Pioneer Industries Program,
  207n39
"Pipe Dreams and Ponzi Schemes,"
  91–92
piracy and privateering, 15, 95,
  210n8
plantation agriculture, 55–58,
  203n19
the planter's chair, 176, 214n12
Playing History video game, 202n5
positionality in the field, 39–42
poststructuralist critiques, 19
PricewaterhouseCoopers, 77, 79
privatization of space, 21–22
privilege: color linked to, 53–54,
  59, 158–60; of EDC people, 90;
  nature and impact of, 41–42, 44
property tax increases, 1–2,
  130–32, 143

Puerto Rican Industrial
  Representatives, 76–77
Puerto Rico: emigration and,
  192; foreign capital on, 68–69;
  industrial development on, 62;
  manufacturing on, 205n30;
  migrants from, 65, 104–5;
  in the "native" debate, 145;
  unemployment on, 64; relations
  with U.S., 16; USVI compared
  to, 5. *See also* Operation
  Bootstrap

Queen Mary Thomas, 52
queen shows, 59

racial capitalism: the EDC as, 70,
  71–72, 161–63; historical aspects
  of, 45; nature and significance
  of, 8–10; spectral time in relation
  to, 14–15; Taylor on, 211n12.
  See also the economic history of
  the U.S. Virgin Islands
racial hierarchies: "dem deh," 108,
  113–16, 210n3; due to foreign
  capital, 7; global circulations and,
  22–26; in industrial development,
  61–62; long term whites and,
  121–26; racial classification
  systems, 52–54
racial violence, specter of, 93,
  115–16, 120
"ragga," 121, 211n11
Ramos, Agapito, 104–5
real estate and land use, 1–2,
  21–22, 130–35
Recharting the Caribbean (Maurer),
  67
The Repeating Island (Benítez-
  Rojo), 13
residential segregation, 109,
  126–28